A Russian Looks at America

Foreword by Henry Steele Commager

Introduction by Arnold Schrier

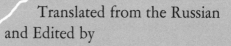

Translated from the Russian
and Edited by

Arnold Schrier

Joyce Story

A Russian Looks at America

The Journey of Aleksandr Borisovich Lakier in 1857

Lakier, A. B.

The University of Chicago Press · Chicago and London

The University of Chicago Press, Chicago 60637
The University of Chicago Press, Ltd., London
© 1979 by The University of Chicago
All rights reserved. Published 1979
Printed in the United States of America
83 82 81 80 79 5 4 3 2 1

ALEKSANDR BORISOVICH LAKIER (1825–70),
a landless member of the Russian provincial
gentry, was the first Russian to travel to
America on his own initiative since the 1780s.
This account of his journey, published in Russia
in 1859, constitutes the first comprehensive
description of the United States written by a
Russian.

ARNOLD SCHRIER is the Walter C. Langsam
Professor of Modern European History at the
University of Cincinnati. He is the author of *Ireland
and the American Emigration* and is coauthor of
two additional works, *The Development of
Civilization* and *History and Life*.

JOYCE STORY is assistant professor of Slavic
languages and literatures at Ohio State University
and has published in the *Slavic and East
European Journal*.

Library of Congress Cataloging in Publication Data

Lakier, Aleksandr Borisovich, 1825–1870.
    A Russian looks at America.

    Translation of Puteshestvīe po Sīèvero-Amerikanskim
Shtatam, Kanadīè i ostrovu Kubīè.
    An abridgement by the translators of the original
two-volume work.
    Includes index.
    1.   United States—Description and travel—1848–1865.
2.   Lakier, Aleksandr Borisovich, 1825–1870.   I.   Schrier,
Arnold.   II.   Story, Joyce.   III.   Title.
E166.L2317   917.3′04′6   79–11205
ISBN 0–226–46795–3

For Susan, Jay, Linda, and Paula
and
For Wayne

Contents

Foreword

Historians as well as artists know that the view depends upon the point of view. Much of the value of Aleksandr Lakier's report on his journey to the United States in 1857 derives from the elementary fact that his was a fresh and novel point of view. Most of the hundreds of foreign commentators who wrote about the United States in the first half of the nineteenth century came from Britain, France, or Germany—from a Europe, that is, which had provided the New World republic with most of its population, and with most of its religious, cultural, scientific, and political heritage as well. Inevitably a William Cobbett, a Harriet Martineau, a Charles Dickens from Britain; a Crèvecoeur, a Tocqueville, a Chevalier from France; a Johann Schoepf, a Francis Lieber, a Francis Grund from Germany, looked at the United States through familiar glasses. They knew English America even before they left Europe, for America was an extension of their own society, and most of them judged it—harshly or sympathetically—by the standards and customs of their own societies. Most of them, too, had already made up their minds about the character of the new nation, and the nature of the democratic experiment in which it was engaged. Their concern—as so conspicuously with Cobbett and Tocqueville—was not primarily with America, but with the lessons America might teach their own nations.

In his interpretation of the American scene, Lakier represented something new: his background was the Russia of the Iron Czar, Nicholas I, and the as yet untested Alexander II—a Russia which had contributed nothing to the making of the United States, a Russia which was a century behind western Europe in social or political sophistication, a Russia with a long tradition of censorship, Siberia, or the gallows, as means of silencing criticism or discouraging unfavorable comparisons.

Lakier's *Journey* was, for all practical purposes, the first serious

and substantial Russian report on America: there had really been
only two predecessors, Svin'in's charming but superficial "Picturesque
Journey," and Petr Poletika's *A Sketch of the Internal Conditions of
the United States,* denied publication in Russia. Lakier's two volumes,
published in 1859, constituted, therefore, the only critical and comprehensive introduction to the United States available to Russians until
after the American Civil War. Unlike his predecessors then, Lakier
could and did write for a Russian audience; what is more, thanks to
Alexander II's brief flirtation with enlightenment, he could write
without fear of censorship or penalty.

Lakier had come to maturity in a Russia heavy with the air of op-
pression, and he was a bureaucrat in a government still absolutist.
Somehow he overcame these handicaps. He was no provincial, but a
cosmopolite, fluent in French, German, and English; he was learned
in many fields—law, history, economics, even heraldry. He was no
aristocrat, but was socially acceptable: he had married the daughter
of the rector of St. Petersburg University, and had moved in the best
social circles. He belonged to the Russia which somehow produced
Gogol and Pushkin and Turgenev, and clearly he shared some of their
liberal views.

A quarter-century separated the America which Lakier described
from that which Tocqueville had surveyed in his magisterial *Democracy in America.* A short time in history, yet, as both visitors discovered,
everything changed more rapidly in America than in the Old World,
and the America of Jackson was indeed different from the America
of Buchanan. It was still agricultural, but on—or over—the threshold
of the industrial revolution: Lakier, for example, was able to go everywhere by railroad or steamboat, and to note, everywhere, the mecha-
nization of agriculture. It was an America still predominantly rural,
but with a score of cities growing with spectacular speed: no theme
in Lakier more recurrent than this, that what had yesterday been a
prairie was today a bustling metropolis of a hundred thousand. It
was an America still committed to social equality but with slavery
not only more widespread but more ardently defended than ever, and
its defenders ready to fight for its preservation. It was an America
whose sections were still New England, the Middle States, the South,
and the Middle Border, but with California in the Union and Oregon
ready to come in: an America where sectionalism dictated disunion
and railroads cemented union. Yet when we compare the Lakier with

the Tocqueville interpretation of this America what is most impressive are not the differences but the similarities.

The personal parallels are not without interest. Both observers were young when they came to America—Tocqueville was twenty-six, Lakier thirty-two. Both were jurisprudents, both historians, both committed to a career in public service. Both were in the United States less than a year and both managed, *mirabile dictu,* to see almost everything that was to be seen. More important is that both seized, at once, upon the same seminal principle that appeared to explain American society—the principle of equality. Tocqueville was already prepared for this even before he embarked on the *Havre*; Lakier learned it as soon as he boarded the (more symbolically named) *Europa.* Both, it might be added, were fascinated by many of the same features of American life and institutions. Both, for example (it is sobering to recall), studied American prisons in order to instruct Europe in a more humane penal and prison system. Both were enormously impressed by the independence of juries and of judges. Both were astonished at the high standards of public and of private morality, and, particularly, at the respect and authority accorded women, and at the exalted moral position which they enjoyed. Both, too, were immensely impressed by the high standards of public education, and by the literacy of all classes in society: there was no one in the whole of Boston who could not read and write, declared Lakier somewhat wildly.

The differences in the two commentators are no less illuminating than the similarities: they are rooted, perhaps, in the point of view rather than in the view. The initial difference was in the resources which each enjoyed. Tocqueville, who was a great swell, came with overpowering credentials. He was able to see everybody who was anybody—presidents, senators, judges, university presidents, scholars, men of letters. He managed, in the brief time that he was here, to interview statesmen like Albert Gallatin, John Quincy Adams, and Edward Livingston; jurists like Chancellor Kent and Joseph Story; politicians like Joel Poinsett and John Spencer; scholars like Edward Everett, Francis Lieber, and Jared Sparks; luminaries like Daniel Webster and William Ellerry Channing, and his thinking was profoundly influenced by what these distinguished men told him. Lakier came on his own, and depended on fortuity for his interviews. He talked with the most miscellaneous people— shipboard acquaintances,

workingmen, petty officials, soldiers, farmers, fur traders, newly arrived immigrants—a pretty good cross-section of American society.
He saw more, and more indiscriminately, than Tocqueville; Tocqueville saw deeper. Lakier was a superb reporter, Tocqueville a
philosopher.

Yet, occasionally, the reporter saw farther than the philosopher:
thus Lakier observed with something like incredulity the phenomenon
of abundance, and he never tires of telling us of the groaning boards,
for breakfast, dinner, and supper— something beneath Tocqueville's
notice, but not beneath the notice of a Russian who knew how serfs
lived. He saw, too, more clearly than Tocqueville, the significance
of the westward movement and of the frontier as a melting pot, a
safety valve, and a school for democracy, and he recounts for us his
fascination with the German immigrants, the French who were prepared to accept slavery, the Indians and Indian agents. He was more
revolted by slavery than Tocqueville, but less concerned: the moral
revulsion is there, but not the desperate conclusion that slavery would
break up the Union.

There was a pervasive melancholy in much that Tocqueville wrote,
a conviction that though democracy was indeed the wave of the future,
that wave would drown out much that was precious—that democracy
would expose every Old World society to the threat of cultural
mediocrity, majority tyranny, and the ultimate subversion of liberty.
Lakier, who was by nature more sanguine and more buoyant, looked
with confidence to the future—a future which would see the triumph
of equality and a closer friendship between the United States and his
own nation. In the end both sounded the same note—with Tocqueville
muted, with Lakier loud and confident. Listen to Tocqueville's conclusion as he contrasts the roles which Russia and the United States
are destined to play in history:

> All other nations seem to have reached their natural limits . . . but
> these are still in the act of growth. . . . The conquests of the Ameri-
> can are gained by the plowshare; those of the Russian by the sword.
> The Anglo-American relies upon personal interest to accomplish
> his ends, and gives free scope to the unguided strength and common
> sense of the people; the Russian centers all authority of society in a
> single arm. The principal instrument of the former is freedom; of the
> latter, servitude. Their starting point is different, and their courses

are not the same; yet each of them seems marked out by the will
of Heaven to sway the destinies of half the globe.

Lakier saw, too, that the example of America could not be confined
to the Western Hemisphere, but would sweep around the globe, but
he had few misgivings about the result:

> Must Americans be confined to America [he asked] or are they fated
> to return to Europe, bringing with them the institutions that were
> regenerated on new soil and were cleared of those excrescences which
> clung to them for centuries in Europe? Young, active, practical, happy
> in their enterprises, the American people see no reason to answer the
> question negatively. They will have an influence on Europe but they
> will use neither arms nor sword nor fire, nor death and destruction.
> They will spread their influence by the strength of their inventions,
> their trade, and their industry. And this influence will be more
> durable than any conquest.

HENRY STEELE COMMAGER

Acknowledgments

This book is the outgrowth of a trip to the Soviet Union in the summer of 1970, a trip made possible by a grant-in-aid of research from the Charles Phelps Taft Memorial Fund of the University of Cincinnati. It was during that summer at the Lenin Library in Moscow that Lakier's *Puteshestvie* first came to my attention, and it was there I discovered that no translation had ever been made. I was encouraged to undertake an English translation by N. N. Bolkhovitinov and V. A. Tishkov, both of the Institute of General History, USSR Academy of Sciences. Valerii Tishkov was especially helpful in making available a number of important sources that were unobtainable in the United States, while the staff of the Lenin Library was extremely cooperative in microfilming needed materials.

Joyce Story joined the project after the first rough draft translation had been completed. It is her mastery of Russian and her extraordinary sensitivity to the nuances of both Russian and English usage that are largely responsible for the smoothness and fluency of the final translation.

I am also grateful to colleagues who, while not directly involved in the project, have nevertheless been generous with their time, advice, and information. They include Nancy O. Lurie, Curator of Anthropology at the Milwaukee Public Museum; Michael J. McAfee, Museum Curator, West Point Military Academy; Bruce Lincoln, Northern Illinois University; Richard Wortman, Princeton University; and Ray Allen Billington, Huntington Library. At my own university, colleagues have borne with patience and good humor my ceaseless efforts to exploit their expertise. Those to whom I am particularly indebted are Daniel R. Beaver, Zane L. Miller, George B. Engberg, Alfred W. Scheide, and Beth W. Dillingham.

American libraries and institutions that have facilitated my research include the Library of Congress, the Boston Public Library, the

New York Public Library, and the Smithsonian Institution. Especially helpful have been the staffs of the University of Cincinnati Library, the Cincinnati Public Library, and the Cincinnati Historical Society.

To my wife, Sonny, who for more than six years has had to endure the presence of another man in the house, if only in spirit, go my heartfelt thanks. Indeed, her growing enthusiasm for Lakier matched my own, and as critic and editor she made invaluable suggestions. If the better book that resulted still has flaws, the responsibility for them is mine.

A. S.

Introduction

Foreigners have long been interested in the United States. Even before the American colonies achieved independence there were those
who came to observe and marvel at a new nation in the making. After
independence the Republic attracted an ever widening stream of visitors who wished not only to satisfy their personal curiosity but also
to inform their fellow countrymen about the largest functioning, constitutional democracy in the world. Their efforts produced an impressive array of travel literature, the perceptions and insights of
which have been as enlightening to Americans as to foreign readers
for whom they were intended.[1] Many would argue that the best single
work ever written about the United States is Tocqueville's *Democracy
in America,* published in 1835. But less exalted travel literature also
has its value for Americans, by "making explicit and vivid what local
residents take for granted," and by providing "a kind of color, detail,
and human interest available in no other historical source."[2]

Most foreign travelers to nineteenth-century America came from
western Europe, principally from England, France, and Germany;
few came from Russia. Hence Russian travel literature on the United
States in the nineteenth century is exceedingly sparse. The first comprehensive description by a Russian who visited the United States on
his own initiative was not published until 1859. The author of that
work, Aleksandr Borisovich Lakier, was also the first Russian known
to have traversed nearly the entire length of the Mississippi. It is his

1. Frank Freidel, ed., *Harvard Guide to American History,* rev. ed.,
vol. 1 (Cambridge, Mass.: Harvard University Press, 1974), pp. 141–51,
lists no fewer than four hundred published travel accounts for the period
1790–1900.
2. Ibid., p. 137.

account, which originally appeared in St. Petersburg in two volumes, that is the basis for this abridged and edited English version.[3]

This does not mean, of course, that Russians were totally ignorant of America until the mid-nineteenth century. Russian awareness of the New World dates back to the sixteenth century. In the 1530s a Greek monk living in Muscovy wrote a theological commentary in which he made brief mention of the discovery of Cuba. Five decades later the word "America" made its first appearance in the Russian language, in a 1584 translation of a Polish work entitled "A Chronicle

3. The full title of Lakier's travel account is *Puteshestvie po severo-amerikanskim shtatam, Kanade i ostrovu Kube* [A journey through the North American States, Canada, and Cuba]. There is no evidence that Lakier's work was known to any American writer or scholar. Neither the *Harvard Guide to American History* nor the Library of Congress's *A Guide to the Study of the United States of America* (1960) has any references to the *Puteshestvie*. Neither do two major anthologies: Henry Steele Commager, ed., *America in Perspective: The United States through Foreign Eyes* (New York: Random House, 1947), and Oscar Handlin, ed., *This Was America* (Cambridge, Mass.: Harvard University Press, 1949). Henry Theodore Tuckerman's *America and Her Commentators,* published by Scribner's in New York in 1864, mentions French, British, Italian, and North European travelers, but no Russians. For the entire period from 1790 to 1900, the *Harvard Guide* lists only one Russian travel account, P. A. Tverskoi, *Ocherki Severo-Amerikanskikh Soedinennykh Shtatov* [Essays on the United States of North America] (St. Petersburg, 1895), which Hans Rogger claims was essentially the first Russian account to describe America "in such concrete and knowledgeable detail." "America in the Russian Mind—or Russian Discoveries of America," *Pacific Historical Review* 47, no. 1 (February 1978): 41. Yet a decade earlier Rogger acknowledged that Lakier's *Puteshestvie* was "one of the very few works published in nineteenth-century Russia whose author had first-hand knowledge of his subject" and observed that the radical critic N. A. Dobroliubov had welcomed it in March 1859 for "its wealth of detail about American institutions and material achievements." Although Rogger also noted Dobroliubov's criticism that Lakier "had neither understood nor conveyed the democratic and egalitarian quality of life in the transatlantic republic"—an impression not shared by other contemporary reviewers—there is no evidence that Rogger himself had actually read the two-volume *Puteshestvie*. "Russia and the Civil War," in Harold Hyman, ed., *Heard Round the World* (New York: Knopf, 1969), p. 179.

of the Whole World." That there were only two short, widely separated references to the New World throughout the sixteenth century
is a measure of Muscovy's isolation from the West during the Renais-
sance. Not until the mid-seventeenth century did this intellectual isolation begin to break down. At that time a number of outstanding
Western geographical works, including Mercator's *Atlas,* were translated into Russian; these Dutch and Latin atlases and cosmographies
contained small sections on America. The Russian renditions were all in
manuscript and had limited circulation. Accessibility to such information was increased during Peter the Great's reign (1689–1725), when
three Western geographical works were printed in Russian translation.
Although none of them contained maps, they did have reasonably
accurate information about America and for the first time gave
American place-names such as New York, Jamestown, and Louisiana
in Russian transliteration. In the second half of the eighteenth century thirty additional geographies were published in Russian, mostly
for use as textbooks in the secondary school attached to the Academy
of Sciences. Many of these did have maps along with descriptions of
the New World. Information about America increased significantly
during the reign of Catherine II (1762–96). Between 1765 and
1797 half a dozen travel books dealing wholly with America appeared in Russian translation.[4]

The decisive event in raising Russian consciousness of America
was the War of Independence. After 1775 there was an increase in
the number of articles on North America published in the leading
Moscow and St. Petersburg journals. Newspapers became the principal source of information for Russians on the American struggle
for independence.[5] Interest in America also prompted the publication

4. The information in this paragraph is drawn largely from Avrahm
Yarmolinsky, "Studies in Russian Americana," *Bulletin of the New York
City Public Library* vol. 43, no. 7 (July 1939), pp. 539–43; vol. 43, no.
12 (December 1939), pp. 895–900; vol. 44, no. 9 (September 1940),
pp. 643–48; vol. 46, no. 4 (April 1942), pp. 374–78; vol. 46, no. 5
(May 1942), pp. 451–57.

5. Nikolai N. Bolkhovitinov, *The Beginnings of Russian-American
Relations, 1775–1815* (Cambridge, Mass.: Harvard University Press,
1975), p. 35. The only two newspapers in Russia at the time, both gov-
ernment-sponsored, were the *Sankt Peterburgskie Vedomosti* [St. Petersburg gazette] and the *Moskovskie Vedomosti* [Moscow gazette]. Ibid.,
p. 37.

in 1784 of a Russian translation of William Robertson's *The History of America,* which had first appeared in England in 1777.[6] In addition to translations, works in German and French were available to educated Russians. The ten-volume account published by Abbé Raynal in 1780 was especially popular and widely read, even though Catherine II was highly critical of its sympathy for the American Revolution.[7]

For all the relative abundance of information on America accessible to literate Russians in the late eighteenth century, most of it came via foreign intermediaries. Books were either in French, German, or English, or translations from them. Even news reports in the journals often originated in London.[8] There were no firsthand, eyewitness accounts of America written by Russians. Few Russians had reason to undertake a costly, arduous, even dangerous journey across the Atlantic. One exception was Fedor Vasil'evich Karzhavin (1745–1812), one of the first Russians to visit America on his own initiative. Traveler, man of letters, son of a rich Moscow merchant, Karzhavin had studied at the Sorbonne as a young man. In 1776, having received an appointment as interpreter from the French government, he was sent to Martinique, where he remained until 1788. Karzhavin, a son of the Enlightenment, was strongly attracted to the cause of the Americans. During his dozen years in the New World he visited the United States on three separate occasions (1777–80; 1782; 1784–87) and may even have been a munitions supplier in the War of Independence.[9] Karzhavin's memoirs, however, were not published in Russia until 1875.[10]

A true Russian travel literature about the United States did not develop until the early years of Alexander I's reign (1801–25) and was facilitated by the young tsar's sympathies toward the Americans.[11]

6. Ibid., p. 33.

7. Ibid., p. 34. The full title of Raynal's work is *Histoire philosophique et politique des établissements et du commerce des Européens dans les deux Indes.*

8. Bolkhovitinov, *Beginnings,* p. 38.

9. Eufrosina Dvoichenko-Markov, "A Russian Traveler in Eighteenth-Century America," *Proceedings of the American Philosophical Society* 97, no. 4 (September 1953): 350–55.

10. Ibid.

11. Alexander carried on a three-year correspondence with Jefferson

This travel literature, in the form of "letters from America," was published in a number of Moscow and St. Petersburg journals. They purported to inform Russian readers about various aspects of life in the new republic, although the authors were not identified.[12] The most widely read of these "letters" appeared in *Vestnik Evropy* [*Messenger of Europe*], a journal founded in 1802 by Nikolai Karamzin (1766–1826), the leading Russian historian of his day. Designed to enlighten Russian readers about cultural and political developments generally in the West, *Vestnik Evropy* also included reports on the United States.[13]

Probably the earliest book-length account of the United States as seen through the eyes of a Russian was written by Pavel Svin'in (1787–1839), an artist-diplomat who served as secretary to the Russian consul general in Philadelphia from 1811 to 1813. Shortly after returning to Russia, Svin'in published an article on the United States,[14] which he expanded into a book in 1815 entitled "A Description of a Picturesque Journey in North America."[15] The book seems to have been fairly popular, for a second edition was brought out in 1818. Svin'in published two more articles on the United States: one in 1820 on trade with Russia, and another in 1829 on the fine arts in America.[16] Svin'in may merit the accolade of "the initiator of Russian

---

between 1804 and 1806. Nicholas Hans, "Tsar Alexander I and Jefferson. Unpublished Correspondence," *Slavonic and East European Review* 32, no. 78 (December 1953) : 215–25.

12. Dieter Boden, *Das Amerikabild im russischen Schrifttum bis zum Ende des 19. Jahrhunderts* (Hamburg: Cram, De Gruyter and Co., 1968), pp. 50–52; Bolkhovitinov, *Beginnings,* pp. 133–34.

13. Richard Pipes, *Karamzin's Memoir on Ancient and Modern Russia* (New York: Atheneum, 1969), p. 55. By 1803 *Vestnik Evropy* had over six hundred paid subscribers.

14. "Vzgliad na respubliku Soedinennykh Amerikanskikh oblastei" [A glance at the republic of the United American States], *Syn Otechestva* [Son of the fatherland], nos. 37 and 38 (1814).

15. In Russian *Opyt zhivopisnogo puteshestviia po Severnoi Amerike* (St. Petersburg).

16. Both articles are cited in Avrahm Yarmolinsky, *Picturesque United States of America, 1811, 1812, 1813, Being a Memoir on Paul Svinin, Russian Diplomatic Officer, Artist, and Author, Containing Copious Excerpts from His Accounts of His Travels in America, with Fifty-two Re-

publicist writing on America,"[17] but his information was rather limited. During Svin'in's twenty months in the United States he never left the Atlantic seaboard and never went south of Virginia. While his book discusses general American conditions, it does not do so in detail.[18] Still, the significance of Svin'in's book is that it began a tradition of direct Russian reporting on nineteenth-century America.[19]

That tradition was continued by another diplomat, Petr Poletika (1778–1849), who served as counselor to the Russian minister in Philadelphia (1809–11) and then as minister (1817–22).[20] Although critical of slavery and the treatment of the Indians, Poletika admired American institutions. The book he wrote in 1821 openly defended constitutional government and for that reason could not be published in Russia. By then the political atmosphere in Alexander's last years had turned reactionary, and, since Poletika still held an official post, he thought it best to have his book published in London, in French.[21] It is ironic that while Poletika's book came out in an English translation in Baltimore in 1826, and was even favorably reviewed in the *North American Review*,[22] the Russian audience for whom it was intended was never able to read it in Russian. In 1830 Poletika did manage to publish in Russia an influential essay on the United States, but it turned out to be the last he ever wrote on the subject.[23]

---

productions of Water Colors in His Own Sketch-Book (New York: William Edwin Rudge, 1930), pp. 32–33.

17. Max Laserson, *The American Impact on Russia, 1784–1917* (New York: Collier Books, 1962), p. 176.

18. A summary of the book's contents is given in Yarmolinsky, *Picturesque United States,* pp. 11–32.

19. Boden, *Das Amerikabild,* p. 69.

20. Ibid., p. 74.

21. *Aperçu de la situation intérieure des États-Unis d'Amérique et de leurs rapports politiques avec l'Europe, par un Russe.*

22. Bolkhovitinov, *Russko-amerikanskie otnoshenie 1815–1832* [Russian-American relations 1815–1832] (Moscow: Nauka Publishing House, 1975), p. 535. The English title was *A Sketch of the Internal Conditions of the United States and Their Political Relations with Europe. By a Russian.* It is odd that neither Svin'in's book nor Poletika's appears in the *Harvard Guide* (pp. 141–51), the more so since Poletika's work had an American edition.

23. Boden, *Das Amerikabild,* p. 75.

For nearly thirty years after the publication of Poletika's article, not a word of Russian reporting on America appeared in print. Those were the years of Nicholas I (1825–55), "the most consistent autocrat" of nineteenth-century Russia, when merely to question the Russian autocracy was considered subversive.[24] Constantly fearful of revolution, Nicholas was particularly concerned that the gentry might lead a movement for a constitutional monarchy, or, worse yet, a republic, just as the Decembrists had vainly tried to do at the very beginning of his reign. The tsar's profound abhorrence of all things constitutional prompted him not only to abrogate the Polish constitution after the abortive revolt of 1831 but also to prohibit all writing dealing with constitutions or constitutional regimes. In his determination to preserve autocracy, Nicholas imposed limitations and prohibitions on the Russian gentry for travel and study abroad.[25] Censorship became so strict and all-pervasive by 1850 that one of the tsar's own censors lamented there were more officials in charge of censorship than there were books published that year.[26] In the last seven years of Nicholas's reign there existed a veritable "censorship terror."[27]

No political press could exist in this climate of repression. Neither books nor magazines nor newspapers were permitted to comment on political events at home or abroad. Publications in the Russia of Nicholas I were limited to purely literary, philosophical, and scientific works, subject always to heavy censorship. In those circumstances literary criticism came to play an increasingly influential role in the cultural life of the country, since reviews of foreign as well as Russian books permitted insights into other styles of life. In this sense literate Russians were not wholly isolated from cultural developments in Europe and the United States. These were the years when Russians became acquainted with the novels of James Fenimore

24. Nicholas Riasanovsky, *Nicholas I and Official Nationality in Russia, 1825–1855* (Berkeley: University of California Press, 1959), pp. 184, 186.

25. Exceptions were made for teachers and students, but with the widespread European uprisings of 1848, which badly frightened Nicholas, they too lost the right to travel abroad. Ibid., p. 218.

26. Ibid., p. 222.

27. Daniel Balmuth, "Censorship in Russia: 1848–1855" (Ph.D. diss., Cornell University, 1959), passim.

Cooper and Washington Irving, as well as with the short stories of
Edgar Allan Poe. And there was hardly a literate Russian who did
not know of Harriet Beecher Stowe's *Uncle Tom's Cabin*. But for information on American government and society, Russians were forced
to rely on western European intermediaries, since they themselves
were prohibited from visiting and writing about the United States.
As in the eighteenth century, such intermediaries "were still indispensable for bridging the informational gap between Russia and
the United States."[28] The single most important bridge was Alexis de
Tocqueville's *Democracy in America,* which was accessible to the
French-reading Russian public.[29] No Russian translation was published until 1860, five years after Nicholas I's death.

Members of the Russian intelligentsia were acutely aware of the
dearth of Russian reporting on America. Yet nothing could be done
until the advent of Alexander II in 1855 brought an easing of restric-
tions on foreign travel and a relaxation of the censorship. Among those
who took advantage of the new, more permissive climate was
Aleksandr Borisovich Lakier. His journey to America in 1857 was
the first made by a Russian visitor on his own initiative since that of
Karzhavin in the 1780s. The two-volume account of his trip that he
published in 1859 became the first comprehensive description of the
United States ever written by a Russian. The significance of that fact
was recognized by even so severe a critic as Nikolai Dobroliubov
(1836–61), who reviewed the work and recommended it "to every
Russian reader who has no way of acquainting himself with America
through foreign sources."[30]

Lakier was thirty-two when he visited the United States in 1857.
Well educated, fluent in English, French, German, and Spanish, he
was a landless member of the provincial gentry. Little is known of his
early life save that he was born in 1825 in the South Russian city of
Taganrog.[31] At the age of twenty he graduated from Moscow Uni-

28. David Hecht, *Russian Radicals Look to America, 1825–1894*
(Cambridge, Mass.: Harvard University Press, 1947), p. 217.

29. Alexander Herzen was given a copy in 1837 by the new governor
of Viatka, where Herzen was in exile. Ibid., p. 22.

30. *Sobranie sochinenii,* vol. 4, *Stat'i i retsenzii, ianvar'—iiun' 1859*
(Moscow-Leningrad: Gosudarstvennoe Izdatel'stvo Khudozhestvennoi
Literatury, 1962), p. 219.

31. A port city on the Sea of Azov, Taganrog was founded in 1698

versity with a degree in law and then entered government service in the Ministry of Justice in St. Petersburg.[32] He went on to earn a master's degree in history in 1848 at Moscow University.[33] By 1851 he had risen to the eighth class (collegiate assessor) in the Table of Ranks and had become a section head in the central administrative office of the Ministry of Justice in St. Petersburg.[34] Lakier's career typified the new social group which was emerging toward the end of Nicholas I's reign, an administrative-legal elite whose members' positions in the administration determined their status in society and whose livelihood depended upon their administrative work.[35] Lakier remained with the Ministry of Justice until 1857, when he left government service to travel in western Europe and America.

By then he was fairly well known among the Russian intelligentsia. He had gained widespread attention in 1848 with the publication of his master's essay on hereditary and service landholdings in Russia.[36]

---

by Peter the Great. In 1825 it had a mixed population of less than thirty thousand, which included Greeks, Germans, Jews, and Armenians, as well as Russians and Ukrainians. Commerce and fishing were the major activities, and until overtaken by Odessa in the first half of the nineteenth century, Taganrog was the principal port in the Black Sea area for the export of grain to western Europe. The town was bombarded and in part destroyed by an Anglo-French fleet in May 1855. "Taganrog," *Encyclopaedia Britannica*, 11th ed., vol. 26, p. 355.

32. *Entsiklopedicheskii slovar'*, vol. 17, no. 33 (St. Petersburg: Brokgauz-Efron, 1896), p. 261.

33. Lakier's career pattern was characteristic of members of his social class. Since the private practice of law did not yet exist in the Russian empire, the only option open to a nobleman lacking independent wealth and trained in law was to pursue a career in government service. Indeed, for landless noblemen such as Lakier the very success of a career in administration depended on education. By the mid-nineteenth century higher education had become "the chief determinant of rank" in the civil service. Walter Pintner, "The Social Characteristics of the Early Nineteenth-Century Russian Bureaucracy," *Slavic Review* 29, no. 3 (September 1970): 441.

34. *Adres-kalendar' ili obshchii shtat rossiiskoi imperii*, 1851, pt. 1, p. 273.

35. Richard Wortman, *The Development of a Russian Legal Consciousness* (Chicago: University of Chicago Press, 1976), p. 88.

36. *O votchinakh i pomest'iakh* (St. Petersburg, 1848).

The book was reviewed in four of the leading journals of the day, from the radical *Sovremennik* [The contemporary] and *Otechest-vennye Zapiski* [Annals of the fatherland] to the more conservative *Moskvitianin* [The Muscovite] and *Zhurnal Ministerstva Narodnogo Prosveshcheniia* [Journal of the Ministry of Education]. The stature accorded the book may be gauged by the fact that the reviewer in *Sovremennik,* K. D. Kavelin, then a well-known professor of civil law at Moscow University, wrote a thirty-six-page review essay.[37] The reviewer in *Moskvitianin* was its publisher, M. P. Pogodin, the noted nationalist historian and journalist, whose essay ran to eighteen pages.[38] While Kavelin and Pogodin were highly critical of Lakier's historical interpretation, they both agreed that the value and significance of his master's essay lay in its rich collection of source materials.

Meanwhile in 1846, two years before the publication of his master's essay, Lakier had become a regular reviewer for the Ministry of Education's *Zhurnal.*[39] Between 1846 and 1856 he annually published one or more lengthy reviews, some running to over seventy pages; the reviews were of a scholarly, critical nature, reflecting Lakier's legal and historical training. The books he reviewed dealt with such topics as Pskovian legal charters, legal manuals, the position of captives in medieval Russian law, the history of financial institutions, and the history of Russian civil law. In the early 1850s Lakier also published a number of shorter historical studies concerning government service in pre-Petrine Russia, Anglo-Russian relations in the sixteenth and seventeenth centuries, and counterfeit coins in the pre-Petrine era.[40] But the work that brought him the greatest

37. *Sovremennik* 10, no. 8, sec. 3 (1848): 57–93.

38. *Moskvitianin* 3, no. 6 (1848): 78–96. The other two reviews were much shorter: *Otechestvennye Zapiski* 59, no. 8, sec. 6 (1848): 59–68; *Zhurnal Ministerstva Narodnogo Prosveshcheniia,* 59, no. 6 (1848): 308.

39. A "formal and pedantic" government periodical, the *Zhurnal* appeared continuously from 1834 to 1905. It contained official orders, regulations, and administrative summaries, as well as specialized, scholarly articles and reviews. Riasanovsky, *Nicholas I and Official Nationality,* pp. 76, 92.

40. *O sluzhbe v Rossii do vremen Petra Velikago* (St. Petersburg, 1850); *Obzor snoshenii mezhdu Anglieiu i Rossieiu v XVI i XVII*

eminence was a two-volume study of Russian heraldry.[41] It quickly became the standard reference in its field in the prerevolutionary period.[42]

Lakier's personal life can be only dimly limned. Never so prominent a writer as to merit a full-scale biography, or even an obituary in any of the leading journals, he was one of those literary figures known to the intelligentsia of his own generation but forgotten or ignored by the next. The paucity of information is further compounded by the fact that Lakier apparently left no personal papers. Moreover, shortly after publishing the account of his American journey, Lakier completely disappeared from public view. From 1859 until his death eleven years later in 1870 at age forty-five, he never published another book, essay, or review. Silence shrouds the last decade of his life, even as it does the first two.

Only for a brief time in his twenties, when he went to St. Petersburg in 1845 to serve in the Ministry of Justice, do we catch glimpses of the man behind the name. Lakier quickly gained entrée to a group of scholars and writers centering around P. A. Pletnev (1792–1865), the rector of St. Petersburg University. Pletnev, a poet, critic, and professor of Russian literature at the university, served as rector from 1840 to 1861.[43] Lakier's introduction probably came through his uncle, Baron F. F. Korf (1803–53), a writer of minor novels and a journal editor, who was a friend of Pletnev.[44] For six years, between 1845 and 1851, Lakier became a frequent visitor at Pletnev's home, where small groups of writers and friends often gathered on Saturday and Sunday evenings. The university rector was impressed with the young civil servant, all the more so when, in the fall of 1845, Lakier,

---

stoletiiakh (St. Petersburg, 1854); *Istoriia poddelki monety do Petra I* (St. Petersburg, 1855).

41. *Russkaia geral'dika,* 2 vols. (St. Petersburg, 1855).

42. Two of the major prerevolutionary encyclopedias stress the importance of *Russkaia geral'dika* in their entries for Lakier. See *Entsiklopedicheskii slovar'*, vol. 17, no. 33, p. 261, and *Russkii biograficheskii slovar'*, vol. 9 (St. Petersburg, 1914), p. 45. For a Soviet acknowledgment of its value, see N. A. Dobroliubov, *Sobranie sochinenii* (Moscow-Leningrad, 1962), vol. 4, p. 458 n.

43. *Entsiklopedicheskii slovar'*, vol. 23A, pp. 874–75.

44. Lakier was a nephew of Korf's wife. K. Ia. Grot, ed., *Perepiska Ia. K. Grota s P. A. Pletnevym,* vol. 1 (St. Petersburg, 1896), p. 587. See also *Entsiklopedicheskii slovar' slovar'*, vol. 16, p. 356.

"despite his indigence," undertook to bring up a poor, eleven-year-old French lad. Such "youthful enthusiasm" made Lakier a "marvelous fellow" in Pletnev's eyes.[45] One may wonder whether Lakier's visits were motivated solely by intellectual considerations, for in January 1851 he married the rector's twenty-year-old daughter.[46] Tragically, Lakier's young wife died in October 1852 after giving birth to a son.[47] Both Lakier and his in-laws were grief-stricken by the loss. The young widower continued working at the Ministry of Justice in St. Petersburg until 1856, when he resigned his position to travel in western Europe, America, and, in 1858, Palestine. After his return to St. Petersburg he taught civil law in a law school for the sons of noblemen, worked on statistical matters in the Ministry of Internal Affairs, and served briefly as an editor on the Commission for the Liberation of the Serfs. In 1859 he married again and moved to Taganrog, the city of his birth, where he died in January 1870.[48]

When Lakier left Russia in 1857 for western Europe and America, he was leaving a homeland whose political and social realities varied sharply from those he had gone to observe. Russia was a land where autocracy and serfdom still held sway; where an educated elite lived worlds apart from an illiterate peasant majority; where an underdeveloped economy stagnated in backwardness and inefficiency; where an entrenched, arrogant, often corrupt bureaucracy monopolized the administrative machinery of government; and where there was no public education for children of all social levels. It was also a land where the judiciary depended completely upon the executive; where in both civil and criminal cases proceedings were secret and inquisitional; where courts and procedures were maddeningly complex and intricate; where the majority of judges were illiterate or almost illiterate; and where bribery among judicial personnel had assumed "monstrous dimensions."[49]

These circumstances of Russian life shaped Lakier's perceptions

45. Grot, *Perepiska,* vol. 2, p. 638.

46. Ibid., vol. 3, pp. 531–32.

47. Ibid., pp. 610–11.

48. G. N. Gennadi, *Spravochnyi slovar' o russkikh pisateliakh i uchenykh* (Berlin, 1876–80), p. 431.

49. Samuel Kucherov, "Administration of Justice under Nicholas I of Russia," *American Slavic and East European Review* 7, no. 2 (April 1948): 125–38.

of America. His perceptions were also influenced by the fact that, while he looked at America through the prism of Russian experience, he did so as a mid-nineteenth-century Russian liberal. His liberal attitudes were probably formed during his student days at Moscow University in the early 1840s, when the juridical faculty contained several dynamic professors who imbued their students with a love and enthusiasm for law born of Hegelian idealism. A contemporary of Lakier has recorded the central idea that inspired them all:

> We learned to see in the state not only an external form, a protector of security, but the highest goal of juridical development, the reali- zation of the principles of freedom and justice in a supreme union, which does not devour individuality, but gives it sufficient expanse, directing it to the common good.[50]

This view of the state as an instrument and initiator of progress characterized all Russian liberals, however much they might have differed in the particulars of their programs. It set them apart from the classical liberals of western Europe, whose faith in social spon- taneity and individual action rested upon the solid reality of a large, energetic, and ambitious middle class. In the absence of any similar social class in their own country, Russian liberals depended upon the state to originate and implement reforms. Chief among those reforms was the abolition of serfdom, which was held to be wrong on moral and practical grounds.[51] Beyond that, Russian liberals looked to re- forms in the educational and judicial systems. When it came to repre- sentative government and a laissez-faire economy, however, not all

50. B. A. Chicherin, *Vospominaniia Borisa Nikolaevicha Chicherina: Moskva sorokovykh godov* (Moscow, 1929), pp. 37–38, as quoted in Wortman, *Development of a Russian Legal Consciousness,* pp. 226–27.

51. Daniel Field, "Kavelin and Russian Liberalism," *Slavic Review* 32, no. 1 (March 1973): 60. When Lakier was a student at Moscow University, these ideas were propounded by K. D. Kavelin, who was professor of civil law from 1844 to 1848 and who wrote the long review in *Sovremennik* of Lakier's master's essay. In 1848 Kavelin left Moscow University for a minor government post in St. Petersburg. His subsequent efforts to rally all educated men behind reform, regardless of their differ- ences in political and philosophical outlook, proved disastrous to his career. See W. Bruce Lincoln, "The Circle of the Grand Duchess Yelena Pavlovna, 1847–61," *Slavonic Review* 48, no. 112 (July 1970): 379–80; also Field, "Kavelin," pp. 62–78.

were convinced of the virtues of these arrangements in a country dominated by the nobility.[52] Lakier himself admired the way the system operated in America—that much is clear from his *Puteshestvie*. What is less clear—in the absence of private papers—is precisely the degree to which he felt the system adaptable to Russian conditions.

Seen against this background, Lakier's *Puteshestvie* provides an intriguing double perspective. On its face it presents a view of antebellum America in 1857; on a more subtle level it offers a distinctively Russian reaction to America. What he chose to tell his Russian readers about American society—indeed what he thought it significant for them to know—was conditioned by the cultural context of both author and audience. That Lakier had a special purpose in writing the *Puteshestvie* is evident in his lament that, while there might be whole libraries of foreign literature about America, in Russian there was "not a single serious essay."[53] His journey to America thus became a mission of enlightenment for himself and for his audience. On the one hand he wished to discover "the core of American democratic equality"; on the other, he hoped Russians might derive useful lessons from "the great experience of the Americans."[54] In light of Lakier's general admiration for the United States, that hope may be read as a statement of liberal purpose. If praise of particular American institutions—slavery excepted—was meant to suggest models worthy of emulation in Russia, then the entire *Puteshestvie* may be thought of as a message for reform in Russia. To be sure, it was a muted message, which exasperated at least one of his liberal critics,[55] for Lakier's vehicle of communication was a huge compendium of information. His two-volume, eight-hundred-page *Puteshestvie* is extremely detailed and highly factual. Judgments and comments on American life and institutions, scattered throughout the work, were never brought together in an overall analytical essay. Readers were left to draw their own conclusions about the core of American democratic equality and the lessons that might be applicable to Russia.

Nevertheless the value of the *Puteshestvie* for Russian contemporaries lay in its having been designed to instruct and inform. Lakier

52. Field, "Kavelin," p. 60.
53. *Puteshestvie,* Preface, p. 2. All references concerning the *Puteshestvie* are to the Russian original.
54. Ibid., p. 2.
55. Dobroliubov, *Sobranie sochinenii,* vol. 4, p. 219.

assumed his audience would be composed mainly of Russians unable to read foreign-language accounts of America. Hence they would be almost totally ignorant of the United States, knowing neither its history and government nor its institutions and people. In that circumstance the *Puteshestvie* had to be as full and complete a source of information as possible because it was likely to remain the only one in Russia for some time. (It turned out that a Russian translation of Tocqueville's *Democracy in America* appeared in 1860, the year following publication of the *Puteshestvie*.) Lakier, true to his didactic purpose, included two chapters, totaling over one hundred pages, on the history of the American colonies and the Constitution of the United States. These chapters have been omitted from this abridged edition, as has a good deal of statistical material and information on groups, such as the Mormons, whom Lakier did not personally visit. In addition, two lengthy chapters describing side trips to Canada and Cuba have been omitted. What has been retained is the essential core—the eyewitness report.

In his quest for information Lakier became the first private Russian to travel widely through most of the United States east of the Mississippi. For five months during the summer, fall, and early winter of 1857 he moved by coastal steamer, railroad, horse-drawn carriage, and river steamboat from the Northeast to the Old Northwest, from the Upper Mississippi to its mouth, and from Florida up along the southeast coast. He visited many of the great and soon-to-be-great cities—Boston, New York, Philadelphia, Pittsburgh, Cincinnati, Louisville, Chicago, St. Louis, Memphis, New Orleans, and Washington. With unquenchable curiosity and energy to match, he asked questions; struck up friendships; got invited to farms, factories, and mines in the North and Midwest, and to plantations in the South. Wherever he went he took copious notes and kept a careful diary. For depth and background he read the works of Tocqueville, Laboulaye, Bancroft, Robertson, and Story, as well as newspapers, magazines, and government reports.[56] He was a meticulous reporter and an informed

56. For Tocqueville's *La Démocratie en Amerique,* Lakier used the translation by Henry Reeve, *Democracy in America,* 4th ed., 2 vols. (New York, 1845). Titles of the other works are: Edouard de Laboulaye, *Histoire politique des États-Unis depuis les premiers essais de colonisation jusqu'à l'adoption de la constitution fédérale, 1620–1789,* vol. 1 (Paris, 1855); George Bancroft, *A History of the United States, from the Dis-*

observer, and strove to provide his readers with as complete a description of American reality as he could. While not always accurate in details, he did succeed in portraying the immense diversity of a vibrant young nation that on the whole he found to be enormously appealing.

The institutions Lakier selected for special emphasis and the ways he reacted to various aspects of American life reveal the nature of his liberalism and the essence of his Russianness. He attached the greatest importance to the American system of constitutional government, with its separation of powers, checks and balances, guarantees of civil liberties, personal freedom, and trial by jury. He saw it as a system that worked exceedingly well in providing peace, order, and freedom for Americans. Indeed the very genius of the Constitution lay in the means by which it successfully reconciled the diversity of the individual states with the need for national unity. As if to impress the idea upon his fellow Russians, he pointedly noted that "a people grow and develop freely only when left to themselves."[57] Yet for all its implicit criticism of autocracy, Lakier's work left unanswered the question of how much of America's experience with constitutional government was adaptable to Russian conditions.

More certain was his oblique but forceful condemnation of Russia's greatest social evil—serfdom. He chose to do so by emphasizing his genuine abhorrence of American slavery, that "hateful ulcer in a free society."[58] Not only did he find slavery a horror on moral grounds, he also saw it as the chief deterrent to economic growth and development in the South. He sought to demonstrate how wasteful and inefficient unfree labor was by unfavorably contrasting conditions in the

---

covery of the American Continent, vol. 1 (Boston, 1834); William Robertson, The History of America, 2 vols. (London, 1777); Joseph Story, A Familiar Exposition of the Constitution of the United States (New York, 1857). Lakier also used the Census of 1850; George Tucker, Progress of the United States in Population and Wealth in Fifty Years, as Exhibited by the Decennial Census (New York, 1843); Edwin Williams, comp., The Statesman's Manual containing the Presidents' messages, inaugural and special, from 1789 to 1851, 4 vols. (New York, 1852); Christopher Morgan, comp., Documentary History of the State of New York, vol. 1 (Albany, 1849); Rules of the School Committee and Regulations of the Public Schools of the City of Boston (Boston, 1857).

57. Puteshestvie, vol. 1, p. 30.
58. Ibid., vol. 2, p. 216.

South with those in the North. In St. Louis he was convinced that, were it not for slavery, the city would prosper "even more than Cincinnati or Chicago."[59] In Maryland and again in Kentucky he commented on the haphazard tilling of plantations as compared to the careful cultivation of farms in Pennsylvania and Ohio. He was appalled by the prodigal use of Negroes and contrasted that with the high productivity of free whites. Serfdom in his own country had sensitized him not only to the perniciousness of bound labor but to the inefficiency of communal agriculture as well. He called attention to the fact that the first settlements in Virginia and New England began to flourish only when the settlers abandoned communal farming and adopted private ownership of land. For him it was an accepted rule that "large estates [tilled by unfree labor] cannot prosper as quickly as small farms cultivated by their owners."[60]

If praise of free farming and condemnation of slavery in America were meant to promote the abolition of serfdom in Russia, a similar ploy to promote reforms was used with respect to other major American institutions. It is no coincidence that trial by jury and public schools, neither of which existed in the Russia of 1857, occupied a good deal of Lakier's attention. He made an effort to observe the courts and the schools in most of the major cities he visited. In his meticulously detailed description of a trial he witnessed in Boston, he was at pains to emphasize the independence of the judiciary and the efficiency, openness, and fairness of trial by jury. This procedure stood in stark contrast to the cumbersome, corrupt, and secretive procedure of the Russian judiciary, which was not independent of but directly subordinate to the government administration. Lakier's training in law and his experience in the Ministry of Justice may explain the special intensity with which he examined and lauded the American court system. It was clearly a model worthy of emulation in Russia.

Lakier's message struck home with his reviewers, all of whom called attention to his description of American legal procedure.[61] The

59. Ibid., p. 204.
60. Ibid., p. 69.
61. *Severnaia Pchela*, vol. 31, February 9, 1859; *Russkii Mir*, vol. 1, no. 11 (1859), pp. 256–60, and no. 12 (1859), pp. 285–87; *Sovremennik*, vol. 3, no. 3 (1859), pp. 25–48; *Otechestvennye Zapiski*, vol. 123, no. 4 (1859), pp. 135–50.

reaction of one reviewer is particularly revealing of the system then prevailing in Russia:

> [In America] no one finds himself in prison unjustly; there are no innocent sufferers. With general publicity of court proceedings and a well-developed sense of citizenship, there can be neither partiality nor malice nor predetermined charges. . . . An American goes to court with faith that he will find justice: one who is innocent does not fear the judge and one who is guilty fears only the law. . . . the judicial process exists for the litigant and . . . all means [are open] for him to utilize it.
>
> Neither the state nor any public institution can make use of special privileges in court; the judge is no partisan of the organ of power. . . .[62]

Equally worthy as a model was the American system of public education. Lakier saw American public schools as instruments for the training of citizens and as inculcators of basic democratic values. "Straight from school," he remarked, "[pupils] bring into real life the principles of democratic freedom and the ideas of self-government which will guide them for the rest of their lives."[63] He was impressed with the fact that, unlike in his native Russia, girls as well as boys attended primary and middle schools, and that in the primary grades they did so together. In visiting several middle schools in Boston he was amazed that the girls knew as much about American history and government as did the boys. "According to our way of thinking," he commented, "this would be unnecessary for women, whose sphere is limited to domestic matters."[64] Russian girls belonging to the gentry and daughters of rich merchant families received their secondary education in exclusive private institutes where, if Gogol can be believed, the main concern was to teach them how to speak French, play the piano, and knit purses.[65]

Wherever he visited public schools, whether in Boston, New York, Philadelphia, or Chicago, Lakier noted that the emphasis was always on training for the practical life. A common grammar-school education

62. *Russkii Mir,* p. 286.
63. *Puteshestvie,* vol. 1, p. 160.
64. Ibid., p. 162.
65. *Dead Souls,* trans. by B. G. Guerney (New York: Holt, Rinehart and Winston, 1961), p. 24.

enabled any young American "to follow a profitable trade or to be elected to office."[66] Lakier stressed the virtues of an educated citizenry to his compatriots in Russia, where primary schooling was virtually nonexistent. His reviewers agreed and one, at least, was fully in accord with the proposition that public education was the basis for civil well-being in America.[67] While the reviewer strongly implied that a comparable condition was highly desirable in Russia, he made no mention of the complexities that had to be faced in transforming serfs into citizens.

American prisons took as much of Lakier's time as did courts and schools, and he made special efforts to visit them in the South as well as in the North. He was particularly interested in the Pennsylvania and Auburn systems, which had already received considerable attention in Europe and Russia.[68] The novel principle that underlay both systems was rehabilitation; incarceration was meant to make penitents of malefactors and through useful work to prepare them for return to society. Here was further evidence, along with public schools, of the "civic-mindedness of Americans."[69] Unlike in Russia, the law in America did not permit exile or corporal punishment. American authorities did not seek vengeance by throwing prisoners into damp, stifling rooms and serving them rotten food. There were no personal insults to prisoners, no binding of the hands, no use of shackles. The purpose of imprisonment was to deprive criminals of the opportunity to harm other citizens and to retrain them to resume useful social roles. It was an appealing model, one in which "America may take pride . . . no less than in its schools."[70]

In the course of his peregrinations Lakier was continually amazed at how quickly and easily he, a foreigner, gained access to public buildings and institutions, whether schools and courts in Boston, prisons and welfare institutions in New York, the Military Academy at West Point or the White House itself in Washington. America was an open society and there was a minimum of red tape. In Russia

66. *Puteshestvie,* vol. 2, p. 34.

67. *Russkii Mir,* p. 258.

68. Blake McKelvey, *American Prisons: A Study in American Social History Prior to 1915* (Montclair, N. J.: Patterson Smith, 1974), pp. 11 and 16; Laserson, *American Impact on Russia,* p. 179.

69. *Russkii Mir,* p. 259.

70. Ibid.

permission always had to be sought from a formidable phalanx of sus-
picious officials and petty bureaucrats, which usually meant either
interminable delays or outright refusals. Lakier recorded not a single
instance of his being denied permission by an American to visit any
public institution he wished.

Lakier's reactions to various aspects of the American national character, while perhaps similar to those of other foreign visitors, were
nevertheless uniquely expressive of a Russian sensibility. The "core
of democratic equality" that he had come to discover was found not in
any single activity but in the ways Americans behaved in particular
situations. Illustrative is his discussion of the difficulties encountered
by New York City residents in their attempts to establish schools for
black children. The New Yorkers finally succeeded but only after
strenuous exertions. It was the manner in which they accomplished
their mission that impressed Lakier. He told his Russian readers that
the New Yorkers acted "privately and through organized societies,
through books distributed to people and through agitation at public
meetings until the noble . . . goal [was achieved]." And in that, he
wrote, lay the "greatness of the American character."[71]

Lakier did not generalize his observation into a principle, as
Tocqueville had done. The Frenchman had pointed out that the true
advantages of democracy were "not in what the public administration
does, but in what is done without it or outside of it. Democracy . . .
produces what the ablest governments are frequently unable to create:
namely, an all-pervading and restless activity, a superabundant force,
and an energy which . . . may, however unfavorable circumstances
may be, produce wonders."[72] In his own way, Lakier, writing some
twenty years later, also perceived voluntaristic action as the inner
dynamic of American society. The history and traditions of his own
country relentlessly militated against any and all forms of social spon-
taneity. Manifestations of individualism were distrusted. For centuries
the only effective public force in Russian society was the state, and
Russians had long since come to think of the state as "the sole agency
responsible for getting things moving."[73] The absence of voluntaristic

71. *Puteshestvie,* vol. 1, p. 229.
72. *Democracy in America* (New York: Knopf, 1945), vol. 1, p. 252.
73. T. H. Von Laue, *Why Lenin? Why Stalin? A Reappraisal of the
Russian Revolution, 1900–1930* (New York: Lippincott, 1964), p. 41.

action in Russia made its operation among Americans all the more striking to Lakier.

Voluntarism was to be seen in the most common occurrences of everyday life in America. Observing how fires were fought in New York City, Lakier noted that ordinary citizens hurried to the scene and pitched in to help the firemen. He commented that "The duty of everyone to run to a fire is incomprehensible to a . . . [Russian]. But in this lies the difference between American society and ours, that no one can, no one must, and no one wants to refuse labor for the common good."[74] One reviewer was convinced that the national character of Americans was best expressed through their mutual cooperation in fighting fires. Conversely, his comment on what Americans did not do on such occasions etched a grim picture of Russian behavior when fires occurred:

> such citizen-firemen do not take it upon themselves to break open cupboards and chests with axes and crowbars for the purpose of filling their pockets or boots with all the valuables they can find; and of course every citizen can easily get to his own burning house if he was absent when the fire started—no sentry's rifle butt forces him to watch from a distance as his property burns. Rarely is there looting and disorder. And although police are on the scene, there is no fracas or fisticuffs, for no American would have carried away a single thing. In a civil matter, citizens themselves manage to keep order without the constant interference that always leads to troubles or paralyzes freedom of action. The police in America are only concerned with disturbances of the public peace, not in appearing beforehand as guardians, which is always an irritant to grown men and arouses their instinctive antagonism.[75]

Labor for a civic cause, however, was not to be confused with communal labor. The American was a determined individualist and neither understood nor approved of the principle whereby "all work for all and no one owns anything." For the American, work was the road to personal success and individual equality: "he achieves independence through work and work alone, and he does not want anyone to stand in the way of his attaining that goal."[76] Lakier was distressed by the

74. *Puteshestvie,* vol. 1, p. 263.
75. *Russkii Mir,* p. 287.
76. *Puteshestvie,* vol. 2, p. 192.

American's constant "running after the golden idol." He acknowledged that America had many poor people but noted that "nowhere
do they strive so for the realization of . . . [self-enrichment] and nowhere do they achieve it more frequently."[77] If Lakier's Russian gentry
sensibilities were sometimes offended by the self-assertiveness of
Americans, coming as he did from a status-conscious society, he nevertheless paid tribute to "the naturalness with which everyone [in
America] thinks he has the right to do as he pleases."[78] However
personally distasteful he sometimes found the spirit of egalitarianism
to be, as when he had to dine at a common table on a Mississippi river
steamboat, still it was "impossible not to submit to the general principle of equality."[79]

The desire for self-improvement and a belief in its attainment
went hand in glove with a pervasive restlessness and optimism among
Americans. In New York City Lakier noted how easily Americans
switched from one job or occupation to another. On a steamboat that
was going down the Ohio from Pittsburgh to Cincinnati he met a
Pennsylvanian who was moving his whole family to the Far West, to
try his luck where land was ten times cheaper and where he hoped
to become a rich farmer. There were no limits to an American's enterprise, Lakier observed. The American "loves his dream as if it were
actuality because he is convinced of its realization."[80] There was no
comparable spirit of individual enterprise and optimism in the serf-
bound society of Russia.

Perhaps the most revealing of Lakier's observations concerned the
role of the police in America. He came from a country where for thirty
years Nicholas I had insisted on strict discipline and order, where
street crowds were always suspect, and where the police kept constant
vigil over any activity deemed potentially dangerous. It is not surprising then that, upon seeing the hustle, bustle, and seeming chaos of the
crowds on Broadway, Lakier asked: "Who keeps order? How does
all this move about and disperse without a word?"[81] His answer was
as simple as it was alien to Russian experience: the American himself
kept order. There were no police in America to maintain quiet and

77. Ibid., vol. 1, p. 211.
78. Ibid., vol. 2, p. 224.
79. Ibid.
80. Ibid., p. 73.
81. Ibid., vol. 1, p. 209.

tranquility. The American, he noted, wanted the police to keep order only so that he and his neighbor were not disturbed. In an open society there was no need for special surveillance of public activities. Preserving the peace was a by-product of individual self-discipline. "The American," he observed, "keeping order himself, sees to it . . . that his neighbor does not disturb the peace either."[82]

In the final analysis, the essence of the American system lay in its being a society of activist citizens. That concept of citizenship was alien to a society dominated by autocracy and serfdom, where all were subjects of the tsar and where obedience to the will of the state was the highest virtue.

The number of literate Russians who knew of Lakier's *Puteshestvie* is difficult to determine. What can be said with certainty is that the work was reviewed in the most widely read journals of the day. *Severnaia Pchela,* [The northern Bee], the most popular daily newspaper in Russia, hailed the book as "new, fresh, and inexpressibly interesting" and praised it not only for providing a "full and true picture of America," but also for allowing the Russian reader to look at the country through Russian eyes and to comprehend it through a Russian mind.[83] It is ironic that such praise appeared in an arch-conservative newspaper whose editors abhorred representative government. Yet *Severnaia Pchela,* despised though it was by the small Russian intelligentsia, had an empire-wide readership that included bureaucrats, military officers, shopkeepers, landowning gentry, literate bourgeois circles, and members of the highest society.[84]

82. Ibid.

83. *Severnaia Pchela,* February 9, 1859.

84. Thomas Louis Koepnick, "The Journalistic Careers of F. V. Bulgarin and N. I. Grech: Publicism and Politics in Tsarist Russia, 1812–1859" (Ph.D. diss., The Ohio State University, 1976), p. 54. A copy of Lakier's *Puteshestvie* was obtained by a rich, self-made merchant named Yudin in the Siberian city of Krasnoyarsk. A fanatical bibliophile, he built up a collection of a hundred thousand volumes, "one of the most remarkable libraries in the Empire" in the late nineteenth century. When Lenin was exiled to Siberia in 1897, he spent two months in Krasnoyarsk and was permitted by Yudin to use the library "practically every day from morning till night." Adam B. Ulam, *The Bolsheviks: The Intellectual and Political History of the Triumph of Communism in Russia* (New York: Collier, 1968), p. 129. There is no evidence that Lenin ever read

Of the liberal and radical literary magazines read by the intelligentsia, the three that carried reviews, *Russkii Mir* [Russian world], *Otechestvennye Zapiski* [Annals of the fatherland], and *Sovremennik* [The contemporary],[85] and especially the latter two, were the most popular "thick journals" in Russia in the late 1850s and 1860s. These "thick journals" played a unique role in the formation of Russian public opinion by spreading throughout the vast empire information and ideas that otherwise might have been confined to Moscow and St. Petersburg.[86] All three journals welcomed the *Puteshestvie* for providing Russians with a wealth of hitherto unavailable practical information on America. They called attention to the prison, judicial, and public school systems, sometimes by means of lengthy excerpts. While *Sovremenik* hoped the *Puteshestvie* would engage the public's sympathy, *Otechestvennye Zapiski* outspokenly declared that "It might be very useful for our pedagogic administrators to borrow from . . . [Lakier's] remarks."[87] In fact the purpose in reviewing the book at all was "to suggest, if not the solution of many social problems, then at least to make a case for pondering them, and Mr. Lakier's book is extremely rich in such information."[88]

The pondering of social problems was pursued in earnest during the late 1850s. Russia's disastrous defeat in the Crimean War had publicly exposed her "social sores,"[89] and the relaxed censorship of Alexander II's first years made it possible to debate them in the press. A movement for reform started to gather momentum. In the spring of 1859 the Editorial Commission began its work of reviewing proposals for the emancipation of the serfs. At the end of the 1850s the

---

the *Puteshestvie.* In 1907 the Library of Congress acquired eighty thousand volumes of the Yudin collection, including the *Puteshestvie.* The only other extant copy in North America is in the Columbia University Library.

85. See n. 61 for full references.

86. Richard Pipes, *Russia under the Old Regime* (New York: Charles Scribner's Sons, 1974), p. 264.

87. *Otechestvennye Zapiski,* p. 143.

88. Ibid., p. 150.

89. Richard Stites, "M. L. Mikhailov and the Emergence of the Woman Question in Russia," *Canadian Slavic Studies,* 3, no. 2 (Summer 1969): 179.

first projects for court reform were advanced.[90] In 1860 a system of secondary schools for women of all classes was established for the first time.[91] Soviet scholars have gone so far as to argue that a "revolutionary situation" existed between 1859 and 1861.[92] While that is an exaggeration, what did exist was an expectant climate of reform, a propitious historical moment for the appearance of the *Puteshestvie*. When Lakier told his readers that, although "one may not love certain particulars in America, . . . one cannot help loving America as a whole or being amazed at what it has that Europe cannot measure up to,"[93] he surely had Russia in mind more than Europe. It is likely that his readers drew the same inference, for in 1859 many Russians felt the opportunity was at hand to try to measure up.

ARNOLD SCHRIER

90. Richard Wortman, "Judicial Personnel and the Court Reform of 1864," *Canadian Slavic Studies* 3, no. 2 (Summer 1969): 228.

91. Stites, "M. L. Mikhailov," p. 181.

92. Charles C. Adler, Jr., "The 'Revolutionary Situation 1859–1861': The Uses of an Historical Conception," *Canadian Slavic Studies* 3, no. 2 (Summer 1969): 383–99.

93. *Puteshestvie*, vol. 1, p. 284.

A Russian Looks at America

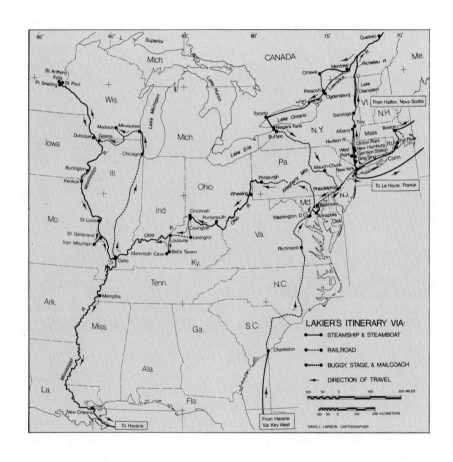

LAKIER'S ITINERARY VIA:

●——● STEAMSHIP & STEAMBOAT

●--●--● RAILROAD

●····●····● BUGGY, STAGE, & MAILCOACH

← DIRECTION OF TRAVEL

100 50 0   100   200 MILES

100 50 0   100   200 KILOMETERS

DAVID L. LAWSON, CARTOGRAPHER

Preface

Having begun my journey through America from Boston, where I arrived from Europe in 1857, I traveled through the eastern states of the North American Union, moved through the central states, and ended up at New Orleans by way of the Mississippi. From there I went to have a look at Cuba, returned to North America and finished my travels with a stay in Washington. That, with the addition of Canada, briefly encompasses those parts of the New World whose description I offer to Russian readers.

Excerpts from my travel sketches already published in magazines have indicated the point of view from which I looked at the countries described.[1] Here I should add that my main concern was to study the institutions and to acquaint myself with the internal way of life of one particular country, the United States. With this concern in mind I went deep into the interior of the country, lived on plantations and farms, and talked with Americans. Personal observation served as my principal source of information. At the same time I could not overlook newspapers as well as certain official and private sources, although my rule was always to describe only what I saw and could ascertain on the spot.

The exception I made was in presenting the history of the colonies, the North American states and their war with England, and, finally, a general account of the advantages and significance of the contemporary American Constitution.[2] Such a digression from what was stated

1. In 1858 Lakier published six articles based on his travels in North America and Cuba. Two were descriptions of New York and one was a description of Congress in 1857. The other three dealt with Cuba and Canada. All were incorporated virtually verbatim as separate chapters in his two-volume *Puteshestvie*.

2. For published works on America used by Lakier, see Introduction, n. 56.

above is explained by my desire to express just once what otherwise would have had to be repeated in various places. Then too, the subject itself is so important and so little known to us that an insufficiently detailed examination of the Constitution of the North American Union, in an essay whose main purpose is to acquaint readers with that country's institutions, could quite justifiably be considered a serious shortcoming.

In any case, if the "Journey" has no other virtue, it will remain as our first description of a young and sparsely populated country that has much in common with Russia and that has many interesting features. In foreign literature, whole libraries have been written about America, its history, geography, laws, and institutions. Our literature can display not a single serious essay about the New World. A closer acquaintance with it will be both engaging and useful.

A. L.

I

Voyage to America

At last, I thought to myself standing on the deck of the steamship *Europa* in Liverpool, I will get to see the land I have wanted to see for so long. To travel in America had long been the object of my dreams. Nevertheless it was perfectly natural for my fellow countrymen seeing me off to ask: Why was I going across the ocean? Was this trip simply the result of curiosity? If so, was it worth the inconvenience, expense and dangers that—even under favorable circumstances—accompany a twelve-day ocean voyage? Couldn't my curiosity be satisfied by reading the travel accounts of others? My questioners did not in the least dispute my point that the country I planned to visit was of extraordinary interest; they agreed that they were ready to follow my example. But still I had not clearly explained why I was going. I saw that I could not talk my way out of it with generalities such as wanting to see how the Yankees live, how they use their freedom to shoot each other with revolvers, or how they get rich. As we stood on the broad Mersey waiting for the tide, I was able briefly to develop for them my thoughts and reasons.

I could not say that I was crossing the ocean on a commercial venture, or to open new lands, or to establish colonies in the Far West; nor was I particularly interested in the vegetation of a land little known to us. Although any one of these purposes would be a perfectly sufficient reason for leaving the Old World for a time, nonetheless all of them, I maintained, had to be subordinated to one overall goal: to answer for myself the question of how this youngest member in the family of humankind had managed to leave its older brothers so far behind in trade, shipping, and general productive activity. Why was it that the North American States were already serving as a model for Europe when from the first existence of America to the present day only a century and a half had elapsed? What promise did the future hold for this enterprising country? What could we derive for our own benefit and edification from the great experience represented by America, a country with which relations—if not yet begun because of the distance involved—would in time, one could foresee, assume enormous dimensions across the Pacific Ocean?[1] And how in that period of time had the American Union arrived at its institutions? How were they working out? Where was the core of that democratic equality which is quite incomprehensible to a European? Even after a visit to England these issues remained unresolved for me. Meanwhile history was clearly saying that America was predestined to give its people those institutions toward which Europe had been striving but had been unable to attain. Of course the settlers who had gone to the New World belonged to that same race which peopled the northern and central regions of Europe, a race which had always stood in the vanguard of humanity's movement toward enlightenment, moral development, and material advancement. But the way forward on the old continent was not always easy. On the contrary, there were historical obstacles from the past, a past which had allowed many attitudes and relations to become so complicated that one had no choice but to renounce his own past and transfer activity onto new soil, to a country not yet begun, where each living thought could take root unhindered and could bear fruit. The land was uncultivated but rich, and nature herself meant for the plowman, with his work, his steadfastness and patience, to extract her buried treasures from the soil.

Whether or not this notion was true—at the time of my departure from Europe it was still only a theoretical assumption—will have to be shown by my essays on the North American States. At that time, at any rate, America seemed to me a distant shining point which would shed light on much that neither Europe's past nor its present could explain to a searching, inquiring mind.

The arrival of the English post in a small steamboat was the signal

1. Lakier may have borrowed this idea from Alexander Herzen, who, writing in 1858 and observing Russia's eastward expansion across Siberia and America's westward expansion to California, thought that the major link in trade relations between the two nations was destined to be the Pacific Ocean, "the Mediterranean of the future." As quoted in Alexander Kucherov, "Alexander Herzen's Parallel between the United States and Russia," in John Shelton Curtiss, ed., *Essays in Russian and Soviet History in Honor of Geroid Tanquary Robinson* (New York: Columbia University Press, 1963), p. 36.

for the imminent departure of our big one, which was making ready to sail across the ocean after who knows how many times before. Like an impatient, spirited horse, our steamship waited for that moment when the reins would be loosed and, tireless creature that it was, it would be free for a full ten days. The captain's mate took a full hour and a half with the bags, trunks, bundles, stacks of newspapers, letters, and packages. What a pile! And all this had accumulated in three, four days, or maybe even less. England as well as the American States uses every voyage of a steamer for transporting dispatches, letters, and packages. The Bremen, Le Havre, Hamburg, and Southampton lines all transport mail, but the line to which the *Europa* belongs has a special government contract to carry mail. The ship is called a "Mail-steamer," a circumstance from which the passengers gain a great deal of security. It is maintained better than others, the captain is more careful, and consequently one travels with less risk. The steamship was indeed huge and excellently constructed: comfort, cleanliness, and luxury were visible everywhere. As luck would have it, there was a young American on board who was returning home. My compatriots introduced me to him and he promised to guide this novice through the new realm where fate was taking me. After a preliminary inspection of the ship, it turned out that all two hundred berths in the first class were taken. But one had nothing to fear about the well-being of the passengers during the crossing, not after seeing the enormous stocks of vegetables, fish, and meat, and hearing at every turn the bleating of sheep, the bellowing of oxen, and the cackling of the most varied poultry, chickens, and turkeys, all waiting their turn to feed the huge company. A milch cow stood quietly chewing its cud in the place of honor on the deck, apparently as accustomed to a sea voyage as a herd of sheep are to the whistle of a locomotive in the populous counties of England.

We were still in the harbor, the English postal official in a red coat was still counting out the packages and parcels, when my new acquaintance, Mr. M., took me to the dining room located in a special arbor on deck, and explained to me that it was necessary to reserve a place for dinner for the entire period of the journey, that later they would all be taken and it would be impossible to get one. I decided to follow his example. My guide was a native of Ireland who had already crossed the ocean more than once to set up business in New Orleans on the southern Mississippi. Home for him was New Orleans, but in

order to avoid the danger of yellow fever, which ravages the southern
United States every summer, and at the same time be able to strengthen
commercial contacts with the continent, Mr. M. crossed the ocean
every year. He was as used to a steamship as to his own office. His
Irish origin was already obscured by a compulsive and constant demand
for activity, by which one could take him for a pure Yankee. But then,
he had a kind, cheerful disposition and a ready laugh. Mr. M. called
himself an American because he had been in the States for more than
two years and had become a naturalized American citizen.[2]

I wholeheartedly thanked the Russians, whom I left in Liverpool,
for introducing me to this guide, who, indeed, did me more than one
service during my journey through the United States. Another bow,
another last word of farewell, another wave of the handkerchief, and
then for some days we were out of sight of land. Now, when all this
is past, I have no wish to recount the grim thought I had about what
might happen on the way, or to recall the fear that crept into my
heart when from all sides—especially in the first days of the voyage—
stories flew around about recent misfortunes on one or another steamship and when gasps and cries were the signs of oncoming sickness.
The waves played with the ship at their will and it seemed that one
more splash and the fragile shell in which were entrusted the lives of
hundreds of people, of whole families, might fantastically. . . . But
one gets used to everything and soon life on the steamship became
more varied and tolerable. The dividing points of the day were breakfast, lunch, and dinner—for which we took as much time as possible so
that there would be less time for getting bored. In the intervals some
passengers strolled on the deck, some sat and played chess or cards, and
some had a passion for books and used the ship's well-stocked library.

For the most part our shipboard society consisted of Americans.
But what is an American? Could this word convey any notion of the
character of a people, as for example the names French, Russian, or
German do? My cabin mate, who was by birth a German and who
spoke English badly, called himself an American from Chicago. I
not jokingly said to him that in my opinion an American was either an
original native, whom the whites inappropriately called an Indian,

2. Lakier erroneously assumes that only two years of residence were
required to apply for citizenship. This was true only between 1790 and
1795. In 1795 the period of residence was raised to five years.

or a European offspring born in the New World. But no! No one
relinquishes the honorable name "American" and everyone in calling
himself a son of America values the rights from which he profits as an
independent and free citizen. But then, can a person be blamed for
preferring a name that is both dear and advantageous to him? This
drive to become an American citizen explains why American society
presents such a confusion of various levels of education, ideas, and
opinions—a situation, of course, not found in any other nationality.
And what was even more noticeable on the steamship was that all are
as one, that no differences divide society into fossilized strata, that all
consider themselves equal in social rights and consequently no one
expects to be deferred to in accordance with his honors, service, or
wealth. In his own circle each person will have his place but in society
all are equal; everyone has the right, neither more nor less than that of
his fellows, to be respected. In this jumble a poor worker will sometimes express himself as forthrightly and independently on a topic of
prime importance as will a venerable and learned fellow citizen, and
there would be no greater insult for an American than to interrupt him
with the remark that his discourse was beyond his competence and
understanding. Can one get used to this jumble? Can this mishmash
be agreeable to a person who has carried over from Europe well-
established notions about caste and distinctions? That remains a
question, but the fact is that each person is equal to every other in his
right to discuss and interpret. There are no people inferior to others,
there are only the rich and the poor, and the latter serve the former
until they themselves become rich. In Europe there are differences
from the cradle to the grave, and there are some boundaries one
cannot even think of crossing. In America those obstacles do not exist
and will not, at least not for a long time.

As happens always and everywhere, on the steamship, too, circles
were formed of people similar in upbringing and views. But the mutual "Good morning, sir!" "Very fine day, sir!" was long heard in
the morning on the deck, in the dining room, and in the corridors.
Sometimes a whole conversation consisted only of these greetings,
but as a result of that same basic principle of equality these fixed
phrases were uttered without fail to everyone.

Citizens from both the northern and southern American states were
to be found aboard the *Europa,* and their interminable arguments over
slavery were all the more heated since the daughters of [Harriet]

Beecher Stowe, author of *Uncle Tom's Cabin,* were traveling with us.[3] While the slaveowners of the southern states could not indifferently pass by a daughter of the woman who in *Uncle Tom* portrays what plantation owners do to the Negroes belonging to them, the abolitionists, the Yankees—inhabitants of the northern states—respected the daughters for the gifted talent of their mother. Even on board ship, as everywhere else, this live issue was the apple of discord, but the majority was for the suppression of slavery. Since we were still on the high seas, the southerners had to yield. But as always those on both sides clung to their own opinions and found it impossible to retreat from them without feeling personally threatened.

The monotony of life aboard ship was broken by the changing of sleeping places from cabin to deck, necessitated more or less by bad health conditions. I passed the time studying maps of America. On board were several Americans who for various reasons and at various times had traveled through the United States. Thanks to their guidance I was able while still on the ship to decide what itinerary to follow and where to stop off. Americans trying to persuade a European not to be daunted by distance do not like to admit that the Mississippi is far from Boston, or New Orleans from St. Louis, although these places are more than two thousand miles [sic] from each other. "Well," one of them told me, "you should have seen how they traveled in the old days when there were no steamboats or railroads, and here and there in the forest you could see log cabins that the first pioneers built and covered with twigs and leaves; you crawled over plank roads in an antediluvian stagecoach pulled by a pair of nags or, what was still worse, you had to make your way on horseback over long distances. What then passed for roads! Now things are different: you can travel easily, comfortably, and rapidly. Railroads serve everyone's needs and you can travel day and night. And isn't it ingenious that merchants can come out from New York to Chicago to transact business in person with farmers in the Far West? That's why all the trains are always full, why companies are making profits, and why the whole Union is covered by rails."[4] My companion spoke even

3. The publication of *Uncle Tom's Cabin* in 1852 gained Harriet Beecher Stowe (1811–96) an international reputation.

4. By the end of the 1850s the United States had thirty thousand miles of railway track; Russia had less than eight hundred miles. Railroad con-

more glowingly of steamboats, and there was no end to his praise.

This information was important to me because I could consider seeing all or at least the major American states, risking nothing except injury or even perhaps my life. But then, where isn't one exposed to danger?

Toward evening, if illness spared us and people were in a pleasant mood, songs and games would begin and the dining room was turned into a salon where everyone amused himself as best he could. Of course, the most interesting conversations always revolved around how many more miles it would be to the Newfoundland Banks, followed by arguments and bets about when we would arrive, as if somehow this could really push us on more quickly. Encountering a ship was an event that drew everyone up on deck; whistles blew, signals sounded . . . in a word, after voyaging for days every one of us turned into a sailor, forgetting that there was another element besides water. Since the weather was reasonably calm for nearly the whole trip, almost everyone felt fairly good. In general our voyage across the ocean left no bad impressions.

On Sundays all other books were put away except bibles, missals, and prayer books. Cards, chess, and other games were banned as unworthy amusements and immediately after breakfast the captain in full-dress uniform took his place in the center of the dining room. The seamen who were not on watch entered the hall and took their places. The service began with prayer, to which the congregants responded. But even after prayers a large part of the day was spent in reading Holy Scripture. The silence that reigned on the ship was the kind that could be found on Sundays in any populous city in England or North America.

On the ninth day we began to approach the shores of Newfoundland, and although there were still more than twenty-four hours to Halifax, our place of debarkation, the joy on every face was, I imagined, the kind experienced by Christopher Columbus upon seeing the New World for the first time. One of the passengers had his home here, another had come to meet his family, a third had in

---

struction did not become a permanent feature of the Russian economy until 1860. Edward Ames, "A Century of Russian Railroad Construction, 1837–1936," *American Slavic and East European Review* 6, nos. 18–19 (December 1947): 58–59.

mind a profitable money-making operation, and for everyone the end of the voyage was the culmination of anxious expectation. No wonder the whole ship was on its feet, despite the fact that it was in the wee hours of the morning when we began to enter the deep harbor of Halifax, the main city of Nova Scotia, which is one of the English provinces in North America.

Approaching the town, we saw how the gas lamps were beginning to light up the sleepy streets and how the customshouse and post office were being opened. The captain announced that we could go ashore but that in two hours we would get under way. We used the time to satisfy our urge to stand on solid ground, we wandered about the streets, we even climbed a cliff with a fortress on it. In general we could ascertain in the semidarkness only that the city served as the chief fortification for English holdings in America and that there were many ships in the port of Halifax, one of the most convenient and best protected against winds and storms. Why there were forts scattered around the entire bay and why the Halifax fortress was guarded so carefully is easily explained by England's fear that, if she ever again engaged in hostilities with America, the closest of the states would turn against this neighboring possession of Great Britain to strike a blow at its rival.

Leaving the city at daybreak, we were able to make out its advantageous and beautiful location. A large number of houses in the lower commercial section are of wood but there are also huge government buildings of stone. There are many of those here since the central administration of Nova Scotia is concentrated in Halifax. The main building, the so-called province building, contains the chambers of the provincial parliament, the supreme court, various government departments, and the public library of the city. The church steeples of various denominations and styles and the general coloring of this city, which in no way differed from those in any small town in England, automatically carried one's thoughts back to the Old World on the other side of the ocean. It was only black people who were startling, at least to the eyes of one not used to seeing colored skin. Incidentally, an American from the United States does not at all include an Englishman from Nova Scotia, Newfoundland, or New Brunswick in the category of Americans. Here, says an American from New York, on different soil and in a different latitude, lives England, that same old England in contradistinction to which the nearby North American states called themselves New England.

The trip from Halifax to Boston, which was our ship's destination, was relatively short, and after only twelve days' sailing from Europe we saw the heights that form the entrance to Boston Bay. Behind them soon appeared Boston itself, the capital of Massachusetts. It serves if not as the governmental then as the moral center for the northern states, known by the general name of New England. Its influence on the destiny and organization of the entire Union of North American States has been extremely important. It was in Boston where the ideas were conceived that then spread to all the states, were enthusiastically accepted everywhere, and were adapted to national life.

Different climates in the two halves of the North American continent could not but have an influence on the character of their inhabitants. In the northern half, where the climate is cold and severe and where there are great forests extending almost from one end of the continent to the other with alternating stony or rocky areas, the people are industrious, sober-minded, venturesome, and enterprising. In the southern half, protected by mountains from the north wind, the land is luxuriant, the vegetation is lush, and the climate pampers and weakens people. Instead of the feverish activity of the New England Yankee who never knows rest and always wants work and business, there is indolence, delicacy, and backwardness. While I do not in the least mean to excuse the Negro system here, which is repulsive to godly and human law, one more readily understands its existence in the southern than in the northern states. Although in the latter slavery has already long since ceased to exist, it is still holding its ground in the former and will do so for a long time to come. Thus, for all the unity of the political system, there are points of dissension between the two halves of the American Union which cannot be resolved.

2

Boston

An argument over the advantages of Boston harbor versus New York harbor divided the passengers of the steamship *Europa* long before it entered Boston harbor. Of those who knew both, some took the side of New England and others defended the Empire City. I could only listen attentively to the arguments of both sides. Each passionately defended his birthplace or place of residence as only Americans can, sparing neither witticisms, ridicule, nor sharp words. Bostonians were accused of being dull Yankees, New Yorkers of sacrificing the rules of honor and conscience in their passion for the dollar. This obviously was totally unrelated to defending the advantages of the port, but the disputants were carried away by provincial rivalry and each wanted to prove to the other not that his origins were better or his status higher but that his city had done more to promote the development of the American people and their activities and had taken a greater part in defending the fatherland. . . . A worthy contest! This argument spread like fire across the whole deck of the ship, and God knows how it would have ended, if we had not then entered the straits between the deserted islands at the entrance to the port of Boston.

The islands, covered with greenery, were like emeralds emerging from the waters of the Atlantic that reflected the hot summer sky of America. Here and there fortifications were visible, remains from the War of Independence. Now they appeared to be deserted and unprotected, or at least one could not make out any soldiers or cannon on them. And why should there be? An invasion could possibly be feared only from the English, but Americans are convinced that that will not happen. Existing commercial ties between them are too close, and the damage that would be inflicted on a city such as Boston or

New York would bring on bankruptcy not only in America but perhaps even more so in England.

During the war with England, Boston benefited from the batteries built on the islands scattered around the port, fortifications which prevented ships from entering the harbor. Now, however, these islands have huge wharves and piers for ships sailing here from all countries of the world. I was amazed at how the sea had carved out thousands of bays and coves in the shoreline, and man has made use of every one of them. Everywhere there is commercial activity, everywhere piers extend far out in the water. On one island a huge hospital towers up, on another a large school building, on a third a lighthouse, and as soon as one enters the port one feels himself among a commercial and enterprising people that knows no fatigue and needs no rest. I was especially confused by the steam ferries that glided across the quiet bay: white in color, they were distinctive in their shape and construction compared to those I had seen previously. The rocker shaft of the engine was thrust up far higher than the highest deck or, more correctly, than the superstructure on it. Two levers of the rocker shaft, like two gigantic arms, worked tirelessly and the little boat went about its business, flying from island to island. For me this was all new, and my companion on the trip had not forewarned me of such marvels.

Finally the steamship's last joyous whistle rang out and the passengers disembarked. I am sure that if none of us wished immediately to repeat the twelve-day ocean voyage, many did not want to part so quickly with acquaintances and fellow travelers. But then, everyone was forced to stay in Boston for two days. The next day was Sunday, a day of rest for people, steamships, locomotives, horses, and even the streets they rode on, and no earlier than Saturday evening was it to be hoped that we and our baggage would pass through customs. Exhortations to look after my things, not to lose sight of them, were incessantly repeated by the experienced Mr. M., and I saw how everyone dragged his belongings together however and wherever he could. A Negro on the embankment yelled out "massa," which is how he pronounced the word "mister," and pointed at his back to indicate he was a porter. Coachmen were already on the ship trying to seize novices, but I was repeatedly told to remain deaf and cold-blooded to all entreaties. I promised to obey but it soon turned out that that was easier said than done.

Meanwhile the ship drew close to a wooden scaffold on which a steam engine had been fitted, and within ten minutes everything was pulled onto dry land and transferred to customs. The official at the customshouse had already inspected the suitcases, placed white chalk crosses on the lids and carried them out, when my friend, who was indeed quick and adroit, "very smart" as the Americans say, tracked me down while I was still waiting for my things to be pulled out of the hold. He managed to tell me in passing about the experience of one of our fellow passengers, a Frenchman who, not knowing English and thinking that, as in France, he had to present his passport, sought out a gendarme or *commissaire de police.* When he met instead with general laughter, he became angry. I, too, laughed, not foreseeing the grief that would come to a person unused to local customs, or to one who would not heed what his guides told him.

While I was waiting, my things had already been transferred to customs, and there I found one of my suitcases. Assured there was nothing forbidden inside, the official scribbled a St. Andrew's cross on it and the matter was over without any difficulty. But the other suitcase could not be found. Whom do you ask? There was no ticket for it, no kind of proof, indeed no one who was responsible for it. As to your questions, anyone can answer by asking why you yourself were not watching your luggage. Perhaps, I thought, it had been taken off at Halifax, where several passengers had disembarked, and I requested that a telegram be sent there. They wired, the answer was no, and they took two dollars from me. They "consoled" me with the fact that in a free land such as America, as I could see from my own experience, a European's way of thinking was invalid: having the key in my pocket gave no grounds for hoping that my uninspected suitcase could not leave customs and be carried off by just anyone. Adding to my misfortunes was the fact that my New Orleans acquaintance was already gone; he had long since left for the city to reserve rooms for us at a hotel.

It was already getting dark when the carriage of the hotel where I wished to stay left customs. What was on my mind could be guessed by anyone who has ever in his life experienced a similar incident. In the four-seater carriage or large coach, somewhat larger than our carriages, there were three benches: two along the walls of the carriage and a third in the middle. In all there were places for squeezing in nine people. It was pitiful to see the ladies suffering with their bags, bundles, boxes, and other unavoidable trifles. Constrained in

body and soul, and all this in free America! I thought to myself as
we rode from distant East Boston to Boston proper. I was ready to
put the whole blame on anyone except myself, but there was no escaping the fact that I alone was at fault, and I told myself to be quicker
and more attentive in the future. That's how the nation here was
formed: if a guardian or watchman had stood over each person, if
it had been possible to trust that someone else would weigh and
evaluate every action and would as a last resort deliver one from
injury and ruin, if, I say, the people had not been constantly left to
themselves, to their own mistakes and virtues, could this active, independent, and self-reliant nation have been formed, a nation that
labors always and everywhere, a nation that, guided by its lucky star
and its own strengths, will not be afraid to go to the end of the world
and that will always get what it wants? "Go to the wilderness of the
American Far West," my traveling companion told me in the evening,
"and you will find them cutting down forests and clearing a road for
rails. Think about the other side of the world: who is raising the ships
from the bottom of Sevastopol Bay, who is found along the shores
of Africa, who is on the Amur?[1] Ask and you will see that it is almost
always the American mechanic, merchant, and seaman. Oh the Yankee
is *very smart,* cunning and energetic, and it is not likely that the European will become like him. After all, what is there in the Old World
to meet the challenge of his youthful courage?"

Our coach with its passengers seated within and baggage lashed
on top crossed the bay on a steam ferry. It was already dark when we
rode onto the streets filled with noisy people, brightly lit signs, stores,
various saloons, theaters, and establishments. At last we were at the

1. In 1857–58 an American company using undersea divers was engaged in raising Russian ships sunk in Sevastopol Bay during the Crimean
War. *Harper's Weekly,* January 9, 1858, p. 20. Small brigs and schooners
from Salem, Massachusetts, traded along the west coast of Africa in the
1850s, bartering rum, gunpowder, tobacco, cottons, wooden clocks, and
brass pans for ivory, gold dust, palm oil, and peanuts. S. E. Morison, *The
Maritime History of Massachusetts, 1783–1860* (Boston: Houghton
Mifflin, 1921), p. 221. An American named Perry Collins descended the
entire length of the Amur River in the summer of 1857, seeking to assess
the region's trade potential for the United States. Perry M'D. Collins,
"Explorations of the Amoor River," *Harper's Magazine* 17, no. 97 (June
1858): 221–32.

hotel. My savior, the New Orleanian, acted as if he were at home here and had a room ready for me. The porch and lobby were crowded with people. Americans were sitting like statues, quiet and motionless. Some, lost in thought, rocked silently, waiting, breathing in the fresh evening air, completely oblivious to everything going on around them, to the new arrivals fussing, searching, unpacking. . . . Amid all this my New Orleans friend heard the story of my suitcase. "What was in it?" Books, a suit, notes, and a travel journal, I replied. I thought he would cry out about the loss of such valuables but instead his response was a cold-blooded *"Nothing at all! It can all be bought again."* He uttered it so quickly that I wasn't able to say anything in defense of my manuscript journal, which he also included among the items that are commonly bought and sold. "Where was your money? You didn't lose that too, did you? No? Well then it's *all right,* everything's in order!" Nevertheless when we had rested a bit we thought of ways to search for the lost item. We obtained the help of an attorney known to my friend but he concluded that there was not even a probability of finding the lost suitcase. How and where could we make inquiries at all the hotels? Nor could we hope that a "driver," the coachman who transports luggage and passengers, had noticed my suitcase, which was no different from all the others. Moreover, tomorrow was Sunday and no driver in Boston would want to be bothered with trying to remember what happened yesterday. I had to forget about the suitcase and I must confess I had lost all hope of ever seeing it again when (to conclude quickly the tale of my ill-fated loss) on Monday evening I was idly looking out the hotel entrance at how they were tying down suitcases to the top of a carriage about to set out for God knows what part of the United States. "Stop!" I instinctively called out, when I saw my lost suitcase in a Negro's black hands. To prove it was my suitcase was simple: my name was on it and I had the key. But no one even asked for proof. The Negro found the two men in whose room my suitcase had been. The men, saying "Beg pardon, Sir," handed it over to me and casually explained that after having become acquainted on the ship they took a single room at the hotel. And up to the moment when the real owner of the suitcase turned up, each had thought it belonged to the other. There was nothing implausible in this story, given the haste with which everything is done in this country, especially during departures and arrivals of travelers. I would have been happy with any explanation to regain what I had given up for lost. I imagined how my suitcase might have wandered had I gone out the entrance two or three minutes later, or had I gone searching for it among the hotels. It was under the same roof as I, waiting humbly for its owner, and did not betray him at the final moment of parting.

"Very lucky!" my American kept repeating as I told him about the find. Perhaps he was annoyed that the lesson turned out so cheaply for a European, or perhaps he thought that I would soon forget it. But I could assure him of the opposite: once burned, twice warned. This event stuck in my memory throughout the entire visit in America, and I never again forgot or lost my suitcases.

II

The day after my arrival in Boston I was left completely free to become acquainted, if not with the inhabitants, who could only be seen going to and coming from church, or with the Bostonians' style of life, which dies on Sundays, then at least with the American House, the hotel in which I was staying. It was based completely on the American plan. That plan is distinguished from the European not merely in name or some insignificant features. It is a different system altogether. American hotels are such a distinctive type, they reflect so much of the American, that there is hardly a place where one might become more closely acquainted with his character and aspirations. In Paris there is the quasi-American Hôtel du Louvre but it least of all provides any understanding of real American hotels. There is a similarity in terms of the grandeur and magnificence of the Paris hotel. But the innumerable bureaus, the paper-shuffling between offices, and the multitude of servants that in essence are superfluous, though in reality are necessary so that the complicated and intricate administrative machinery does not come to a halt—all these inconveniences are piled on in the Paris hotel because such are the requirements of the country and the tastes of its inhabitants. In Europe they think the more forms there are, the more complicated the administration is, and the more checks and inspections there are, the fewer are the deceits and the abuses. The American thinks just the opposite: he feels that the less complicated, the cheaper, and the less distrustful the administration, the fewer the deceits and the more honest the man. Generally pettiness, stinginess, and fussiness are far removed from the American. He likes to do everything on a large scale, to demand round numbers, to be as brief as possible with words, and to make haste in business. If someone becomes expansive and drags things out, or asks a great many questions, listen to his speech and make sure he is not a German or a Frenchman.

You enter the hotel and silently sign your name in the guest book. Next to your name they silently write the number of the room you will occupy, and silently hand the key to a Negro. He by innate talkativeness interrupts the silence, takes the traveling bags and guides you to the assigned room. There is no appeal if the room is too expensive. It means the other rooms are taken or are reserved for ladies who may yet arrive and who necessarily get the best accommodations. No matter when you arrive the room is ready, and there is nothing more for the Negro to do in it. In winter the room is heated by steam, in summer it is ventilated. If it is in the sun, the jalousies are lowered. It is evident that careful hands worked on the arrangement of these rooms where the occupants change daily. Rules are attached to the door for the guidance of the guests. These rules do not contain the repetitious phrases *it is forbidden, it is required, it is requested* pertaining to various matters. Instead they contain a daily schedule giving the hours for breakfast, lunch, dinner, tea, and supper, and, finally, inform one that the total cost for a one-room lodging, including the room, maid service, a bath, and illumination, is two and a half dollars per guest. That is not much compared to the three silver rubles twenty-five kopeks in our country, especially considering that you are taken care of for the whole day.[2] The hotel owner, of course, loses nothing in these rates, otherwise he would not bother to build this huge palace and decorate it lavishly. Everyone knows beforehand what expenses he will encounter. Only wine is kept on a separate account.

A gas jet hangs from the ceiling of every room and you can light it any hour of the day or night. No one controls how much or when to burn it. Everyone knows what he needs and is free to use as much as he wants. In precisely the same way, there is running water in every room. You turn on the faucet and enjoy the benefit of clean, clear, fresh water. Multiply the consumption of gas and water by a thousand guests, not considering the servants, to say nothing of the lobbies, parlors, and men's and ladies' rooms on various floors, and

2. In 1857 the rate of exchange was $1 = 1 ruble 30 kopeks silver. There are 100 kopeks in a ruble.

you come up with not inconsiderable expenditures. But they are
absorbed by a great number of users, a fact that becomes even clearer
when one considers how many guests stay at the hotel daily. For
clarity I should indicate that people travel a great deal in America.
Hotels throughout the Union, from the poorest in small towns of the
Far West to the richest in New York or New Orleans, vary in their
magnificence, size, wealth of conveniences, and price, but they answer
the tastes and needs of Americans to such a degree that in essence they
are the same.

The morning begins with breakfast at eight o'clock. On his way to
the dining room everyone considers it his duty to buy a morning paper.
Papers here are sold by young boys, with the indulgence of the servants
and the hotel owners. Depending on the party to which an American
belongs, he selects a paper and finds time, while the food is being
served, to read the news of interest to him in the area of politics and
in the financial and commercial world, to consider what he should
buy and sell and generally what would be profitable for him. Meanwhile he has already been given a breakfast menu prepared that same
morning. This contains roast meats, fish, and a whole list of dishes
which would be about right for a good dinner. Depending upon the
selection, he can order coffee, green or black tea, chocolate or milk;
and whatever bread he wants, wheat, rice, or corn; various fruitcakes,
toast (i.e., toasted bread), and, strangest of all, our Shrovetide pancakes.[3] They are liked so much that they are served to everyone even
if not requested. After such a breakfast it seems one could wait for
dinner, but at midday there is a second breakfast ("lunch") of cold
food; then from three to six is dinner, which, as everywhere, is the
meal that most of all reflects the character of the cuisine. What kind
of cuisine do they have in the United States? It, too, has been influenced by the mingling of various ethnic elements in America.
French cooking is too refined for a population that has so many
English in it, and English cooking is too plain. I do not speak of the
private homes of the wealthy, where French cooking prevails. In the
hotel where I stayed dinner was a display of cooking from every con-
ceivable nation. There were soups, fish, roast beef, and sauces of the

3. Lakier uses the Russian word *bliny,* which are thin flat cakes of
light batter cooked in a pan. Orthodox Russians eat them on the Sunday
before the beginning of Lent.

most varied names, preparations, and compositions. There were salads, roasts, pastries, and fruits. It was difficult to think of something that would not have been on the dinner menu or on the table. Portions were unlimited, measured only by one's own appetite. It is a shame that I cannot list here the complete "bills of fare," or menus. These are large sheets printed especially for dinner, and on the reverse side are various useful advertisements and notices. Tea is at seven o'clock and again there are cold cuts. Finally from nine to midnight is supper, so that the dining room is always lit and the tables are almost always covered.

But how is it all controlled? Who is a hotel guest and who is a stranger? To sort them out would be difficult and would require that documents be shown and questions be asked. Therefore whoever wants to take advantage of the hotel's largesse would find nothing simpler, though I was assured that this seldom happens. All the other rooms of the hotel, however, are at the disposal of any American. The newspaper reading room is open; it is a warm room where one can read and rest. But the Americans' favorite place is what we call the front or Swiss room, an especially large room arranged with couches, chairs, and rocking chairs along the walls. The most important business is conducted and settled here: who is to be elected to what office, whom to vote for, and what positions to support. Here is where companies are organized, friends are introduced, acquaintanceships started up. And since the entrance is from the street, it is open to all Americans. After dinner there is a whole bazaar here. Youngsters burst in with the evening papers, together with flower sellers, peddlers of various knick-knacks, and sometimes musicians. There is also a side door to the barroom where whiskey, wine, and various soft drinks are sold. The most common and frequently asked question among Americans is: will you have something to drink? They repeat it at any suitable occasion, out of courtesy, upon closing a profitable deal, or to celebrate, and to refuse would be an insult. For ten cents they give you a glass with ice, place before you granulated sugar and a bottle of whiskey, gin, or wine. You pour as much as you like—they don't bother with that trifle. In summertime the guests are offered various soft drinks, soda water, and sherry cobblers (made of sherry and ice), and when the barroom is open it is always filled with guests. Eventually the lobby and barroom get crowded, stuffy, and hot. An American who wants to rest or feels a need to ponder and reflect

A Russian Looks at America

Boston, from East Boston, 1857

"I was especially confused by the
steam ferries that glided across the
quiet bay. . . . For me this was all new,
and my companion on the trip had not
forewarned me of such marvels."
(p. 15)

Illustrated London News,
January 9, 1858

The Boston Common, 1858

"... after dinner he took me to the so-called 'Common,' a public park which is the Bostonians' pride and joy and where they love to stroll. There are shady walks, a great fountain, and places for strollers to rest." (p. 29)

Harper's Weekly, May 22, 1858

The Emerson School for Girls, ca. 1850

"In one of the girls' schools [in Boston] I chanced upon a history lesson. . . . The girls freely answered the purely governmental questions as if they had been trained for political office. . . . According to our [Russian] way of thinking this would be unnecessary for women, whose sphere is limited to domestic matters. But in America women are looked upon differently." (pp. 40–41)

The Metropolitan Museum of Art, Gift of I. N. Phelps Stokes, Edward S. Hawes, Alice Mary Hawes, Marion Augusta Hawes, 1937

The St. Nicholas Hotel on Broadway, 1855

"I chose the most American hotel, the one most American in style and preferred by Americans themselves over the others in New York. It was even bigger and more luxurious than the one in Boston. . . ." (p. 63)

Museum of the City of New York

Broadway Crowd, 1870

"Despite the wide sidewalks, the
crush is so great that one cannot
take a step without poking someone
with elbows or body. . . . Who keeps
order? How does all this move about
and disperse without a word?"
(p. 66)

Library of Congress

Launching of the *General-Admiral,*
the Largest Wooden Ship in the
World, September 21, 1858

"I will never forget how I was among
those invited to the keel-laying of this
enormous steamship, heard a Russian
prayer read on foreign soil by a fellow
Russian officer, and how . . . I
expressed a wish to see this new
warrior in our waters." (p. 82)

Harper's Weekly, October 2, 1858

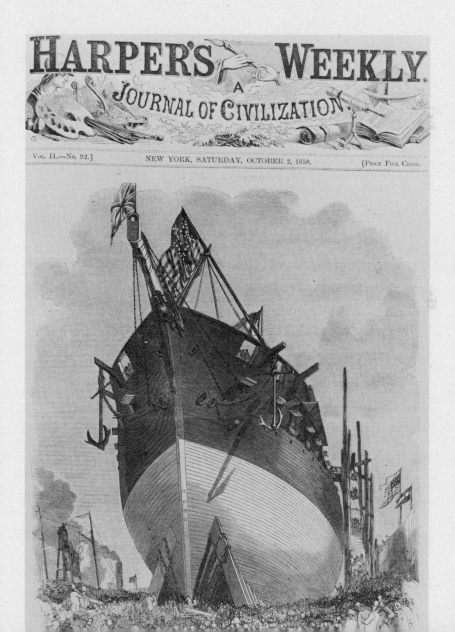

HARPER'S WEEKLY.

A JOURNAL OF CIVILIZATION.

VOL. II.—No. 92.]   NEW YORK, SATURDAY, OCTOBER 2, 1858.   [PRICE FIVE CENTS.

Triennial Parade of New York City Fire Department, Broadway, 1856

"... when the anniversary of its founding comes, [a fire-fighting company] takes advantage of the occasion to dress up in red fire-jackets, to take hoses, hooks, ladders, and buckets, and to parade down Broadway past the decorated balconies and houses to the accompaniment of music, fireworks, and happy, thankful shouts from the people." (p. 86)

Frank Leslie's Illustrated Weekly, October 25, 1856

Female Workshop, Sing Sing Prison, 1854

"Americans have managed to make the work of criminals productive for the criminals.... [and for] the country, compelling them to produce whatever is generally needed and required." (p. 100)

Gleason's Pictorial Drawing Room Companion, October 21, 1854

West Point Military Academy, 1856

"... my eyes had somehow grown unaccustomed to military uniforms and glittering epaulettes, which one sees neither on the street nor in society, and I looked with curiosity upon military braid and buttons I had not seen for such a long time." (p. 103)

I. N. Phelps Stokes Collection, Prints Division, New York Public Library, Astor, Lenox and Tilden Foundations

Crossing the Alleghenies on the Pennsylvania Railroad, 1853

"For the most part the train headed through the valleys, and, where it could not escape the inclines, the cars were pulled to the top by means of chains attached to several engines positioned in various places on the mountain." (p. 115)

Gleason's Pictorial Drawing Room Companion, October 22, 1853

Quakeresses at Friends Meeting,
Philadelphia

"[In Philadelphia] one continually
encounters the Quakers' ever-present
black wool hats, their long, peculiarly
cut black frock-coats, and the old-style
attire of their wives and daughters;
moreover, the predominant type of
face remains one constantly sunk in
serious thought." (pp. 120–21)

Westtown School, Pennsylvania

Girard College, Philadelphia

"Girard College . . . is an excellent example of a Greek marble temple and . . . were it not for the fact that every column represents the sighs and tears of those orphans who will not get an education because of the money thrown away on ornamentation, the Greek Corinthian-style temple would be appropriate." (p. 129)

J. T. Scharf and T. Westcott, *History of Philadelphia,* 3: 1945.

A Midnight Race on the Mississippi, 1860

"Despite the dangers of navigating these changeable rivers and despite the constant encounters with other steamboats, the captain never refused to sail at night. . . . The trouble comes when another steamboat wants to pass: the captain never refuses a race with a rival." (p. 141)

Inland Rivers Library, Cincinnati Public Library

Alexander B. Latta's Second Steam
Fire Engine, "Citizens' Gift," Built
in 1854

". . . a steam engine flew by
harnessed to four strong horses, the
engine belching dense clouds of
smoke and leaving a trail of hot
embers on the roadway. I did not
know what it was." (p. 153)

The Cincinnati Historical Society

*Alexander B. Latta, an inventor of
genius and a volunteer fireman
himself, successfully designed the
world's first steam fire engine,
which could outperform six of the
old hand-pumpers. (Oil of Latta in
the Smithsonian Institution)*

Fighting a Fire in Cincinnati with
Steam Fire Engines, 1858

"As soon as the machine stopped, the
horses were unharnessed and the hose
was connected to the water reservoir;
instead of by human hands, the water
was pumped by steam. An enormous
stream of water soon appeared. . . ."
(p. 153)

Harper's Weekly, October 30, 1858

Bloody Affair in the Courthouse at
Hawesville, Kentucky, 1859

". . . after seeing a revolver in his
belt, [I asked the Kentuckian] why
it was impossible to manage without
firearms here. [He replied:] 'The
slightest offence, disagreement, or
caustic remark leads to a fight or a
revolver. When something is to be
judged here, we do it ourselves
through lynching. It's quicker and
more effective.' " (pp. 161–62)

Frank Leslie's Illustrated Newspaper,
March 19, 1859

Illinois Land Sale Advertisement

"To make the [Illinois Central Railroad Company's] lands as attractive as possible, their virtues and advantages are described in detail [in the free brochure]." (p. 172)

ILLINOIS CENTRAL RAILROAD COMPANY
OFFER FOR SALE
ONE MILLION ACRES OF SUPERIOR FARMING LANDS,
IN FARMS OF
40, 80 & 160 acres and upwards at from $8 to $12 per acre.
THESE LANDS ARE
NOT SURPASSED BY ANY IN THE WORLD.
THEY LIE ALONG
THE WHOLE LINE OF THE CENTRAL ILLINOIS RAILROAD,
For Sale on LONG CREDIT, SHORT CREDIT and for CASH, they are situated near TOWNS, VILLAGES, SCHOOLS and CHURCHES.

For all Purposes of Agriculture.
The lands offered for sale by the Illinois Central Railroad Company are equal to any in the world. A healthy climate, a rich soil, and railroads to convey to market the fulness of the earth—all combine to place in the hands of the enterprising workingman the means of independence.

Illinois.
Extending 380 miles from North to South, has all the diversity of climate to be found between Massachusetts and Virginia, and varieties of soil adapted to the products of New England and those of the Middle States. The black soil in the central portions of the State is the richest known, and produces the finest corn, wheat, sorghum and hay, which latter crop, during the past year, has been highly remunerative. The seeding of these prairie lands to tame grasses, for pasturage, offers to farmers with capital the most profitable results. The smaller prairies, interspersed with timber, in the more southern portion of the State, produce the best of winter wheat, tobacco, flax, hemp and fruit. The lands still further South are heavily timbered, and here the raising of fruit, tobacco, cotton and the manufacture of lumber yield large returns. The health of Illinois is hardly surpassed by any State in the Union.

Grain and Stock Raising.
In the list of corn and wheat producing States, Illinois stands pre-eminently first. Its advantages for raising cattle and hogs are too well known to require comment here. For sheep raising, the lands in every part of the State are well adapted, and Illinois can now boast of many of the largest flocks in the country. No branch in industry offers greater inducements for investment.

Hemp, Flax and Tobacco.
Hemp and flax can be produced of as good quality as any grown in Europe. Tobacco of the finest quality is raised upon lands purchased of this Company, and it promises to be one of the most important crops of the State. Cotton, too, is raised, to a considerable extent, in the southern portion. The making of sugar from the beet is receiving considerable attention, and experiments upon a large scale have been made during the past season. The cultivation of sorghum is rapidly increasing, and there are numerous indications that ere many years Illinois will produce a large surplus of sugar and molasses for exportation.

Fruit.
The central and southern parts of the State are peculiarly adapted to fruit raising; and peaches, pears and strawberries, together with early vegetables, are sent to Chicago, St. Louis and Cincinnati, as well as other markets, and always command a ready sale.

Coal and Minerals.
The immense coal deposits of Illinois are worked at different points near the Railroad, and the great resources of the State in iron, lead, zinc, limestone, potters' clay, &c., &c., as yet barely touched, will eventually be the source of great wealth.

To Actual Settlers
the inducements offered are so great that the Company has already sold 1,500,000 acres, and the sales during the past year have been to a larger number of purchasers than ever before. The advantages to a man of small means, settling in Illinois, where his children may grow up with all the benefits of education and the best of public schools, can hardly be over-estimated. No State in the Union is increasing more rapidly in population, which has trebled in ten years along the line of this Railroad.

PRICES AND TERMS OF PAYMENT.
The price of land varies from $7 to $12 and upward per acre, and they are sold on long credit, on short credit, or for cash. A deduction of ten per cent. from the long credit price is made to those who make a payment of one-fourth of the principal down, and the balance in one, two, and three years. A deduction of twenty per cent. is made to those who purchase for cash. Never before have greater inducements been offered to cash purchasers.

EXAMPLE.
Forty acres at $10 per acre on long credit, interest at six per cent., payable annually in advance; the principal in four, five, six, and seven years.

Stephen Bishop, the Guide at
Mammoth Cave in the 1850s

"Mr. Bell recommended that we take
with us the Negro Stephen, who . . . .
is known to everyone for his knowledge of the caves." (p. 166)

Horace C. Hovey, *Celebrated American Caverns* (Cincinnati: Robert
Clarke Co., 1896), p. 59.

House-moving in Chicago, 1859

"You continually see houses here
being moved from one place to
another.... [House-movers] lift a
house with all its furniture, stove, and
utensils from its original place, put
it on a kind of sledge, lay rollers
underneath, and move it over planks
to the new place." (pp. 175–76)

Chicago Historical Society

CHICAGO ADVERTISEMENTS.   xi

J. S. McINTIRE,

HOUSE RAISER & MOVER

Has unequaled Apparatus for the above Purpose.

Grain Elevators in Chicago, 1866

". . . more than 18 million bushels of grain were brought to the Chicago market during 1857 . . . and all of this huge mass of grain is going to compete with our [Russian] wheat in European markets. . . . In Buffalo I had been struck by the huge wooden structures used for grain storage. In Chicago they are even more colossal, usually five stories high." (p. 179)

The Library of Congress

A Sioux Encampment, Upper Mississippi, 1858

"These accounts by a [half-breed Indian agent] who was well acquainted with the way of life of his forebears were extremely absorbing, especially since he promised to show me the Indians in their native dwellings at St. Paul where they were coming to meet him." (p. 196)

Illustrated London News, April 10, 1858

Thresher Powered by Sweep Horse-power, 1855

"America is particularly proud of its agricultural machines. . . . I saw a threshing machine in an open field threshing grain and pouring it into sacks. In one day that machine with eight horses and six men can harvest up to six hundred bushels of grain. . . . Because of these machines the price of grain in America is kept low." (pp. 186–88)

The J. I. Case Company

Big Eagle, A Sioux of the Fort
Snelling Region, 1830s

"I was particularly delighted when
[a Sioux] Indian ... boarded our
steamboat for St. Paul. . . . His face
and arms were painted in a most
fearsome way. . . . For a long time I
peered at the markings. . . . I must
confess that I tried in vain to get at
their meaning and significance. . . ."
(pp. 197–98)

George Catlin, *The Manners,
Customs, and Condition of the North
American Indians* (London, 1841),
1 : 134.

Sioux Medicine Bags (g), 1830s

"On the belt of the young Sioux was
fastened a snake skin which ... the
Indian would let me look at only with
great reluctance. He accorded it some
kind of special respect and honor.
That, explained [the Indian agent],
is the Indian's talisman, which he
guards with his life." (p. 200)

George Catlin, *The Manners,
Customs, and Condition of the North
American Indians* (London, 1841),
1:38.

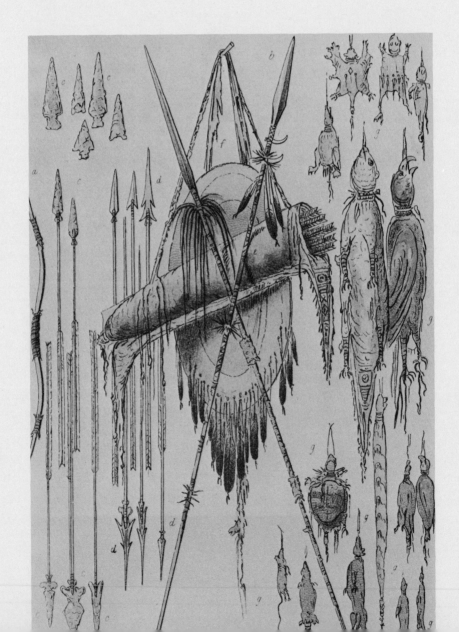

Fort Snelling, Upper Mississippi,
1858

"Fort Snelling was close to the place
where we had met the Indian chiefs.
... [it] was built about forty years
ago when all of Minnesota was
Indian territory and it was impossible
even to foresee a time when the
impassable forests and limitless
plains would be ceded to whites for
settlement." (p. 203)

Illustrated London News, April 10,
1858

A Planter's Home and Sugar
Plantation on the Mississippi, 1852

"The planter's house . . . was almost
always visible from the steamboat. . . .
Behind [the house] is a series of low
squat little houses for the Negroes
who comprise the planter's wealth
and enable him to wallow in luxury
and comfort." (p. 228)

*Gleason's Pictorial Drawing Room
Companion,* May 8, 1852

The Levee, or Landing, at St. Louis,
1857
". . . it is amazing that hundreds of
steamboats arrive here and are strung
out along a three-mile-long levee."
(p. 207)
Missouri Historical Society

Sale of Estates, Pictures, and Slaves
in the Rotunda of the St. Louis Hotel,
New Orleans, 1857

"I thought . . . I would attend these
auctions more often, but they so
revolted my soul that I did not go
back again." (p. 241)

The Historic New Orleans
Collection

Presentation of Pawnees, Poncas, and Potawatomies to the President of the United States, at the White House, January 1858

"... plenipotentiaries from the Pawnee, Ponca, and Potawatomie had arrived in Washington. With all my heart I wished that these poor people ... be satisfied in their expectations and petitions." (pp. 255–56)

Illustrated London News, February 13, 1858

The White House, 1855

"There are neither doorkeepers nor
glittering liveries, and if you were to
enter the White House by mistake, not
knowing who lived there, it would be
difficult not to think it was a middle-
class home." (p. 254)

*Ballou's Pictorial Drawing Room
Companion,* March 17, 1855

takes his chair out onto the hotel porch, calmly places his feet on the railing or a nearby chair, or rests them on a pillar, unconcerned about showing the soles of his boots to passersby. But the picture of an American hotel would not be complete if some attention were not paid to the fashion stores for ladies, the hairdressers for men who are fussy about their appearance, and the other stores that spring up in a hotel lobby as if in some lively Paris arcade.

An American hotel is a whole world, but managing it is easy and uncomplicated. Behind the desk in the lobby stands a gentleman who keeps a book on all arrivals. He knows who is at the hotel and who has left. To keep accounts is simple: multiply the number of days by two and a half dollars and add the price for wines and any special bills and tickets that have the user's signature and room number. Moreover each one of the thousand rooms in the hotel is connected to the front office by a telegraph, and consequently there isn't an intolerable and incessant ringing of bells for servants. Since it would be difficult for a servant to run to all six floors of the hotel every time someone needs him, the manager lets him know through a speaking tube the floor and the room number requesting service. It takes but a moment for the servant to appear and to satisfy your wish. The organization is a model of simplicity and attentiveness. You can get whatever you request at any hour of the night and it is all done promptly. Here is an example: in the evening you place your linens outside the door of your room and in the morning you find them washed and ironed—thanks again to the use of steam. It is with steam that one cooks in the kitchen, cleans the building, and washes and irons the linens. Wherever possible, human hands are replaced by a power that works tirelessly and runs with uniform diligence. Indeed it is difficult to point to an activity where steam or machines in general are not employed. If machines are not used, it means there is no possibility of doing so.

Bookkeeping in America is generally reduced to extreme simplicity, though all precautions are taken so that the owner of a business does not lose by its simplicity. The word "checks," in the sense of reckonings, bills, or counters, is heard everywhere. Let us say you go to breakfast in a restaurant and order two or three dishes. In other countries, in order to present the bill, a piece of paper with the name of the establishment is required; it is then necessary to dip pen in ink, write down the entire addition, sign it, acknowledge the receipt, etc.

In America you are given a little printed ticket with the price of your order designated on it; as you eat more, the figure is increased. At the restaurant's exit you hand your check to the cashier, pay as many dollars or cents as it written on it, and the matter is finished. On railroads, in banks—everywhere—there are printed checks; Americans abhor needless writing and copying.

III

Along with the others I too went to church on Sunday. I do not know whether it was obvious that I was of another country and faith or whether such actions are typical in America, but I had not taken ten steps when, out of a group of women walking toward me, one came forward and handed me a rolled up piece of paper with something printed on it. I was certainly not expecting any such message, as I was busy reflecting on the independence of women walking alone, without escorts, and looking as boldly at the men as the men looked at them. What, I thought, did this female messenger want of me? She was well dressed, her features were delicate and not bad at all. The young girl did not have the appearance of a suppliant; on the contrary, everything about her suggested she was not one of the poor. Automatically I took the paper from her hand and, while I looked at her face, she turned and went on her way. I unfolded the paper and saw that there were several printed sheets on the necessity of observing the Sabbath. Very well, I thought, and placing the Sunday exhortation in my pocket, I continued on my way to Old South Church. I had been told a lot about its antiquity and style. Again I met a girl and I thought that this one at least would not want to give me a lesson on how to conduct myself on Sundays. Imagine my surprise when even she could not pass me by without slipping a brochure on temperance into my hand. This exhortation on temperance was absolutely unnecessary and I would have been ready to return the philanthropic gift to the young straw-hatted Bostonian had I had a chance to catch up with her bold stride before she disappeared into the crowd. No, I thought, I will not take any more brochures on anything, and I turned into the First Methodist Church. The congregation was already seated and singing a melodious hymn. All were sitting decorously and quietly. Once having entered, one had to be seated and listen to the entire service, which included singing all the prescribed hymns and then ended with a sermon. Here, as in England, to interrupt the dead silence would be against the custom of the country. The church was full of people. The men had substituted round black hats for their daily large-brimmed gray ones. They were not carelessly dressed, as was customary on weekdays, but rather had their hair combed, wore black tailcoats, and sat with great solemnity. The women were dressed neatly and cleanly, although not ostentatiously, their eyes fixed on the preacher, heads inclined toward their prayer books, and even if they raised their heads, their hats covered their faces.

When I returned to the hotel carrying with me a free spiritual library, I was afraid that my American, with whom I had arranged to have dinner, would not want to talk about Sunday. But I steered the conversation to spiritual subjects and edifying books. I gave him the brochures the young girls had handed me and asked him to explain the reason and purpose for the generous distribution. He assumed the solemn American pose that a son of the New World adopts in thinking over an important matter or settling upon an absolute truth. I had found my American on the porch of American House, rocking on a chair near the pillars, with his boots on the back of another chair. "Of course the Boston girl realized that you were a stranger," said my companion. "Probably from the way you looked at her hat or maybe from the way you watched her walking, she guessed that you were not going to church for prayer at all. And on this day, Sunday, a Puritan girl wants to be all for God and in God, and she immediately reminds anyone who interrupts her tranquility that one does not be-have that way and gives him a book for his edification."

"Yes, I saw only how the young girls were walking alone, without any escorts, mothers, brothers, or fathers. My European eyes were not admiring their hats or ankles, particularly since neither struck me as anything special, but rather what to a visitor from Europe is simply the fantastic freedom of the woman, her independent gait, and on the other hand the politeness and courtesy with which she is treated by men. At any rate, on whose behalf are those brochures printed with which Americans are so lavish, who composes them?"

"Well," said my friend with a particular American intonation, "do you know what a Puritan is? There was a time when he was hounded in Europe and, believing that his was the true explanation of Holy Scripture, he fled to this wilderness to escape the influence of England and to praise God in his own way. Down to the present day he, as everyone else, considers piety, moderation, sobriety, and morality as necessary for the people's good and for the well-being of the institutions he supports as his own personal creation. It would pay to have a chat with a Bostonian some time about New Yorkers, and better yet about the people in New Orleans who defend slavery. You can then confirm for yourself the opinion he has of anyone who does not observe Sunday so strictly and does not talk so much about religion as he does."

I saw that we were embarked upon a real Sunday conversation, so I drew my chair a bit closer to that of my American friend. And although I was simply unable to find room for my feet the way he did, I began to listen attentively to his talk.

"A Bostonian," continued the American from New Orleans, "is a strange individual. He is still an Englishman in America. His governor is addressed as 'Your Excellency,' as if he were still living in London. For all of his good qualities, industriousness, and determination, the Yankee is not an American. In his house and in the streets it is still England. Smoke a cigar on the street and you pay a fine. The Yankee is straightlaced and certainly no friend of freedom. He is a slave of public opinion and custom, and, despite the fact that old England did more harm to New England than to any other part of the American colonies, he has no objection to emulating it in attitudes and customs. It is strange that down to the present day the constitution of the state of Massachusetts compels each one of its officials to take an oath renouncing submission and obedience to the British government,* as if the former bond between colony and mother country were still in existence."

I remembered that the Puritan who fled England brought with him across the ocean his intolerance for other faiths. Not knowing to what faiths the many churches scattered all over Boston belonged, I asked my companion about it. On the way to America I had frequently heard Americans of various parties and political persuasions say that an American generally has access to all the most abstract questions about the conditions and way of life of his country; that being well informed about the state where he lives and works, he is also equally acquainted with the other sections of the Union because information about them is quickly disseminated through hundreds of organs—newspapers, travel books, acts of the legislative assemblies, etc. And indeed, the

* "I renounce and abjure all allegiance, subjection and obedience to the King, Queen or Government of Great Britain." [Footnote in original.]

question about churches in Boston troubled my companion as little as if I had asked him about the New Orleans cotton presses, or the Negroes on his plantation.

"Once," replied Mr. M., "Massachusetts in its Puritan exclusiveness and zeal to spread the teachings it considered the purest, drove out everyone who was not a Puritan. As a consequence, those who were persecuted separated from the main colony and today it is they who comprise the totality of New England. Obviously those separations could only weaken Massachusetts, but later, when unlimited freedom of religion was declared, the other smaller states grouped themselves around Boston as a center. At the present time Boston is the American Athens, governing public opinion for all New England. As for religion, everyone can freely maintain whatever faith he considers most suitable and in accordance with his own convictions and understanding, provided that the adherents behave peacefully. It follows that each sect must provide its own pastors and teachers, and usually in the unpopulated areas and newly created settlements the matter is managed even more simply and cheaply. A clergyman wishing either to spread the existing faith or introduce the people to a different interpretation of Holy Scripture, builds a church either with stockholders or with the help of his followers. He tries to gather his parishioners around the church: he sets up a Sunday school, teaches the children free of charge, and attracts attention through his sermons. In the free hours when the church is not used for divine service, it becomes a hall for concerts and public lectures. And there is nothing at all reprehensible if the preacher or teacher becomes convinced that his views are not quite just, if he substitutes new ones, and if his brethren follow him."

"Consequently there must be as many sects as teachers?"

"That is just about the case. In Boston alone there are more than one hundred religious sects and congregations.[4] They get their names from the founder of the sect or from its principal distinguish-

4. In 1870 there were over two hundred churches in Boston representing some twenty-five different religious denominations. If one takes into account variations among the many churches of the same denomination (e.g., Baptist, Congregationalist, Methodist, Unitarian, Episcopalian, and Universalist), a claim of "more than one hundred religious sects and congregations" is not unreasonable. A comparable situation existed in 1857. Oscar Handlin, *Boston's Immigrants: A Study in Acculturation,* rev. and enl. ed. (Cambridge, Mass.: Harvard University Press, 1959), p. 263.

ing dogma. Citizens have the same freedom in religious matters as they do in private life. The governor of a state, for example, is only required to declare himself a Christian, no more. Each independent sect, sometimes only slightly different from the other with which it is closely tied, has its own periodical publication and tries to spread its ideas by distributing brochures and pamphlets among the people. These publications are written either by the pastors themselves or by one of the parishioners. It is not surprising that a European should be struck by the variety of religious faiths, sects, and teachings, their churches, parishes, and mentors, and the printing and distribution to the public of edifying brochures. But we consider it useful to have freedom of religion," concluded the American, "because, as a result, no one has imposed on him beliefs and ideas he does not agree with. A doctrine that is not good will fall of its own accord, it will merit general distrust. The proof of that is the Mormons: the government did nothing to weaken their doctrine and what happened? The Mormons were chased out by the people themselves. The church in which they thought to gather all mankind is now a pile of rubble, and they must seek escape from persecution in the far plains and deserts. The government wanted only that the sect, in occupying territory, recognize the higher authority of the Union; it was the people who persecuted the Morman polygamists![5] But then, read over those pages the generous Boston girl gave you today and you will find much that will be of use to you."

[Lakier quotes at length from the pamphlet dealing with Sunday observance and describes the strict Puritan blue laws.]

Impose similar demands on any people in matters of conscience and morality, I thought to myself, and there would be objections and complaints, but a people who have imposed these constraints on themselves readily submit to them. Free in law, the Puritan is a slave to custom and public opinion. While not tolerating government interference in the administration of community, city, and state as a whole, he does not exclude it from participation in domestic, everyday affairs.

[Lakier recounts the exhortations of the second pamphlet for moderation and temperance.]

5. The "pile of rubble" was the Mormon Temple ruins in Nauvoo, Illinois. The Mormons established a new community on the shores of Great Salt Lake in 1847.

Although at present Bostonians in their civil laws are not so strict in matters concerning morals as they once were, nevertheless, a certain severity remains stamped on their faces and a kind of taciturnity and abstemiousness is evident in their whole behavior. An American thinks precisely of that kind of person when calling someone a "Yankee" or "Yankeelike."

It is obvious that under those conditions the New England legislatures could not be inattentive to laziness, idleness, and the use of hard liquor. Long before the state of Maine raised the banner against rum, gin, and whiskey, and long before the so-called antiliquor law, the law and public opinion in Boston punished anyone who gave himself up to drunkenness. As early as the seventeenth century each foreigner entering a Boston hotel was watched by a person who had no other duty but this. He attached himself to the foreigner without any invitation, and as soon as the overseer for sobriety felt that the guest had had enough to drink, he could refuse to allow the guest another drop of spirits.

I saved the brochure on temperance as a memento of unadulterated Puritan literature. The life and speech of the Puritan are also distinguished by the same severe style and the same brevity and dryness.

"It turns out that one can learn the character of Bostonians much better on Sunday than on any other day, when their activities are the same as those of people in other American cities," I said to the American from New Orleans as I sat next to him at dinner. "Of course," was his answer. "On Sundays the Yankees are in their element. After a full century they are the same Puritans who disembarked at New Plymouth," and as proof he promised to show me the Puritan Sunday public prayer. Indeed after dinner he took me to the so-called "Common," a public park which is the Bostonians' pride and joy and where they love to stroll. There are shady walks, a great fountain, and places for strollers to rest. The main attraction is a huge elm, the so-called liberty tree. More than a hundred years old and witness to the first debates on independence, this tree is preserved by the Bostonians as holy, as a precious monument of the past. This historical elm will long serve to remind Boston of the significance it attained in word and deed in the War of Independence. In appearance the elm is still young, its thick foliage spreads out over one hundred feet and its lower trunk has a circumference of up to twenty feet. But at present no herald of liberty, no protector of autonomy and independence preached under it, only a young clergyman who expounded on the psalms. In the intervals between prayers there reverberated the melancholy sounds of hymns. No great imagination was needed to be carried back in one's mind to the time when the Puritans first hailed the New World as their new native land.

The sermon continued until it got dark. It is one of the ways to attract people away from idleness and boredom on Sundays—a kind of Sunday school for adults.

IV

The next day my American was preparing to leave Boston for New Orleans, but he went to the trouble of seeing to it that I should have a guide during my stay in New England and until I visited his city. Whoever has not experienced the courtesy of an American can have no idea of how obligingly he both recommends you to someone else and accepts another's recommendations. This is perhaps due not to any excessive kindness of heart, nor can it be due to advantages anticipated from a relationship with a person who has no financial transactions and who straightaway reveals that he has no special business and has not come for trade. Rather this courtesy is understandable in a person who wishes that the province he lives in, the city he was born in, and the country he belongs to be well learned by a foreigner. Moreover an American is convinced that there is no country on earth more perfect than the United States in terms of its government and institutions, and he readily reveals to everyone whatever he thinks will be of interest. The American loves the Russian, for whom he predicts a great future and whom he wants to amaze with his own wealth, rapid growth, and present-day riches.

The next morning we set off for the public park where we had been the evening before. It was now a crowded street or square; young and old Yankees were walking through it in all directions. Since it was still early, we met a whole crowd of happy youngsters running to school with books under their arms. My companion suggested I would enjoy visiting the educational institutions and he promised to acquaint me with a young lawyer who was in charge of a municipal school district.

Meanwhile we headed for the capitol, where the senators and representatives of the people meet. The capitol stands on a hill, with pediment directly facing the Common, and is distinguished by a majestic cupola. It resembles all the other capitols in the North American states and is one of the finest buildings in Boston. Since the legislative assembly was not in session, it was possible to see the chambers. There is nothing unique about them; portraits of Washington are the only adornments. His statue stands in the rotunda at the entrance to the capitol. It was put up by his comrades in the Great War of Independence and, though it is said to have cost $15,000, it is not in any way remarkable. Generally in America you quickly find out the length and width of facades, the number, weight, and size of the pillars, as well as the price of buildings, monuments, and refinements. An American who shows you around a building will quickly mention all these details. From his point of view a description without them is impossible; moreover, it would be both incomplete and unworthy of the precise American mind.

Having entered the lobby, I began to look for someone, a doorkeeper, a guard, to take me up into the cupola. But my American burst out laughing, and saying "Come on!" took me to the top. From here it was actually easy to view the entire city and the surrounding islands. When the Puritan immigrants arrived here, my comrade told me, they found the Indian name for this place was "Shaumut," which means "living springs." But three sharply protruding rises in that hilly cape persuaded them to change the name to "Tremont" ("three hills"), which has remained the nickname for old Boston. The three hills were easy to make out. We stood on one and the others were beside it. From the cupola there was a vivid scene of irregular streets seething with people, of Boston squares, church steeples and the columns of public buildings, and of the wharves and activities in the harbor. One recalls with amazement that in the seventeenth century, on the cape where the city is now situated, there still lived only one white man, John Blackstone, and that [John] Winthrop, who was to become governor of the colony of Massachusetts, had not yet crossed over to Boston from Charleston, lying opposite the cape. Land was then so cheap that in 1635 Blackstone sold his Boston cape rights to the expanding town for thirty pounds sterling and moved south to Rhode Island.[6] Today it is another matter. Boston, so named because of

6. In the early nineteenth century "Shawmut," the Indian name for the tadpole-shaped peninsula which was the site of Old Boston, was thought to mean "fountains of living water" or "springs." More recently the term has been translated as "where there is a going by boat," or cross-

the many immigrants from Boston in England, has grown into a great city. Although in 1790 the population was no more than eighteen thousand people, it has now grown to one hundred fifty thousand, that is, it has multiplied eight times in some seventy years.

From the cupola it was easy to discern that a small neck connects the peninsula containing Old Boston with Roxbury to the south. Large embankments and bridges lead to Charleston, and to East and South Boston, with steam ferries, horses, and railroads going off in all directions. The ferry system amazed me. Nowhere in Europe have I seen anything like it, not even in England itself. I can imagine if the Americans owned the Bosphorus, across which people are transported on frail craft, how they would organize steam ferries to cross it! They are on every river and lake in the United States. The deck of a tall steam ferry is turned into a platform for carriages, horses, and heavy weights. Along the sides are special rooms for ladies and gentlemen. The ferries cost only a few cents and cross the broad bay every five minutes. My comrade told me that in winter, when the bay freezes along the shore, they set up transportation by sleighs, which are moved by steam and wind power instead of by horses.

V

Boston's role in the War of Independence, the part the city played in the formation of the Constitution and in obtaining the European powers' recognition for the new nation—all these factors impart a special significance to the history of the New England capital. Its inhabitants, by then already distinguished by their seriousness of purpose and their education, sympathized with those great events perhaps more than did those of any other city. To this day there are several monuments in Boston to that glorious epoch of American history. A foreigner is proudly taken through Faneuil Hall, the so-called "cradle of liberty," where the leaders repeatedly told the people of the sacrifices that had to be made for the common cause and where they guided

---

ing place. Because of its three peaks, the first settlers called the peninsula "Tramount" or "Trimountain." Eventually it would be known as Beacon Hill. In 1634 the Reverend William Blackston sold his forty-four acres on "Shawmut" to Boston for thirty pounds. Darrett B. Rutman, *Winthrop's Boston: Portrait of a Puritan Town, 1630–1649* (Chapel Hill, N.C.: University of North Carolina Press, 1965), pp. 40, 70.

public opinion. Here were frequently heard the voices of people whose memory is dear to America. To this day part of the building is used for public meetings, if not by the people as a whole then by various parties before elections. It is also used when a popular orator wishes to persuade his fellow citizens of some political truth or advance some idea.

Finally it was necessary to look at the monument erected in honor of the era itself. Since America is still a young country, it is generally poor in statues and columns and has little to show in the way of ruins and remains of the past. All its recollections are concentrated around one epoch, one glorious epoch, before which and after which the history of America followed a more ordinary course of development. Boston's soil is especially noted for its historical associations, and that explains why there are almost as many monuments here as in all the rest of America. Here, it is pointed out, is where the American troops stood; there the English troops were beaten and ran off in that direction; here the militia met them, there they defeated them, and so forth. One of the important and decisive victories of the war was gained on so-called Bunker Hill, where a stone pillar has been erected to commemorate it. It goes without saying that for Americans this place is holy, and they are in their glory when showing it to foreigners.

Since the monument is located in Charleston, one has to get there by horse-drawn railway, which in other countries is quite properly called "the American railway." It would be difficult to dream up anything more convenient for a city with a large population. A pair of horses easily and almost at a trot pulls a huge car which can seat up to forty people. But the car is so large that the same number of people can stand in the middle and around the outside. Although the cost of a ride is insignificant in comparison to the spaciousness of the car, the carriage is kept very clean. This is explained by the small expense in maintaining it: a sizeable amount of money is obtained from the many people who use this means of transportation, and, since the wheels move on rails, extra people do not add too much weight. When the rails are not being used by trains, for which they were originally put down, other conveyances can use them. Consequently, far from being a hindrance to circulation in the city, the rails facilitate it. At both ends of the line are places for harnessing the horses; as soon as the car comes to a stop, the horses are changed and the car starts back. In various places there are also collateral lines along which trains travel. Each car has a conductor who is indistinguishable from any other gentleman traveling in the carriage, except for a band on his hat indicating his function. As soon as the car comes to the end of the line, the conductor takes off the band and becomes an ordinary citizen like any other.

We used one of these cars, which leave downtown Boston every ten minutes for Charleston, to get to the Bunker Hill monument. Its size and the hill it stands on make it visible from afar and it is one of the first things to catch the eye when one arrives in Boston. You clamber up three hundred steps to the top but you absolutely forget your fatigue when you reach the summit and there, spread out before your eyes, is a vast panorama of the sea, the naval dockyard, and the piers for ships of various companies and countries. If your eye is sharp and the weather clear, you can make out the snowcapped mountains north of Boston and the craggy cliffs of Maine.

VI

I was delighted with the guided tour in the morning. Later, after returning to old Boston, we went to look for the attorney to whom my companion wished to introduce me. Just as blocks of buildings near the Temple and Law Courts in London are occupied by barristers' offices, so in Boston the attorneys live close to the Court House. It was not difficult to find the person we were looking for. He was a young man who had graduated from Harvard University and had already been handling clients for several years. His entire office consisted of two rooms. A clerk sat in the first, and the second contained volumes of Massachusetts state statutes, books by the best American jurists, Blackstone's essays, a collection of United States Supreme Court decisions, and so forth. The attorney received and advised his clients here. It was here that I was introduced to him and heard the familiar "very happy!" which, judging by his smile and warm handshake, he really meant. The attorney was a member of the city school board and promised to write several recommendations for me to various teachers. In America the latter, properly speaking, are also what in other countries and in our own as well are called directors of institutions.

He advised me to start with the schools for which Boston is famed. He gave me full instructions as to when and in what order to visit each type of school; provided me with published regulations and reports on the educational institutions of Boston; and as befits a practical American, he gave me every opportunity to learn for myself how it was that Boston's schools acquired for the city the epithet of the American Athens.

Why should Boston have such an advantage? I could not help but ask the attorney as I bid him farewell and stocked up with his signed visiting passes that would enable me to enter the various schools. Do other cities really not strive for the same general development of education for the masses irrespective of rich or poor?

"Boston," replied the attorney, "is a city of Puritans who have always believed that morality and education are the twin foundations without which a nation will fall. Those who came to Massachusetts colony were educated people and they tried to impart to their children and descendants the moral quality they themselves possessed. Therefore from the very beginning of the colony's existence laws were passed for public education in a spirit that has not been emulated by a single state." No other country has a phenomenon like Boston, concluded my new guide, and he advised me to investigate the public school system quite carefully. I followed his advice and did not regret the few extra days I spent in Boston.

The basic difference between education in New and Old England stems from the principle of state intervention in family and financial relations for the attainment of social goals. This difference is seen not only in the numbers of pupils but also in the very goal of education. In a country where the holding of public office, the right of election, and generally the exercise of civil rights is a function of class privilege, education cannot be as equally extended to all as in one where everyone either elects or is elected to public office and consequently sees the necessity of being prepared for it. During my visit to England I was amazed at the figures indicating how little education was spread in Great Britain. Illiteracy in England is not uncommon, though in classical education there is hardly a country where the upper class can be compared with the English aristocracy.[7]

To the present day, education in England preserves that medieval,

7. Lakier's vague characterization of illiteracy in England as "not uncommon" masks the fact that adult male literacy in 1850 was well over 65 percent. John R. Gillis, *The Development of European Society, 1770–1870* (Boston: Houghton Mifflin, 1977), p. 216.

monastic character it has had for centuries. The study of ancient
Greek and Latin takes up a large part of the time in English schools,
especially in the universities, and crowds out the living languages and
more practical sciences. Obviously the Americans could not permit
such a circumscribed or one-sided education; as much as possible, the
world of science had to enlighten each one according to his talents
and aspirations for education. Even less could there be thought of
dividing pupils of various social classes not only by institutions but in
one and the same institution by room, dress, and department, as is
done in England.

Each state, being absolutely independent from every other state
in matters of internal administration and structure, has its own school
funds and establishes education on principles it finds the most suitable and useful for its own needs. That is why it is difficult to draw
a picture of a common school system for all the states of the Union.
They share the common aspiration of increasing literacy as much as
possible, but how to achieve this is left to each state and even to each
city. Such are the demands of self-government: each person knows
best his own needs and those of his neighbors and relatives, and each
is thus left to manage his own fate in the best way he knows.

There are places however that shine for their education or, more
correctly, for its availability to all citizens. Ask any American and he
will point to Boston in Massachusetts and Philadelphia in Pennsylvania as the two cities where there are more schools and pupils than
in any others.

Let us look more closely at the education system in the Boston
public schools, which have an advantage even over Philadelphia, first
by virtue of age and second because education is more widespread.
*There is not a single citizen in Boston's population who cannot read
or write.*[8] As far as I know, this is the only example of its kind on the
face of the earth. To be absolutely exact I have used the word "citizen."
As a seaport, Boston receives, after New York, the most immigrants
from Europe. They bring with them to the New World their lack of
education, their poverty, and the resultant attitudes. In order that

8. Lakier's statement is, of course, a gross exaggeration, designed to
impress his Russian readers. It ignores the poor white and black citizens
of Boston, many of whom could not read or write. Stanley K. Schultz,
The Culture Factory: Boston Public Schools, 1789–1860 (New York:
Oxford University Press, 1973), passim.

these newcomers not disturb the general harmony of an educated city, Boston has assumed the burden of their care and sends them to school, even those who would not want to step foot in one. The American Athens has its own school street-police charged with seeing to it that children do not wander about the streets without good reason. There are two officials, "truant officers," who either themselves or on instructions of the school principal track down children not attending school. They make the parents or relatives send the children to the nearest school and insist on seeing that this is done. Of course the ability to read and write is still far from the education that brings a reduction in crime or turns a person onto the right path. But literacy provides a person with an opportunity for further self-development and opens doors to occupations that were formerly closed to him; it also deters him from ignorance and vice, which are inseparably linked.

In other countries the spread of popular education is inhibited by a lack of means to pay for schooling. In Boston schooling is paid for by the city. Special taxes are collected from the inhabitants for this purpose, sufficient to cover expenditures for support of the schools, salaries of the teachers, and the purchase, construction, and upkeep of school buildings. The people who share this burden are those who themselves or whose families benefit either directly from the advantages of education or indirectly from urban well-being and order. In this fashion the obligation to support the schools is divided proportionately, and the rich with their excess wealth share in the education of the poor.

In addition nearly one-third of the proceeds from the sale of land in Massachusetts townships is designated for a special school fund. From last year's account it is evident that the state of Massachusetts collects more than $2,300,000 in taxes from its citizens for the support of schools. At 1 ruble 30 kopeks silver to the dollar, that is nearly three million silver rubles. Moreover, the school fund for the entire state was $1,625,932, from which the interest of $48,600 was distributed among the separate towns for the support of their schools. But in order to share in this revenue the town itself must collect at least $1.50 (1 ruble 90 kopeks silver) for each urban child between the ages of five and fifteen years. Should a community not carry out what the law requires, any father of a family whose children would suffer from such neglect of the public welfare has the right to begin proceedings not only to have the obligation fulfilled but to seek damages in fines and penalties.

In each of the districts scattered throughout Boston there are several primary schools, so that the latter are close to the inhabitants of every district. There were 241 primary schools in 1857 and each had about sixty pupils, children from four to eight years of age. From primary schools children move on to middle or grammar schools. Only one such school is placed in each district of the city. There are eighteen of them in Boston and each has about 650 pupils.

On the lower level are the primary schools. They are compulsory for every city-dweller and no teacher has the right to refuse to accept a child, whether male or female, whose parent is a city resident. Schools must have approximately equal numbers of pupils so that each teacher will have a group of about fifty children. They are distributed among six classes. Textbooks are designated for each, and reading, writing, and arithmetic are taught in all classes. While visiting these schools I was amazed at the speed with which the children answered questions which were quite complicated for their age, and solved arithmetic problems. Every pupil had a slate in front of him and the principal requirement of the teacher was that all be busy at the same time and that no one flag in attention. With the word: change! they exchanged slates with one another and checked each other's work.

In appearance the buildings housing the primary schools are not majestic or in any way luxurious. Nothing is done for the sake of appearances but everything is clean. Each child wears his own clothes and is neatly dressed. For this neatness I think the schools are partly indebted to the women who serve as teachers' assistants. There is a special high school for these assistants in Boston. They are also city residents and were themselves at one time in those same schools. Their moral influence on the children is extremely important, especially on the older ones. Up to two-thirds of the teachers in Massachusetts are of the female sex. If Americans, who never burden women with public employment, have decided to make an exception in the case of education, it is primarily because a woman by her very nature belongs in a school for children, because she has more patience and a greater degree of gentleness. It is from school that a child carries away a respect for ladies that he retains for the rest of his life.

The highest levels of school administration are always left to the men. Teachers are required not to teach in any other public school except the ones to which they are assigned. They are also not to establish private schools and not give lessons on the side earlier than six o'clock in the evening, excluding Wednesdays and Saturdays after dinner, when the pupils are free. Similarly, public school teachers are not to publish either political or religious journals. In general, because they receive a relatively large salary from the city, teachers and school principals belong exclusively to the schools to which they are appointed. From May to October school is open from eight to eleven in the morning and from two to five in the afternoon. During the rest of the year it is open from nine to twelve noon and from two to five in the afternoon. On certain days—a small, definite number—pupils are excused from attending school.

Middle schools ("grammar schools"), as they are defined in the regulations, are designed for teaching "the common branches of an English education," in contrast to a classical education, for which there are special institutions designed to prepare students for the university.

Children of the female sex attend classes together with the boys in the primary schools but are separated in the middle grades. However, their course of study is no less or easier than that for the boys. With a few exceptions the textbooks are the same. . . . In America a woman is as independent as a man; she enters life boldly, moves through it alone if fate does not send her a husband, works as much as is possible, and writes and teaches. Her physical weakness is protected by public opinion. Of course if there is any kind of aristocracy in America it consists exclusively of *ladies,* women for whose social life men have sacrificed everything. And it must be admitted that American women, feeling that men have placed a halo over them, take full advantage of their position. Nevertheless, I think the basic education that girls receive in school explains more than anything else the respect that American men, without exception, accord to women.

Every middle school, or division within a school if it is for both sexes, is divided into four classes, and each class is subdivided according to the number of pupils, so that each teacher has up to sixty pupils. As soon as he has thirty more pupils he is given a woman assistant. The admission of female teachers to schools attended by boys aged eight to twelve has a moral influence on the character of the children. Although these teachers are usually young girls specially trained for this vocation, the boys willingly obey them, not out of fear but from innate bashfulness. While the voice of the teacher might not always be effective, the fear of her becoming unpleasant and of offending her stops the boys. Even in school they are already on their own, being the supreme judge of their actions, and they get used to taking care of themselves. Straight from school they bring into real life the principles of democratic freedom and the ideas of self-government which will guide them for the rest of their lives.

The demands on principals and teachers of middle schools in the cities are great. They must constantly be in the institutions assigned to them, but their labors are appreciated and suitably compensated. On the other hand the absence of a teacher of whatever rank is not tolerated for a single day. As soon as an appointee fails to fulfill his duties for whatever reason, it makes no difference, he is replaced by a candidate chosen by the school committee, or by a female tutor of a normal school. An appropriate deduction is made in the salary of the absentee.

Thanks to the letters of recommendation with which my new acquaintance supplied me, I had no difficulty at all in visiting several middle schools. For 650 pupils, a two-story structure is usually built; if both boys and girls attend the school, they are usually kept on separate floors. I will not repeat how clean everything is, as in a good bourgeois home; cleanliness and order take the place of outward splendor and obvious wealth. The children are in various kinds of attire and each of the girls wears her own little frock. They dress however they can, but quite neatly. They are generally well behaved and it seems to me there cannot be a trace of shyness, let alone fear, among American boys and girls in the presence of strangers. All the pupils in the middle school classes were constantly attentive, all were busy, so that each of the teacher's listeners was ready to answer his questions. Raising the hand is a signal of readiness to answer a question and it is the teacher's choice whether to ask the whole class or only one pupil. In one of the girls' schools I chanced upon a history lesson. The topic was Washington and the American Constitution. The girls freely answered the purely governmental questions as if they had been trained for political office. Hence the knowledge that every American has of his rights and duties is not at all surprising. According to our way of thinking this would be unnecessary for women, whose sphere is limited to domestic matters. But in America women are looked upon differently. I cannot adequately express my amazement at the speed with which ten- and eleven-year-old girls in another school I visited solved quite complicated arithmetic problems. It is true that arithmetic is taught in all classes in the primary and middle schools and is considered to be one of the most essential subjects for people who spend their lives calculating profits. Much attention is paid to the drawing of maps; geography, like the other sciences, is taught by visual demonstration. Pupils are taught how to travel from America to all parts of the world. They must tell the route a steamship takes, what stops it makes, where anything remarkable is to be seen, and what one finds important in the country where it arrives. Of the various parts of Russia they know only the Crimea, from the last war. One pupil in a Boston school went all through Russia, starting at Odessa, and had to name from memory the main cities to be seen on the way. This was no easy task but the little Yankee acquitted himself well, telling what was remarkable about Kiev, what Smolensk was, and what one might see in Moscow and Petersburg. And if among the cities distinguished by their wealth he incorrectly named some little town, an error which his teacher did not correct, it is hardly for us to complain, especially since we know so little about America.

After completing middle school a twelve-year-old Bostonian can read and write; he knows basic English grammar, arithmetic, and enough United States geography and history to serve the needs of any citizen. But if one were not satisfied with this knowledge and wished to be even better prepared for life and commercial activities, there are more schools just as accessible as middle schools. These are the English High School for boys and the Girls' High and Normal School. In the former the course of study is spread over three years and completing that education is considered comparable to having an academic degree. Young people aged twelve to sixteen are taught ancient geography, general history, algebra, geometry, trigonometry as applied to measurement, surveying, navigation, astronomy, more on the United States Constitution, bookkeeping, drawing, French and Spanish. Finally, pupils who might desire to improve themselves further, especially in the mathematical sciences, may stay a year and take lessons in astronomy, philosophy, logic, Spanish, geology, mechanics, the engineering arts, and higher mathematics. Theology and instruction in religion are not offered in any of the various levels of schools. This is mainly because there is no established religion and each person can be a member of any church he chooses. Pastors are entrusted with providing religious instruction to the degree and to the age-level required by the rules of the sect.

The daughters of well-to-do Bostonians receive a primary education at home, but their parents gladly send them to a Girls' High and Normal School. To enroll in the latter, a girl must be no younger than fifteen and no older than nineteen, and is required to pass an examination in reading, writing, arithmetic, English grammar, geography, and history. The course lasts three years and consists of the same subjects that are taught in the boys' high school, not excluding philosophy, astronomy, and algebra. Latin, however, is added at all class levels. For those who wish to teach, there are lectures on pedagogy. Whenever people are needed to fill in for a while for absent teachers' assistants in the middle schools, they are borrowed from the normal high schools. When I visited one, the teacher wanted to give me an example of a young girl's knowledge of Latin, and however strange it was to hear grammatical forms and translations of Latin authors by young girls, I could not but agree with the need for teaching a dead language in order that the students acquire a basic knowledge of English. In the arts the girls learned drawing and singing.[9]

This, then, is the organization of the Boston public schools, whose single goal is educating citizens to carry out the responsibilities placed upon them by the city. Therefore the entire system of education in these schools is completely practical. And since there is a sufficient number of schools and their doors are always open for everyone, it is clear why Boston can proudly say that not one of its citizens is illiterate. This circumstance has a palpable influence on the character of Bostonians, on their tranquility and morality. One must not be at all surprised if a Bostonian asks a foreigner not to stay long in New York, or at least not to use New York as a basis for drawing conclusions about all of America.

9. "There was no higher or professional education for [Russian] women until the 1870's and secondary education, from 1764 to 1858, was limited to Institutes for girls of the gentry class or of the few merchant families who could afford the tuition. In these Institutes (there were about twenty of them in the Empire in mid-century . . .) the atmosphere was stifling and the teaching unimaginative and unrelated to reality." Richard Stites, "M. L. Mikhailov and the Emergence of the Woman Question in Russia," *Canadian Slavic Studies* 3, no. 2 (Summer 1969): 179.

However, the Boston school system would be incomplete if there were not one more institution which educates young citizens and prepares them for higher education in special schools and the university. There exists for this purpose in Boston the so-called Latin grammar school, instituted in the seventeenth century. Latin and Greek are taught there, besides mathematics, geography, history, recitation, English, and French. The teachers must be university graduates; the pupils, no younger than ten years of age, must present recommendations from teachers in schools they attended, be able to read and write, and have a basic knowledge of geography and English. The course of study lasts for six years; besides including the general subjects of education such as history, geography, arithmetic, and English literature, it gives special attention to the study of Latin and Greek; translations from one language to another; compositions in poetry and prose; a detailed study of classical antiquity; and, among the modern languages, French literature and conversation.

VII

The example of Boston serves as a model for the other counties and cities of Massachusetts, and even for all New England, and for this reason in particular the Yankee's opinion about the great significance of Boston is justified. Of even greater importance is the fact that the university which is considered to be one of the best in the United States is located if not in Boston itself then in one of its suburbs. In any case Harvard College in Cambridge is three miles from Boston and is the oldest institution of higher learning in North America. It was founded in 1636, and since Pastor John Harvard promoted the creation and flourishing of this university in its very first years through his own labor and money, the institution is named in his honor. The first printing press in America was built in Cambridge, a town which strongly reflects an academic atmosphere. The presence of the university, students, and professors has not been without its influence on the town.

The American horse-drawn railway line also goes to Cambridge, and after about a thirty-minute ride from Boston I was at Harvard College. But this is not one large multistoried building capable of holding all the students. Instead, about fifteen buildings of various sizes and different architectural styles are spread out over a large area. I had a letter to the president, James Walker, a doctor of theology and former professor.[10] I asked a student where the president lived and he pointed to a small house, a cottage, surrounded by a garden. I found the venerable president, a man in his declining years, puttering about the flowers, and presented my letter of recommendation. Having learned that I would like to become better acquainted with the teaching and general education system at the college, he led me inside his modest dwelling and after some opening inquiries about my own country, he told me the history of the institution. Its purpose and basis are the same as those of the various colleges at Oxford. These are rather higher *gymnasia* where young people study subjects necessary for a university education, for which a large number of the college buildings are used. Philosophy, rhetoric, history, classical and modern languages, and mathematical and natural sciences are taught in the various buildings. Many of the above subjects are not unusual even in the courses of the English High and Latin schools, though in the latter they are taught with an eye to a more practical application to life, and time is not wasted on ancient languages, which are useless for those who do not devote themselves to the learned professions. Relatively few young people attend college compared to the large number who are educated in the public schools. For 1855 there were in all 339 undergraduates, that is, those who did not yet have their academic degrees. But the American is not at all distressed about this. He is concerned about citizens being well enough educated to carry out the will of the people; for him scholars are a luxury. The latter are needed to spread learning; they are the future teachers and molders of youth. But the majority of young people do not attend the university; they stop after middle school, from which they gain a rounded education quite sufficient for life, and leave scholarship to a selected few. Such an attitude toward schools is hardly the most incorrect, especially in a country like America where not a single life-force must be or can be wasted, nor be without some benefit or significance.

There are four professional schools at Harvard University and each has its own building: the Divinity School, Law School, Medical School, and a school for mathematics and the natural sciences. The Divinity School, in which the course of study lasts three years, is

10. James Walker (1794–1874), a Unitarian clergyman who became professor of Natural Religion at Harvard in 1839. He served as president of the university from 1853 to 1860.

divided into three class levels: entering, middle, and graduating. Students in the last class preach in the churches of the city on Sunday evenings. The Law School has three professors who between them cover the subjects in jurisprudence. However, there are few lectures, about ten a week, and they only train the students in how to study and what to pay attention to. The Law School, or as we say in our country, the Juridical Faculty, has its own special law library and a lecture hall. The hall is decorated with portraits of the great American jurists, [Joseph] Story and [Daniel] Webster, who belong to Boston. The former was a professor at Harvard College, the latter a Boston statesman and subsequently an orator in the federal Congress. If an occasion presents itself during a lecture, the professor asks the students questions on topics or cases related to the lecture, and this system of examinations is considered the best and most satisfactory. There are no incentives for students to attend lectures and no testing of their knowledge and information until they take the examination for the academic degree. Twice each week student courts are set up and here the young people learn the lawyer's profession and make speeches in defense of clients. These model courts have the advantage of being supplemented by clubs organized by the Cambridge students for court debates and discussions. There were 125 students in the Law School in 1855 from nearly every state in the Union, as well as from the English provinces in America, Nova Scotia and Canada. The Medical School is located in Boston in order to be closer to the hospital. The school for mathematics and natural sciences is known as the Lawrence Scientific School.

For astronomical observations there is an observatory at Harvard College run by William Bond, the well-known astronomer.[11] The observatory has a refractor which is the same size as the one in the Pulkovo observatory, both having been made in the same workshop.[12] These two are the largest refractors in the world. The cupola erected

11. William Cranch Bond (1789–1859), a self-taught astronomer who was in charge of the observatory in Cambridge from 1839 to 1859. It was during his administration that a fifteen-inch telescope was installed, matching the one newly put into operation at Pulkovo.

12. Pulkovo is a village near St. Petersburg (present-day Leningrad) where in 1839 the Russian Academy of Sciences established its chief astronomical observatory. At the time it was the largest observatory in the world.

over it is enormous and can be opened on various sides. The instrument moves on rails, and for the convenience of the observer there is a special seat which can be raised or lowered, along with various gadgets and auxiliary instruments which make the help of another person unnecessary. While saying goodbye, the venerable director of the observatory handed me as mementos photographs of the moon and other sightings made at the observatory. The president of Harvard College showed me the university library and gave me copies of his reports on the university made during the last few years.

In the evening I spoke with my lawyer-acquaintance about the things I had seen in the schools and my observations of the university. I could not help but share with him my amazement at institutions that provide everyone, even the poorest, with an opportunity to develop his talents as well as his moral and spiritual strengths. There is no question that America is indebted to England for its school system. But the exclusive castes and classes that history created in Europe did not exist in the New World and did not serve as an obstacle to the extension of education to the whole mass of the people. America and Americans can take no credit for this fact. Nevertheless it is impossible not to call fortunate a people who so well understood the general blessings of education and so wisely took advantage of the lessons of other countries and other times.

VIII

After viewing the schools, libraries, and museums, all of which promote the development of the people, I was to visit the courts and prisons. [Lakier describes the structure of city government in Boston, as well as property qualifications for voting and holding office in Massachusetts.]

The constitution of the state of Massachusetts adheres to several distinctive principles in the selection of judges. There are states, New York among them, where judges are elected for short terms, along with other officeholders. The disadvantages of this system are clear: a popular election cannot give a person the experience and perspicacity a judge needs to render decisions on the citizens' most important interests—their property, their honor, and their lives; and a short term of service is one of the main reasons why judicial positions are sought through all sorts of illegal means by people who have no calling for the posts they seek, who see in them only a reliable way to get rich quickly. The public knows this—during elections voices are always raised on behalf of justice and against the corruption of officials— but the election ends with the majority of the voters in favor of the candidate who was able to curry their favor.

The Massachusetts constitution has avoided such obviously harmful disadvantages by having the governor, with the consent of his cabinet, appoint all judges, the attorney general, and sheriffs. And since the cabinet is composed of officials elected of and by the people, Bostonians maintain that limits are set as to the influence of the judges' executive power and actions, all the more so since the governorship changes every year but judges remain in office for life so long as they conscientiously fulfill their responsibilities. In order that judges be quite outside the reach of popular influence, they are provided by law with handsome fixed salaries. The talents of judges are valued extremely highly: while the governor of the state receives a salary of $3,500 (about 4,500 silver rubles) and his secretary of state, who is something like a minister, $2,000, the chief justice of the state supreme court gets a salary of $4,500 (about 6,000 rubles) and the other justices $4,000 (5,200 silver rubles). A judge must devote himself completely to his responsibilities so as to fully preserve his independence: as soon as he accepts office as governor, senator, or representative on the state or federal level, he relinquishes and loses his judicial office.

My new guide, comparing this system with those existing in the other states, gave preference to his own. "A great many lawyers," he said, "cap their careers with a judicial post. The best lawyers are not at all averse to this opportunity for public service, all the more so since it involves a long term in office and at the same time is well compensated."

I could not disagree that, if the courts are truly to administer justice, judges must be persons trained for this important profession. "And that is even truer in America," added the lawyer, "for nowhere else does a judge enjoy such autonomy and independence. His position is absolutely unique: he can even find an act of the Senate and House of Representatives unconstitutional and declare it invalid. The decision of a judge is indispensable in matters involving private individuals against one another or against the state, or in matters between the states. Obviously, enormous responsibilities rest upon the judge, and rather than have him chosen through unrestricted suffrage and popular

passions at election time, it is far better for the people to forego the
right to vote and be assured of a judge who is conscientious and experienced."

It was interesting to listen to the lawyer's attempts to demonstrate
how the abuse that might result from a system of appointing judges
is mitigated by the presence in court of jurors drawn from the people
and of lawyers who are specially trained legal experts.

It turned out that my companion knew in detail the French court
system and could compare it with the English and American courts.
He did not understand why in France they consider a juror drawn
from the people incapable of deciding a question of fact, occurrence, or
the existence of liability; why, in short, they do not want to call on
his common sense and everyday experience in a civil proceeding, when
they have no reluctance to trust his judgment of events in a criminal
case. The lawyer argued differently about the application of the law:
it must absolutely be the prerogative of a person with specialized
knowledge of legislation. The lawyer's advantage is great; since the
judge exists to determine fact, the attorney can completely devote
himself to the legal aspects of the question. Of course, a juror must
also have a natural capacity to comprehend, and if specialized education is not required of him, it is useful that he not be completely
without general education. One can positively say that nowhere in
the world are there such capable jurors as in America. Every citizen
here understands his duties and, precisely because he is educated, values
their execution.

"At any rate," said my companion, "it is also well to have some
definite assurance, as is the case here and in England, that jurors are
capable of understanding the everyday relations of their fellow citizens, that they possess some means and are of good repute. But, unlike
the French, we do not allow the government itself, in the person of a
prefect, to select the jurors. In our country this matter is entrusted to
sheriffs appointed by the governor, who in turn is elected by the
people. In general we think the more freedom left to the litigants
themselves in selecting and rejecting jurors, the more correctly and
completely the lists are compiled, and the earlier the defendant knows
in whose hands his fate rests, the better it is for the litigants. In
short we remember that the judicial process exists for the litigant and
we open all means for him to utilize it.

"Neither the state nor any public institution enjoys special privi-

leges in court. The judge is no partisan of the organ of power, but
rather sees to it that the rights of the accused are fully protected.[13]
At the same time, the prosecutor defends the public interest, and in
this respect neither one side nor the other has an advantage. Even
a person accused of a misdemeanor or a felony is first brought before
a grand jury, and he is turned over for trial only if the accusation
against him is found justified in a true bill voted out by at least twelve
of the grand jurors.[14] Since a trial verdict is valid only when it is unanimously agreed to by the full set of jurors sitting in the court, that is,
twelve men—so that twenty-four men in all have judged the fate of
the accused—there can be no occasion for questioning whether someone underwent accusation and conviction through the enmity and
malevolence of so many of his fellow citizens."

While he explained to me the Americans' view on the necessity of
juries in civil and criminal cases and their faith in the soundness of
the jury system—an institution that was inherited from their fore-
fathers—we arrived at a building that housed the courts. In front of
us was a door with the inscription: Police Court of Boston. Here, the
lawyer told me, cases of misdemeanors and minor offenses are heard.
We entered a spacious chamber full of people. The entrance was
open to all. Take notes, print them if you like—no one minds. If the
decision is correct, there's no need to fear publicity; if wrong, then it
is well that the opportunity exists for pointing out the mistake to the
judge himself, who will be more careful in the future. Everyone
arrested for any reason appears in police court for a preliminary examination. The initial testimony of witnesses is taken here. Since no one
can be taken into custody for more than twenty-four hours without
being informed why he is being held—otherwise his release can be
demanded by any citizen on the basis of a writ of habeas corpus—
every morning the police judge summons those caught and arrested

13. Before the judicial reform of 1864, which established a separate
and independent court system with trial by jury, justice in Russia was an
integral part of the administrative system. Cumbersome and corrupt, it
was based on class status rather than on the principle of equality before
the law, and relied entirely on a written and secret procedure. Most
judges were nobles and had little or no legal training. Richard S. Wortman, *The Development of a Russian Legal Consciousness* (Chicago: University of Chicago Press, 1976), chap. 3.

14. A grand jury may have up to twenty-three members.

the day before and either frees them, imposes a fine, or decides the accusations should be heard by a grand jury and a court. Cases moved quickly, and my companion assured me that seldom are there uncompleted examinations of the arrested or witnesses left over for the next day.

The lawyer escorting me had to defend a case in the [state] Supreme Court, and we headed in that direction. His client was already waiting for him and he sat down beside him. I thought I should stay behind, but he pointed out a seat alongside him. The lawyers are generally grouped around the somewhat higher chair of the judge. A lawyer is inseparable from the person whose case he has taken. They are continually talking things over; the litigant reminds the lawyer what to pay attention to and if necessary stops him and whispers something in his ear. The lawyer himself is not in doubt when to ask his client something. It goes without saying that neither the judge nor the lawyers wear uniforms, or English gray wigs with the classical curls and ringlets, or formal French caps and robes. Everyone comes dressed as is, finds himself a convenient spot, and has in mind only one thing—how to finish the case in the best way possible. It is the lawyers upon whom the whole American and English procedure rests: the judge's only concern is to take brief notes on the testimony of the witnesses, notes that will guide him in the final conclusion of the case; but the means by which the arguments of the two sides are presented—that is the affair of the lawyers. They question witnesses, demand explanations, and raise objections. As soon as a lawyer on one side poses a question that his adversary considers inappropriate, the judge must decide whether the witness has to answer or not. The judge is no more than a mediator at this point, for until the verdict, which must be brought in by the jury, he does not reveal his opinion about the case in any way. Consequently he cannot inhibit the jury, and conversely the opinion of the jury cannot offend the judge. He has only one duty: to apply the law.

The jury decided in favor of the client of my lawyer-acquaintance, and he left the court satisfied at having won the case. His place was taken by other lawyers and other litigants. What could have been simpler and more natural than such a court? It fulfills the purpose for which it was created. Everything is done so that infractions of the law do not go unpunished, and with a minimum of delay, red tape, and paperwork. A case is explained to an American judge by people whose obligation and in whose full interest it is to use all possible weapons and arguments to present their side, and if after this he makes an incorrect decision, it is human nature which is at fault, for man is not perfect. Legislators, at least, have done everything in their power to see to it that such mistakes occur as rarely as possible.

My guide constantly alluded, and he had good reason to do so, to the economy and simplicity of the court system. So did other Bostonians with whom I had a chance to discuss the subject. I could add to these great qualities yet another—the naturalness and fairness in distributing the tasks that necessarily accompany the conduct of legal proceedings. But there was still one question I wanted to ask my companion: was one judge enough for a court decision to be as impartial as possible? Could one always entrust a single official with the fate of one's property, status, honor, and even his life?

"Do you really think," my lawyer replied, "that the number of judges is of any significance? If a judge is an educated and decent man in the broad meaning of that word, then having him work with peers who function as assistants would mean depriving him of that energy and firmness a man must have if he is to act on his own and answer for his actions. He will either be constantly in conflict with those who should be helping him and thus needlessly wasting time that could be usefully applied to the case, or else he will yield to a majority. In both cases justice obviously loses. But more often what happens is what I have seen in French courts: out of five or seven members, the majority of them sleeps, everyone hoping that his neighbor is listening. In any event the one who more readily and clearly understands his duty rules the majority. We have faith in our judges and we believe that two half-educated people do not make one truly educated judge. In ordinary cases it is sufficient to have a single judge who values his opinion and who will not give it before thinking and weighing the meaning of his words. The jurors and lawyers assist him, and the presence of the public and publicity and the chance given to everyone to discuss the judge's actions—all these factors restrain him from violating the trust placed in him. Moreover, if a judge's decision were appealed, it would be considered by a full meeting of the entire court, a 'full bench.' But public faith sustains the verdict of a single judge and makes possible the so-called circuit courts. It is not the custom in our country to elaborately and ceremoniously greet and see off a judge who travels around his district to dispense law and justice, but we have the same system of circuits as in England. Just as it is with the English judges when they meet in Westminster Hall, so only at designated times do our judges gather in the capital city of a state to attend to the cases awaiting them there. The court reaches out to everyone and does not want litigants, witnesses, and lawyers to go looking for it.

"Just as the Federal Supreme Court justices travel around the individual states, except for the too distant ones, so the state justices travel around the counties. The number of members of our Supreme Court is equal to the number of districts into which the state is divided. The civil court—the court of common pleas—operates in exactly the same way. Moreover, justices of the peace travel around the separate townships into which the counties are divided. The gradation between these levels of courts is determined by the value of the property in dispute and the seriousness of the crime in the case, but the procedure is always the same. County and city cases ready for consideration are waiting for the person bringing law and order with him. Juries and witnesses are summoned and the doors are then thrown open to each and every one. I believe," concluded the lawyer, "that there is no better court system."

Seldom have I spoken with such an intelligent and broadly educated lawyer as this one. Even if the system of circuit courts is not suitable for every state (the institution existed in ancient Russia, where it was called "judicial rounds"), and even if it is inapplicable to a large and sparsely populated country where there are no good transportation routes yet, I could not but share my companion's views on the jury system. And I was particularly amazed at the sound organization of lawyers in America and at the understanding of their relationship to the judge and to their clients.

IX

I did not find the Boston prisons as interesting as the courts of the Massachusetts capital. The prisons are built according to the Auburn system, named after a little town in New York State. It was in Auburn that the first prison was established to achieve rehabilitation of criminals by separating them at night and having them engage in congregate labor during the day, when, incidentally, they are not allowed to speak to each other. This system prevails primarily in the northern states of America and New York has built these prisons on a large scale.[15] Hence the lawyer who had been my guide advised that I not form any ideas of the system based upon the Boston prisons but that I give my attention to Blackwell's Island, near New York, which was completely occupied by prisons and correctional institutions. Nevertheless I noted several facts which I will cite.

From four hundred to five hundred criminals are usually housed in the Massachusetts State Prison; they are both whites and nonwhites, including Negroes. According to a report for 1855, there were 483 prisoners, the youngest from fifteen to twenty and the oldest from seventy to eighty. The terms of imprisonment extended from two to twenty-five years, as well as to life imprisonment. Since the labor of the prisoners is hired out to manufacturers, their work does not go to waste. On the contrary, the report claims that all expenses for maintenance were $88,295; income from work was $76,598. The state and its citizens were thus left to pay only the difference, $11,500, for the security of having been freed of criminals. The warden who conducted me around the institution tried to convince me that, compared to the total population of the state, the large number of prisoners was in no way evidence against the people's morality because more than two-thirds of the prisoners were not from Massachusetts. They were either residents or natives of other states or foreigners who had committed crimes in Massachusetts and had ended up in the Boston prison. Bibles had been distributed to all cells and about one hundred dollars is allotted yearly for a library where I found more than seven hundred volumes of different kinds. The prisoners willingly make use of them, and most of the books showed evident signs of a love for reading.

For criminals who are minors, that is, from six to seventeen years of age, there is a state reform school where those guilty of theft, larceny, disorderliness, drunkenness, fraud, and vagrancy are sent. They remain there either until they are of full legal age (are legally adults) or until their terms have expired. The purpose of the institution is to train the young criminals in work and good conduct and to provide them with at least the rudiments of an education. Moreover

15. The Auburn prison system was begun in 1816 and became one of the chief models for the next half-century of prison development in the United States. Blake McKelvey, *American Prisons: A History of Good Intentions* (Montclair, N.J.: Patterson Smith, 1977), p. 11.

all domestic chores are performed by the youngsters themselves. The labor of the prisoners is also leased out to manufacturers. The prisoners' time is divided as follows: four hours daily for instruction, six hours for work, and eight and a half hours for sleep, rest, and various duties. This school can house up to five hundred trainees, and each one is given forty-five dollars a year.

For girls who are depraved, of ill-repute, or without proper supervision, there is a State Industrial School for Girls where again with work and instruction an attempt is made to put children of wanton propensities on the right road. This institution has existed only since 1856 and is built around the family model. There are three buildings housing girls sent here for correction and in each there is a separate family of thirty children, there being ninety trainees in the whole institution. A single complaint by a father or guardian about a girl's disorderly behavior is enough to open a place for her in the reform school. Since evil propensities reveal themselves early and reform cannot be certain later than age sixteen to eighteen, girls are admitted to the institution no younger than seven and no older than sixteen. They remain until they are eighteen, if before that they have not been taken in service in a private home or sent to a farm. Even then, however, the school's supervision over the foster child does not end. The school keeps track of her and continues to have a beneficial influence over her.

Here it is apropos to mention the preventative, so to speak, schools which are established to deter even those who are not, but could be, on the wrong path if left without special supervision and care. Regardless of the fact that municipal solicitude extends to the child of every city-dweller and that free education lightens the burden, there is nevertheless a whole class of people who have no parents or shelter and are helpless. The state is concerned about these unfortunates too and the elimination of all possibilities for poverty. I did not encounter any destitute people on the streets of Boston. Children who are not supported by charity live in state-supported schools which have been established for them. They are from five to fifteen years old and, according to the report for 1855, it appears that there were even 59 children younger than five in such schools, along with 396 between five and ten and 132 from ten to fifteen years of age. In short the resources of the state insure that a poor person needing the community is not forgotten. Those resources comprise mainly taxes on the property of citizens, but they are so great that they cover all the expenses and needs of society.

After having seen and acquainted myself with the municipal institutions in Boston, I set out for its environs. Aside from the islands, the city is surrounded by small towns in the suburbs. The general character of all of them is one and the same: lanes of elms and sycamores of which the Bostonians are such lovers, and roads lined with bright little houses of the kind seen all over London and the other great commercial cities of England. Transportation in all directions is easy and convenient and many families stay in their cottages even in the winter. If America surpasses the rest of the world in quantity of railroads, Boston and the state of Massachusetts, in proportion to its area, has the largest amount of railroad track.

Finally it must be noted that just as history made Boston a center of learning, so its location and the industriousness of its residents could not but be reflected in commerce and industry. Steam factories operate in all parts of the city, and Boston mechanics are renowned throughout the Union and even outside it. Boston serves the same function for production in New England as the port of New York does for that of the western states. The so-called White Mountains and the altitudes generally in New England gave rise to the idea in Boston of carrying ice to the hot countries of India and to the Antilles Islands, and this trade has remained almost exclusively in the hands of Boston merchants.[16] The abundance of timber in the nearby mountains did much to foster shipbuilding and the construction of many wharves in Boston; from a commercial point of view, however, the proximity of such a city as New York renders Boston of secondary importance.

16. Frederic Tudor of Boston conceived the idea of shipping ice to the West Indies in 1805. In 1833 he began shipping ice to Calcutta. By 1850, Tudor, along with other enterprising New Englanders, had extended the Boston ice trade to every large port in South America and the Far East. The ice trade prospered for a generation after the Civil War, until the invention of cheap artificial ice. Morison, *Maritime History of Massachusetts*, pp. 282–83.

3

New York, I

I

There are countries where one encounters difficulties in moving about
from place to place with his belongings. Either roads are nonexistent
or impassable, or horses are generally lacking, and one travels only
because he must or because he feels an irresistible urge to do so. In
America the difficulty is of another kind: one does not know what road
to take, or what railroad or steamship to choose.

They all meet at the same points, the lines are the same or almost
the same length, and prices are identical. Especially for a novice who
only several days earlier has set foot on soil quite unfamiliar to a
European, the answer to the question is not as easy as it seems. One
looks at a map of the railroads and is dazzled by the network that cov-
ers the eastern, most industrialized section of the United States. Every
city is connected by rail with the principal centers of commercial and
industrial activity. To transport anything from city to city by horse,
mule, or camel would be as strange here as to build railroads in the
Far East for just any landing pier or small town. In America the pack
horse will soon be as antediluvian an animal as the mammoth.

The difficulty of making a choice put me to the test when I wanted to
go from Boston, where I had arrived from Europe, to New York. To
every question I asked in the hotel about when the train left for
New York, the luggage carrier or porter, who takes the place here of
the splendid European doorman, asked: "What route do you want to
take?" This answer put me in a quandary. The hotel coach is ready at
all times to take passengers and baggage to any railroad station. I
finally decided to go first by night train on the Fall River Line and
then on to New York by steamship. Leaving by train at six in the
evening, I would spend the night on the ship and be at my destination
early the next morning. At the designated time the hotel coach was

filled with passengers, their things loaded on the roof or chained to the back, and the carriage, driven by a single coachman, set off for the railroad station. I had not yet traveled on American railroads and had no idea what class to go. I was amazed that the schedule showed but one price for everyone. After my trunks had been unloaded, I went to get a ticket. While handing over the money, I stammered something about a class, but the American, not saying a word, thrust a ticket at me for which, incidentally, I was very glad. I saw that the others were impatient and I hastened to take my seat, remembering that here everyone fends for himself. "Help yourself," that is, take care of your needs yourself. An American will say that to you in season and out, and he himself sticks to the same rule, hurrying and rushing to carry out his business unassisted. There is the same kind of rush with the baggage. "Where to?" a gentleman asks, totally indistinguishable from any other gentleman traveling on the train. One thinks he will weigh the luggage, jot down a figure, take extra pennies for the extra pounds—not at all. He attaches copper stamps, "checks," to the handles of the luggage, frowns when he does not find the handles quickly or when he attaches the stamps clumsily, hands the owner stubs with the same number, and does not bother with anything else. If your trunk is sturdy it will arrive safely; if not, it is likely to burst. They return the broken pieces to you and should you say anything, they add the phrase, "Never mind," similar to our "It's nothing!" or "Help yourself." However much baggage you may have, they stow it all, give you five, six, ten tags, and with that the business is finished.

The cars were almost full when I entered one of them. The American passenger car is like a long room accommodating seventy or eighty people, with windows on both sides and two seats next to each window; in the center there is an aisle by which one can go from one car to another. The backs of the seats are made in such a way that they can be turned, allowing one to face the opposite direction and thus sit in the company of acquaintances. For night travel each passenger is given a soft pillow on which he can rest his head. The furniture is clean and covered with velvet, and painted on the walls of the cars is a pretty girl with a tambourine, or some sort of landscape, or a portrait of Washington. At either end of the car are mirrors and the ever present water tanks for everyone to use. But where are the common people? Where are the rich and powerful of this world? Where are the ladies? These were the questions I felt like asking my neighbor, whose pointed beard, lack of mustache and side-whiskers, thin pale-yellow face, soft felt hat, and simple, inelegant attire clearly revealed that he was a pure American. But he himself, probably by the same reasoning having guessed that I was a foreigner, began to speak to me. He asked how I liked the American railroad system and what impression America made on me. The questioner well knew he would be given an answer full of praise. The American accepts praise as pure truth, not for a moment doubting that his state and city are the best in the world, that in America everything is good, the government free, and so on.

It was not at all strange that the American was certain of my eulogies, for no one suffers a foreigner to speak badly of one's country. We are prepared to defend the slightest insult to our nation, but we ourselves perhaps will note one or another of its dark sides and will say what must be done to correct the evil. In this respect the American is even more chauvinistic than the Englishman, who will not permit another to censure England, its system, its ships, or its economy, but who himself will readily expose Parliament, the frauds of the ministers, or the East India Company. In the American's opinion, however, there are simply no evils in his country, and fully convinced that he has nothing to conceal, he readily speaks on any subject.

When you tell an American about class divisions in other lands, he becomes ecstatic about the equal state of each and all, without distinctions of wealth, origin, or connections, in his own country. In America he considers this equality absolutely natural, and he separates out only the colored (with whom whites want to have nothing in common, not even the air they breathe), and ladies (who are considered higher beings deserving esteem and general respect—an aristocracy, if you will). All others have the same rights, the best seat belongs not to the one who is rich and can pay more, but to the one who comes first. For the American, the fact that women are constantly deferred to proves that they are highly valued and that society wishes to protect them from men who, under the mantle of common equality, might behave rudely and embarrass them. A young girl is thus protected by public opinion and every honest man, and without any danger she may traverse the North American States from one end to the other to satisfy her curiosity, fully confident that whoever her neighbor might be, he will be happy to lend her aid and assistance.

After having loaded the train the conductor shouted: "Go ahead!

Forward!" instead of the English "All right! All is ready!" and the cars started to move. How glad I would be if they invented something like life preservers for railroads so that in the event of danger one would have some hope of rescue, as at sea. That wish evoked an unpleasant smile on the lips of the American beside me. He began to tell me that American railroads were slandered in Europe, especially in England, that they were in no way worse than European railroads, that in construction they were simpler and cheaper, that their trains ran faster and more often, and that, if accidents occurred, they did not at all exceed those on European railroads, especially when one took into consideration the length of the lines and the number of riders on them. Maybe so, but the railroad on which we were riding did not quite accord with what my neighbor was saying: one set of tracks, bridges not finished off with guard rails, road beds not raised and unprotected against walkers and animals, and the inevitable "cowcatcher" substituting for the live guards and workers of whom thousands and thousands would be needed in other countries to guard the thirty thousand miles of track that the United States possesses. The cowcatcher is a two-sided contraption attached to the locomotive, is pointed in the front and powerful enough to sweep cows off the tracks (whence its name) and generally anything else that might cause an accident if caught under the wheels of the train. Given our precautions, the cowcatcher would be superfluous. In America accidents would occur fairly often without it or, more truthfully, there would be an increase in the number that take place. That is not to say that human life is cheap here. I think the American is daring, enterprising by nature, and counts a lot on luck. But he does not go to fight wolves in the forest: that is his "Never mind!"

The railroad route through the local countryside was nothing special. At the start it ran along the shore of the bay, then through woods; dwellings quite often flashed by, and short stops were made everywhere. It all went quickly. The conductor, again a gentleman without any special distinctions except for the green tags in his hand, took tickets and gave in return checks on one side of which was written "Put this on your hat" (an action which everyone performed) and on the other side the names of the stations and the distances separating them. By the end of the conductor's round of the cars all the passengers had green stubs behind their hatbands, like cockades. When the time came to collect them, the conductor pulled

them out himself, even if the passenger were asleep. The American
is so serious and so hates to disturb matters with idle pranks that he
will never play jokes on a neighbor by pulling out his stub, and even
less will he appropriate it for himself. The train was huge, and about
nine in the evening I saw that everyone was getting ready to leave,
arming himself with his traveling things. I did the same and my
neighbor admonished me not to delay if I wanted to find a berth on
the ship. We reached the seaside town of Fall River. Everyone actually
broke into a run and, since no one lagged behind, there was neither
a crush nor disorder. Everyone worked silently by himself and for
himself as if the others did not exist.

"Where is the ship on which we are going?" I asked a Negro who
suddenly turned up. "You are on it," was his answer, and I actually
heard the hissing of the engines. The train had drawn right up to
the pier and the ship was pulled up so closely to the gangway that I
had not noticed crossing it, all the more since it was dark. I clambered
up the steps and was startled by an enormous room that served as a
general parlor and sitting room for the passengers. It was all in
carpets and mirrors and the walls were decorated with scenes and
paintings. The room was illuminated by massive bronze lamps that
were reflected in the mirrors. Furniture was spread out in various
corners, there was water for use of the passengers in the middle of
the room, newspapers and bibles on the tables, and a piano in one
corner. I looked at all this magnificence with something like un-
controlled amazement. Everything I had read in guidebooks and
heard in stories about American steamships was as nothing in com-
parsion with what I found on the steamship *Empire City*. But the cool,
eternally busy American had already dragged out the newspaper just
in from California, had put his feet on the marble fireplace or on its
bronze grille, had pulled out some chewing tobacco from the front
pocket of his waistcoat and had managed to savor its taste, spitting
into spittoons placed for this noble purpose by every table, couch,
and armchair. Spittoons here constitute the same essential accessory
as ash trays on German trains.

None of the Americans was surprised at the size of the ship or the
magnificence of the sitting room. Obviously all this was too commonplace for them. Not one of these "gentlemen" paid the slightest attention to the foreigner dumbfounded with wonder, and I could at
my own leisure more closely observe the faces of these people ponder-

ing, constantly calculating something, completely unsmiling and cold
until the familiar dollar came into the picture. Were it not for my
obliging neighbor, I would have sat observing all night. But the American had predicted how surprised I would be at one of the best American steamships and did not miss this chance to delight in the amazement of a novice. "Let's go," he said, "I'll have time before dinner
to show you the different decks of the ship." "Let's go," I gladly
answered, and thought we would immediately leave the room with
which, one might think, I was already familiar. But the American
showed me in detail the great number of paintings and the great
amount of velvet, mahogany, and bronze; evidently he wanted to
initiate me into all the subtle finery of the parlor.

At the other end of the ship on the same level was a room for ladies.
Here, even aside from the splendor of the ladies themselves, the
appointments were even more magnificent and luxurious than in the
room for men; I did not know if it were possible to wish for a better
dwelling on *terra firma.*

Both sides of the enormous deck on which this floating palace had
been built led out onto an open gallery, and we went out onto it. The
ship was moving rather fast, despite the night darkness. First a sailing
vessel poked by, then a steamship; whistles were exchanged on both
sides, and we proceeded safely on our way. Well, and what if there
were a collision? The American would have answered that the one
who survives intact continues on, and the one who does not sinks
to the bottom. But I did not ask such melancholy questions. On the
contrary, in a burst of awe for the intellect, the courage, and the
enterprise of the people, I remarked almost to myself: "What would
the savage Indians who lived along this coast two hundred years ago
have said if they had seen such a wonder!" "Well, not just the
Indians," my neighbor replied; "our steamships can amaze even a
person from civilized Europe."

We had not managed to finish our tour when there was a crash of
a Chinese gong struck by a Negro, and the sound carried far out to
sea. It had been necessary earlier to get a ticket for supper for half a
dollar. The table was arranged with various viands, meats, the pork
without which an American won't sit down to dinner or supper (the
same as with mutton in England), fish dishes, vegetables, and breads
of various kinds. Everyone selected whatever he wanted and asked
the Negro standing behind the food to cut a portion for him. But then

"Help yourself," don't dawdle; hurry, reach, don't offer anything to your neighbor, but take what you like because soon everything will run out, and—"It's all gone," says the Negro serving you. No matter where you look, everything is mixed up on the plates, everyone hurries as fast as he can, and in ten minutes chairs begin to scrape and everyone leaves his place as if having fulfilled an unpleasant duty with which, if he could, he would willingly dispense and which he fulfills only out of necessity. If you're not accustomed to this procedure, you could go hungry, but the example is catching, especially when you are sure to suffer if you lag behind. The ladies, who for dinner were allowed at the head of the line with the captain, sometimes did not follow the general example and remained a little longer at their tables. But no one uttered a word of censure, neither the lowest of the Negroes nor the grandest of the gentlemen, for the woman is the universal idol. A man who indulged too much in gastronomic pleasures, however, would have been subject to censure by his neighbors. Someone has compared Americans at the dinner table to sharks. The comparison is rather good, and the reason for the haste is the same: the desire to get down to business and not waste time.

I awoke early the next morning and went onto the gallery on the third deck. I saw that we were sailing in the middle of the sound, that land was visible on both sides. This was Long Island Sound, separating the mainland from Long Island. The first buildings belonging to New York that strike a stranger are those designed for charitable or correctional purposes. These were hospitals, lunatic asylums, workhouses and prisons which are located all over Blackwell's Island. At last we were in the East River, which flows along the eastern side of Manhattan, where New York is situated, while the Hudson River or northern river is located on the northwest side of the island. Flowing together and emptying into the Atlantic Ocean, these rivers form a harbor which, because of its size and depth, provides an advantageous position with respect to both Europe and the productive provinces of America. There is nothing like it in the entire United States. Having sailed past small blossoming towns spread out over Long Island, past Green Point, Williamsburg, and finally Brooklyn, and constantly encountering the ferries that carry people and cargoes across the wide river, our ship, with the mast swaying over the deck, entered New York harbor proper. It is here that real American enterprise shone through. Ships of various sizes, countries, and nations were going in all directions. Beyond the berthed ships the quays were not visible either in the East or Hudson rivers. On the landing piers, which were supported by wooden pilings and built for different companies, thronged various types of people, white and black, rich and poor, the well dressed and the half-naked. If the embankment was not pretty, not finished with stone, it was nonetheless convenient. No matter how deep a steamship's draft, the ship comes up to the shore itself to be unloaded. On the whole the matter was done quickly and efficiently.

II

Yes, this is a big city, I thought to myself as we pulled up to the pier on the Hudson. I took the checks out of my pocket, handed them to the gentleman looking after the baggage, told him I would be staying at the St. Nicholas Hotel, and boarded a carriage for the hotel.[1] We came out onto Broadway. I was not so interested in the immense—it's true—buildings, covered with signs, posters, and advertisements from top to bottom; this you can see in the large cities of Europe and you do not know who borrowed from whom this idea of attracting customers and visitors with enormous signs and colorful advertisements. I was more interested in the people on the street running about with preoccupied expressions, with not a stroller among them who might have come out for a breath of fresh air, or to admire the clear sky, or to dream a bit. But perhaps they dream on the run here. Broadway promised a lot for an observer, but first I had to get settled in the hotel. I chose the most American hotel, the one most American in style and preferred by Americans themselves over the others in New York. It was even bigger and more luxurious than the one in Boston, but in essence the arrangement was the same, not more than $2.50 per day. On all floors there were spacious rooms, halls, dining rooms, and wide corridors. Whole families stay in these hotels for months and years, attracted by the luxury and relative cheapness, compared at least to what a similar style of life might cost in their own homes. As a result, of course, family home life suffers. But a wife who loves

1. Opened only four years before Lakier's arrival, the St. Nicholas Hotel on Broadway was one of the most luxurious in New York City. John A. Kouwenhoven, *The Columbia Historical Portrait of New York* (Garden City, N.Y.: Doubleday, 1953), p. 277.

finery and outward brilliance is relieved of household cares, and at the same time a hotel gives her husband the chance to be closer to the center of activities. Commerce or a passion to make money devours every other passion, and the American is at home with his family very little. It is as if he is content with preaching general respect for the ladies and this sets his mind at ease. He dresses his wife up in silks and satins and buys her diamonds, but don't ask anything of a heart in which a golden idol is ensconced. Exceptions can not only be found but are even encountered frequently, mainly because in the people we are accustomed to call Americans there has been an influx of many, if not all, of the European nationalities. In the hotels there is a special table for ladies, special parlors, and special entrances. I leave it up to the ladies to decide whether they enjoy being isolated that way, or whether they are offended by the respect which is shown not to their personal qualities, their virtues and beauty, but to their sex, without any distinction. I myself happened to be a witness as a man got off a public omnibus in order to give his seat to his housemaid, only because she was a woman. And this is by no means the sole example.

There are several hotels similar to the St. Nicholas in spaciousness of rooms and luxury of appointments. They are all concentrated on Broadway and give the appearance of marble palaces. Each has its own habitual guests who go there and invite their acquaintances. Broadway is the favorite street of the industrial and commercial classes of the population. Others prefer Fifth Avenue where the wealthy families live. Whereas there is not a house on Broadway without an advertisement on it, on Fifth Avenue there are no advertisements at all, and this part of town reminds one most of all of the fashionable sections of London.

But it is time to get out of the hotel. Let's walk with others on the sunny side of Broadway to the park, one of the centers of city activities. The layout of New York is as easy to learn as the layout of St. Petersburg. It is remarkable that Dutch cities served as models for both, and that in part, at least, their builders were Dutch. The precision with which the American Empire City is divided up into sections, with broad straight streets that, with few exceptions, intersect each other at right angles, is obvious Dutch tidiness.[2] At the time of Gov-

2. New Amsterdam was established by the Dutch on the tip of Manhattan Island in 1626. It remained under Dutch control until surrendered

ernor Stuyvesant[3] the city extended only to present-day Canal Street, where there actually was a canal. In 1656 New York had in all 120 houses and one thousand inhabitants. As late as fifty years ago a large part of Manhattan Island was covered with the flower gardens and kitchen gardens of which the Dutch are so fond. It is remarkable that the streets intersecting Broadway up to Washington Square have historical names but beyond there are numbered from 1 to 131, as if history had become exhausted and refused to serve the imagination.

The streets traverse the city from northwest to southeast and intersect thirteen avenues at right angles. Approaching the tip of Manhattan Island that thrusts out into the sea, some avenues are cut off, and others discontinue their numbers and take on names. Not all streets are populated yet or even paved with stone but they are designated on the map, and when the population grows to about two million all the space from the tip, where the Battery is located, right up to Harlem, where the island ends on the north, will be occupied. In addition, the areas closest to New York, particularly Brooklyn, are being settled and constitute suburbs as it were. Population has multiplied more than tenfold in half a century [from 60,489 in 1800 to 629,810 in 1855]. Brooklyn alone already has nearly two hundred thousand inhabitants. One can easily see that by the beginning of the twentieth century New York will be bigger than Paris and will be second only to London.

Starting in the morning until late in the evening, Broadway and

---

in 1664 to the English, who renamed it New York. Although the Dutch began the rectangular street system, the pattern was more firmly established and extended by the English between 1680 and 1763. John W. Reps, *The Making of Urban America: A History of City Planning in the United States* (Princeton: Princeton University Press, 1965), pp. 148–54. Peter I founded St. Petersburg in 1703, and his strong Dutch leanings dictated the way in which the city was planned. He wished to have a town "on the model of Amsterdam." During the first half of the eighteenth century the straightness of the streets and their regular angular intersections shaped the growth of St. Petersburg. Christopher Marsden, *Palmyra of the North: The First Days of St. Petersburg* (London: Faber and Faber, 1942), chap. 2.

3. Peter Stuyvesant (1610–72) was director general of the Dutch North American colony of New Netherland, with its principal base at New Amsterdam, from 1647 to 1664.

the adjoining streets are crowded with magnificently dressed women and with Americans rushing about on business. Despite the wide sidewalks, the crush is so great that one cannot take a step without poking someone with elbows or body. If you want to excuse yourself or if you wait for apologies, the American has long since flown by like an arrow. It dawns on you that an American cannot tell a lamp post from a person and you end up like him—forcing your way through all obstacles and pushing with no less effort. Meanwhile there is the noise on the street from the thousands of carriages, omnibuses, and loaded wagons, from the din of youngsters hawking newspapers, the rattle of toys being demonstrated by street vendors, from whistles and squeaks and the hoarse shouts of auctioneers by their shops; notices and announcements are thrust in your hands, huge boards pasted with gigantic posters are being carried on their shoulders by men and women hired for this purpose; on some streets there are rails for American horse-drawn cars, and enormous coaches scurry back and forth. In the midst of this whirlpool the pale, lean American walks briskly to the pier at the port, or to the courts, or to Wall Street and the banks and offices of the commercial houses and companies. On the streets along the way American flags are stretched from one house to the other, painted all in long red and white stripes, studded with stars on a blue field. And there goes a detachment of militia in a full-dress parade marching in step to the music, or some kind of procession moving along. Who keeps order? How does all this move about and disperse without a word? To count how many carriages and how many people pass by a given place on Broadway in one hour is positively impossible. Apparently no one pays any attention to the interests of anyone else. Here and there policemen are visible, dressed in the manner of English police. But the main part of their day, it seems, is spent in guiding ladies across the street from one sidewalk to another, protecting the spoiled American woman from jolts and bruises. But then the American, keeping order himself, sees to it, as it were, that his neighbor does not disturb the peace either. Hence there are no police in America for the preservation of quiet and tranquility.

The buildings on Broadway are striking by their height, and the speed with which they have been erected is amazing. The most recently constructed are similar and resemble one another, to the detriment of architecture and art. The American does not want to be bothered with external opulence, and he has devised ways to build houses quickly and relatively cheaply. It is remarkable that when the lower floor is not yet ready, the upper is already available: the whole building rests on cast-iron pillars with floors, roofs, and foundations of the same metal; when people are already living and working in the upper stories, the lower is still a row of columns on which the house sits. They are now trying to build as many fireproof houses as possible, using wood only for window frames and doors. The architecture of public buildings, for which no American will decline to spend the last dollar, is distinguished by an imitation Greek style, and more than one temple resembling the Greek Parthenon houses some kind of bank, insurance office, school, library, etc. The New Yorker is proud of them and with good reason; they have all been built and supported with public funds.[4]

In the evening Broadway presents a different scene, illuminated by gaslight from street lamps and from rows of magnificent stores, confectioners' shops, amusement and entertainment places. It is then that you think the American can, indeed, enjoy himself. The broad sidewalk is again congested with people, in the midst of whom the richly attired ladies appear in bursts of gay colors; couples swing off the main street either to the theater or to a sumptuously lighted confectioner's; at various places of entertainment flags are fluttering and music is playing; everywhere there are immense playbills and dreadful signs with portrayals of beasts and fantastic wonders. Go into any theater (there are about ten on Broadway) and all are full of people and everyone is enjoying himself in his own way. Parades by militia and especially the fire brigades with their equipment, music, flags, and fireworks are also frequent in the evening.

No one better than the American can depict in an advertisement the beauty and sweetness of the most ordinary things. To praise them he will find room for poetry and prose, will call on history for help if only it can bring him a dollar, and will spare no money for spreading the information that there is only one thing on earth deserving attention and that this thing is at his disposal for ten or twenty-five cents. Well, how can one not be tempted, especially when Yankee Doodle rings out from the corner balcony, when it is declared that

4. Lakier has confused private business structures housing banks and insurance companies with public buildings housing schools and libraries.

not for long will New Yorkers have the pleasure of seeing the wonders
of Barnum somewhere in some saloon or theater.[5] The American looks
at an advertisement that attracts a large number of customers as an
enterprise that is successful and profitable thanks to his own efficiency
and industriousness. For advertising purposes, he is helped by newspaper references, which are sometimes merely vague hints, by "testi-
monials," or seeming expressions of thanks for pleasures afforded,
and by ruses of the most varied nature. All the while that the American
is silently and smilingly raking in the dollars his gullible countrymen
bring him, he is perhaps dreaming up some new sort of enticement
for the morrow.

Late at night Broadway becomes deserted, but the next day there
is again the same bustling crowd, the same running after the golden
idol, and, just as there is no limit to man's passion, there is no limit
to his enterprise when the goal is financial security if not self-
enrichment. Not everyone, by far, achieves this desirable state, and
here as everywhere there are many poor people. But nowhere do
they strive so for the realization of this ideal and nowhere do they
achieve it more frequently. There is not a servant who would not hope
in time to become an independent farmer with the honorable right to
elect and be elected in his county. There is not a poor man who
would not plan to have in the future a piece of land of his own. This
very real possibility of achieving self-reliance by means of an independent existence, the broad field of productive activity open to
everyone who comes to American soil, the stories (somewhat embellished by imagination and newspapers) about how people on this
side of the Atlantic become rich easily—all this attracts immigrants,
not only from poor and aggrieved Ireland, but from the rich Rhenish
provinces where the population is too dense, where history has raised
up one class at the expense of another, and where the poor have
despaired of ever achieving an independent life.

The statistics on immigration from Europe to the United States
offer unique and extremely interesting data. The figures speak clearly
and eloquently and their argument is inexorable.

[Lakier points out that, between 1819 and 1855, more than four

---

5. Phineas Taylor Barnum (1810–91), showman and promoter,
opened his American Museum at New York in 1842 and used elaborate
advertising for his bizarre exhibitions.

million aliens came to the United States, mostly from the United
Kingdom, Ireland and Germany.]

At the tip of Manhattan Island where the Battery is located is
Castle Garden. It is designed exclusively for immigrants during the
first moments of their arrival in the States.[6] There is an "immigrant
depot" here where each of the newcomers pays two dollars. On the
day the ship arrives with the immigrants one can see the pitiful,
emaciated, weary faces of fathers, mothers with infants, and youngsters exhausted by an inexpensive, it is true, but long and uncomfortable ocean voyage. They bring various kinds of junk to the New
World where it can prove to be useful. And if there were no hope of
finding a true haven here, as well as jobs and prosperity, who would
pay in order to endure all these privations, who could be compelled to
leave his homeland? A small sum of money collected through the
sale of some land or personal property at great loss is brought here
and serves as the base on which hotheads build castles in the air. But
the dreams disintegrate with the first step on American soil, not because the land is inhospitable, but because the science of making
money does not come easy anywhere. A European from Germany,
indeed from anywhere (except England, of course), good-natured
and hoping only for work, falls into the hands of an American who
looks to see whether or not he can swindle the fellow. And he does
so, because he wants to prove in practice the truth of the principle that
money brought from Europe does not provide happiness and wealth
in America; that, consequently, one must expend it, get to know all
the wisdom of the Americans, and then start anew to work and toil
until enough is acquired to begin a new life. The experience of a
compatriot who arrived here earlier can be of service to an immigrant,
and there is nothing easier than to pay a few dollars for signs and
advertisements that attract the novice's eye and to rush him via an
immigrant train to any part of the United States. At first he will apply
to a farmer for work, and will put aside savings from the large
salary that workers receive (usually a dollar a day). After having
saved up enough to buy several acres of land, he will cultivate part

6. An immigrant depot was set up at Castle Garden near the Battery
in 1855. All immigrants arriving in New York had to be landed there
and were able to change their foreign money, buy railroad tickets, seek
advice about jobs, and even obtain temporary shelter. The 1850s were
years of heavy German and Irish immigration.

of it, fence it in, build a little house and, if the possibility presents itself, resell it for a profit, buy a bigger and better plot or move to the still untouched Far West with its legendary treasures. Then he will acquire a piece of land somewhere on a navigable river, or close to a town and railroads, invite others to build houses and fences through common effort, clear part of the forest, seed virgin soil where it is more convenient, lay the foundations for a small town, and sing the praises of its location and its advantages to settlers. He will then wait until the United States government takes it into its head to sell these parcels of land at public auction, where the lowest bid is a dollar and a quarter for an acre and where even those who already own some land are allowed to bargain. Only then, that is, after the land has already been worked for several years, does the owner begin to pay taxes on it and assume the burdens of which earlier he had been free.[7] But the true seeker of independence and wealth will not stay here. He will fearlessly move on to a still more profitable place, one that promises to yield in time a treasure, a place where the European with knowledge obtained in the Old World under quite different conditions would not have foreseen anything at all, but where his Americanized brother will untiringly set to work again and find his treasure. Then, as a rich man, he will achieve his dream—he will settle in a large commercial city, sit in the senate or legislative assembly of the state, and add "Esquire" to his family name as a title of independence, or he will gain a respected place in commerce, becoming the head of a railroad company or bank or some other enterprise.

But what has happened to the friends of the lucky man? They have stayed in the city and got used to the diversions and glitter of city life. They work when there is work, try to make both ends meet, but cannot achieve the bliss destined for another. If the German immigrants can be upbraided for insufficient practical sense, general opinion about them as exemplary, industrious workers would accord them the right to a bright future. The Irish are distinguished by laziness or rather unconcern about tomorrow; they work diligently for days at a time until they joyfully exchange their hard-earned dollars for

7. The Preemption Law, passed by Congress in 1841, provided that any male adult could preempt a quarter section (160 acres) of the public domain by building a cabin and making certain improvements, then buy the land at the minimum price when it went on sale.

gin and whiskey. Meanwhile their children are without education and earn a living by picking pockets or by standing barefooted with brushes cleaning people's boots; their daughters give themselves up to debauchery wherever they are in domestic service. The same poverty from which the ragged Irishman fled across the sea persistently followed him to the New World. If the German does not have the boldness to throw himself into an enterprise which can ruin or enrich him, if he is content to sit with his stein of beer and tell stories to his friends about the success of some Hans from his village, the Irishman does not have the patience, the perseverance, the amazing constancy of the American to pursue a goal until he reaches it. When there is work, both the German and the Irishman have bread. The slightest whim of fate, a decline in business or trade, or a financial crisis, and the poor man has nowhere to go.

Something like it could be seen in 1857 when thousands of people needing bread and asking for work gathered in front of New York's City Hall.[8] The scene was worthy of the manufacturing district of some old European city. Is it America's fault that workers, who are needed in the central and western states, have piled up at the final stage of production and not at its source? During several days' time there were mass meetings and public gatherings. Speeches were made against the municipal authorities for not looking after the needs of the people and against the rich for using the labor of the people but refusing to provide aid in their hour of need. The beggars and the poor grew in number, crime became more frequent, and the streets at night were not altogether safe. The matter ended with the City Council assigning $250,000 for developing the so-called Central Park, a project which could provide work for a thousand people.[9] On one side the American merchants were becoming impoverished or at least said that they had been ruined by too many bold ventures unprotected

8. Lakier is describing one aspect of the financial panic of 1857 which began in August of that year. Caused by over-speculation in railroad securities and real estate, it also brought on a world-wide depression in shipping.

9. Although plans for Central Park had been proposed as early as 1850, the property for it was not purchased until 1856. Actual work on the park began in the depression year of 1857, when the city instituted a program of work relief for the unemployed. Kouwenhoven, *Columbia Historical Portrait of New York,* p. 295.

by ready capital; on the other side the workers were suffering from
the fear brought on by hunger and destitution. The matter could have
ended with the plundering of the city treasury, and the meetings of
hungry workers could have become disorderly and riotous. But happily
two months after the start of the bankruptcies business recovered and
the poor again had work. The memory of those unhappy times has
been preserved in a touching play, *The Poor of New York,* running
in one of the Broadway theaters.

It is a moot question whether in this instance it was better for the
municipal authorities to provide temporary assistance or to find a
way to provide steady work for the poor in the rural states where
there was a need for workers. It is sad that the rural population is
decreasing and the area of uncultivated land is growing while the
population of the cities is rising noticeably. America may in time reach
the same state of affairs as have the manufacturing and commercial
cities of England, that is, extreme poverty existing alongside extreme
wealth. Americans pay too little attention to this. New York serves
as evidence. In the course of fifty years the number of its inhabitants
has increased more than tenfold.

III

Isn't that kind of population density dangerous for the well-being
of a city? Economic questions can easily and necessarily be transformed into political questions, especially in America where all government is in the hands of private individuals—the citizens. Every city
is governed through elections of its citizens who are entrusted with
executive, judicial, and legislative powers. Isn't the well-being of the
citizens best served by a guarantee that elections are conducted
honestly and without bribery and that elected officials will fulfill their
duties with scrupulous integrity? In other words, could not the poverty
of the urban population that finds itself dependent on the wealthy
class be attributed to errors of administration, however strict the latter was in its beginnings and whatever were the sacred motives of
those who wrote the Constitution? I often happened to be at elections in various American states but nowhere do they present such
a spectacle as in New York. First of all the offices in New York are
especially prestigious and advantageous and those wishing to fill them
are far more numerous than in any other city in the Union. Secondly,
the right to vote is extremely broad according to the state constitution

of New York. Commerce, the great number of administrative departments necessary for a large city, the craving to make a fortune
or to improve one's income, the large number of companies, these
are what attract most people to New York. The vanity of those
hungering for office is gratified by earning the favor of the people,
making speeches at meetings, protecting the interests of the poor
workers, criticizing the other party as much as possible, and in general
propagating their own ideas when elections draw near. The main
thing is that the candidate strive not to be taken for a person trying
to gain influence, or as the American says, a "politician." The American people do not like individuals who have devoted themselves to
government affairs, and they distrust even the educated person with
good intentions as soon as he is reputed to be a politician. In the
speeches of the person anxious for office and in those of his minions,
the "canvassers," as well as in the advertisements nailed up in various
places around the city, the candidate must be put forward as a "man
of the people," and on election day he must go to the polls to see what
passions are agitating the voters and why they wish the election of
one or another official. After it is certified that a person has the right
to vote and that he resides in that section of town where he has come
to do so, the voter drops into the ballot box the name of the official
whom he wants for one or another office, a matter he has agreed upon
earlier with his co-workers, his neighbors, and others. Persuasion is
accomplished through words, whiskey, or money; sometimes it is
accompanied by threats and even ends with revolvers, if all the above-
mentioned means are unavailing. Newspapers, too, play an important
role. Of course not every candidate has his own newspaper, but the
party to which he belongs uses all the contrivances and tricks to en-
sure that its protégé will gain the sought-for office; sometimes there
is recourse to the same lies as appear in personal advertisements.
Whether an election is advantageous or disadvantageous for the
city depends on the moral disposition of the leaders in this affair—the
"leading men," whose voices imperceptibly and invisibly have a substantial influence on the entire government.

[Lakier describes in detail the organization of the New York City
government.]

Each of the enumerated administrative bureaus has its own office
and clerk; the number of deputy clerks is set and chosen by the executive authorities. The clerks see to it that the actions and orders of the

department with which they are concerned are brought to the attention
of the general public. Generally municipal affairs entrusted to a
specific department are not kept secret from the public; in addition to
the fact that the doors of each office are open and that newspapers deal
with subjects relating to city government, at certain times reports are
presented to the mayor by his subordinates and by the mayor to the
City Council. Nevertheless, misuse, especially embezzlement of funds
by public officials, is quite frequent. Everyone talks and writes about
it but the funds vanish, and though the officials are prosecuted justice
is a long way from always being satisfied.

In private life public opinion does not severely chastise the person
who, profiting from someone else's negligence, makes himself a fortune, then ruins himself and drags others into poverty through risky
ventures or a declaration of bankruptcy, only to bide his time to begin
his business anew. The American never despairs. Ruined today, he
can become rich tomorrow. Even if this theory should not apply to
city government, general complaints in America about the existence
of graft and the use of public funds for private purposes by officials,
especially in most recent times, are quite commonplace. It frightens
those who consider the power of public opinion, along with the im-
possibility of concealing even the smallest misdemeanor, one of the
main advantages of government by the people. In New York such
misuse of funds is more frequent than anywhere else. Who is to blame
for such sad occurrences? Could it be the voters themselves and the
frequent change of city authorities? It is unfortunate that, if an American who is elected to office for one or two years foresees that at the
end of his term he will not merit the good favor of the voters, he
will want to enrich himself while in office just as he would have in
private business under fortunate circumstances. Meanwhile the seek-
ers after office in New York are no fewer than in any European city.
They are for the most part Irishmen who know the language and
agree to fixed salaries. With each new mayor there appears a new
phalanx of officials to replace ones chosen by the previous mayor.
Public affection changes and in our day it has been changing as often
as it did in ancient Athens. Whoever is extolled to the skies and praised
for his dedication to the public's welfare cannot be certain that tomorrow he will meet with the same sentiments. In the past year during the elections for a new mayor, instead of support for Mr. Wood,
who was the public idol for two years, voices arose among the people

in favor of another and Daniel Tiemann of the Independent party gained the upper hand.[10] The brevity of service, to say nothing of the passions that play an important role in public elections, explains this phenomenon, one which worries people who truly love the blessings and good fortune of the Union.

The American does not become completely attached to any one occupation: today a farmer, tomorrow an official, then a merchant and a seafarer. This is not because he is fickle but because he is adroit enough, or as the people themselves say, "smart" enough, to accustom himself to any occupation he chooses, either from inclination or necessity. He will finally stay in the one that seems to him the most lucrative. Thus officials who are replaced every two years join the ranks of private citizens and choose occupations according to their taste. But the American considers public education a necessity if one is always to be ready for such a change, a change that by our understanding is abrupt and not easily explained. He is not concerned about being a great scholar. At age fourteen or fifteen almost every young man is left to his own devices; he works, bustles about, and acquires some capital, not so that he has some money for a rainy day, but so that he can pool his modest resources with someone else's to function with the combined strength of two. Trust is innate to the American, and however often a less perspicacious person falls prey to a more far-seeing fellow, he does not cease to acknowledge the strength and power of a partnership or company as opposed to a single individual. In any case I think it is education alone, spread to all classes of the native population, that can explain the phenomenon. The immigrants and their children serve as direct proof of this. The American blames them for all the poverty and debauchery in New York, makes them responsible for misdeeds in public service, and the whole Know-Nothing party howls loudly against the gladness with which America greets its evil—the poor immigrants.[11] It is not likely that this opinion

10. Fernando Wood (1812–81) was one of the three or four leaders of Tammany Hall in the 1850s. He was elected mayor of New York in 1854 and reelected in 1856. Daniel Fawcett Tiemann (1805–99) was a manufacturer of paints and active in local politics. He served as a New York City alderman for five years (1850–55) and tried to stop the sale of liquor in the city. In 1859 he was elected mayor.

11. Officially known as the American party, it was one of the national political parties in the 1850s. The popular name Know-Nothing came

will ever prevail because the United States still cannot manage without Europe, and the claims of the Know-Nothings, moreover, are repugnant to freedom of government. But the very existence of this party, which fields its own candidates in every election, demonstrates to what degree the Old World immigrants are guilty in the eyes of Americans.

"Virtue and morality are indispensable for popular government," said Washington in his Farewell Address. Therefore he bequeathed as a subject of prime importance the consideration of an institution for spreading general education. As public opinion grows stronger, it is essential that it be truly enlightened, and the views of the great citizen-leader and general are shared by Americans. Every district and every township has its own school and church, for which a part of the public lands are set aside, and the inhabitants elect their own governing officials. The township itself has the obligation of seeing that the children receive an education. It knows the value of education, provides funds for the support of schools, and sees to it that the worthy goal is actually attained. New York can point with pride to its schools for the colored, all the more so in that these institutions were built according to the same model as those for whites. But since public opinion in New York, too, cannot abide the Negro's black skin, colored children are segregated. In visits to New York schools I became convinced that the colored are able to learn quickly and, if not better, then at least no worse than whites. On the other hand the southern states cannot forgive New York for an innovation that directly disproves their notion of the incompetence and primitiveness of the entire black race. It is interesting that in New York itself when they began to seek locations for teaching black children and supporting them by charity, it required supreme efforts and donations. But this is the greatness of the American character: it does not give in to the first obstacles, on the contrary it is irritated by them and gains in strength and energy; it acts privately and through organized societies, through books distributed among the people and through agitation at

---

from the fact that members of its secret lodges used "I don't know" as a password. Anti-Catholic and anti-immigrant, the party called for the exclusion of Catholics and foreigners from public office and for a twenty-one-year residence for immigrants as qualification for citizenship.

public meetings, until the noble purpose of the affair ripens and yields rich fruit.

Higher education is available to New Yorkers at a university founded in 1831. Compared to other schools and even to the universities of other countries, New York University does not have a significant number of students. This is largely because the training received at grammar schools is sufficient for the active, independent life that attracts the American. Life itself fills in the rest of his education. A young man necessarily develops when he is left to himself and when he feels the obligations society places on him, and regardless of what is said about American newspapers, magazines, and periodical publications in general, in many ways they exercise a positive influence on the coming generation. One must not be at all surprised if at fifteen or sixteen a young American has formed his own independent views on things, has chosen one or another party, and reflects this party's spirit and direction in his discussion of politics. Even many Americans, and more so foreigners, see an evil in this unrestricted freedom to discuss the needs of their own groups and the actions of the officials they have elected to government. They see the possibility that it will needlessly disturb public tranquility without benefiting anyone. This would be a just concern if it were not for the fact that the opposing side has an equal right to refute and correct errors or blunders. The American, in addition, does not trust the printed word; in newspapers he does not seek out scholarly essays that would tell him what to do and how to do it, but rather a full chronicle of what is happening at home, in Europe, and in other parts of the world.

Literature profits little from the 3,754 newspapers published in the United States (613 in New York alone). But there are many benefits both for foreigners and for Americans in the incredible speed with which one can find out what is going on around him. There is hardly a people who know the most distant parts of their country better than the Americans know theirs. Large newspapers everywhere, both in America and abroad, have their own correspondents. Without reporters not a single official or ceremonial breakfast or dinner could take place, nor a single ball of a minister, consul, or other official. A reporter has time for meetings, too, he mingles in the crowd and listens to opinions, and still he manages to make it in time for a dinner. If there are speeches at the dinner he pulls out his little book and takes notes. He tries to find out who is in attendance, how the ladies are dressed—and if their attire merits attention, he notes it down. The next day the whole country will learn what happened, and if it is interesting, it will be reprinted. It is obvious that one finds everything printed in newspapers, even trifles unworthy of attention. But nothing is concealed, and if society's newsmonger cannot be bribed with the glass of champagne a reporter drinks at a dinner, or by his invitation to a ball, not to invite him is still worse. The whole country will find out not only that there was a ball or a dinner and what rumors there are about it, but also that no reporter was favored with an invitation. Any description of any kind of celebration or meeting appears the day after it took place, and there are as many reporters as there are large newspapers. One cannot take a step or two out of the ordinary that someone does not notice it and publish it. Go out, for example, with a liveried footman and order a coach and four, be a prince or a count, and the next day the whole country will know about it, regardless of the fact that it seems only the holder of such distinctions would be concerned, and regardless of what little importance these distinctions are.

Newspapers have their correspondents in various lands, and how impatiently news is awaited on the day a ship arrives from Europe! A small steamboat is sent to meet the ship which, especially if it is coming from Europe and headed toward Boston, throws a small tarred barrel overboard with the latest news, exchange rates, and prices on the various markets. Before ever touching land the news is already flying over the telegraph to all the United States and by evening is being read in New Orleans and Kansas.

[Lakier describes the leading newspapers in New York City and is incredulous at their huge circulations, each nearly twice as large as that of the London *Times,* "the most widely distributed European newspaper." He also mentions the large circulations of periodicals such as *Scientific American* and *Harper's Magazine,* the cheap reprints of English books, and the many libraries in New York City. This prompts him to comment that "If education were not so widely diffused among Americans this great number of cheap publications could not exist." Education, he points out, is also promoted by the numerous publications of the American Bible Society and the American Tract Society.]

With such resources for the improvement of public morality, it is no wonder that, despite the variety of elements intermingled in the city, everyone observes Sunday as strictly in New York as in England. Even the German, who dislikes conforming to the English custom of observing Sunday as a day devoted exclusively to prayer, rest, and meditation, does not appear on the broad empty streets of a city that yesterday served and tomorrow again will serve—with exemplary zeal—the quest for gold and worldly gain. In what other city, furthermore, could one find the success enjoyed here by sermons on abstention from hard liquor which, incidentally, is quite essential for workers in a cold climate? Thousands of people everywhere have signed petitions for the approval of laws against hard liquor. After the law was adopted by the state of Maine, where it originated, other states began to agitate for it. The Temperance Society now estimates its followers in the hundreds of thousands.[12]

On the other hand, nowhere does phrenology, mysticism, communion with spirits, a belief that what is hidden from us can be discovered in indirect ways from twirling tables and plates—nowhere do these mysterious sciences enjoy such success as in America. Once again these ideas are disseminated by the same means: meetings, public lectures, societies, cheap books virtually thrown at people; even several mediums between the real and unreal wórlds have been discovered. But it must be confessed that Americans are more fortunate in inventions for the material benefit of man, in the telegraph and railroads, than in their deviations from the declared goals of Providence.

12. Maine passed the first statewide prohibition law in 1846. By 1855 thirteen other states had passed similar laws.

4

New York, 2

I

[Lakier describes the natural advantages of New York harbor, the growth of the city as a great depot and market for European manufacturers, and the river, canal, and railroad networks that made New York City a major export center for the grain and raw materials of the western states and Great Lakes region.]

In recent times America has been shipping great quantities of grain abroad and thus may become a dangerous rival for Russia in the future. Meanwhile New York, with its transportation routes and cheap freight charges, is promoting the development of agricultural activity in America. The virgin soil of the western states is not cultivated very intensively, but there is so much of it that the farmer's labor is rewarded a hundredfold. Instead of human hands—expensive in a small population—steam plows and other improved agricultural machines are used. With relatively few expenses farmers thus get larger crops and are in a position to market them more cheaply. What influence that agricultural situation has had on commerce is evident from statistics, which demonstrate how quickly the amount of grain pouring into New York from the western cities has increased in recent times. I take only Chicago, which owes to this branch of activity its rapid and—even in America—almost unparalleled prosperity. In 1844, 6,320 bushels (a bushel equals 1.386 chetverika) of grain were shipped by lake from Chicago; six years later in 1850 this figure had already reached 100,871, and in 1856 it was 169,516. Other cities send forest products, timber, grain, and minerals to New York, and from there they are distributed to Europe and other parts of the world. The southern states also use New York as a main port for foreign trade and thousands of bales of cotton are shipped here by sea from New Orleans to be sent to English factories.

New Yorkers have thus become brokers not only for producers
and merchants of the entire Union, but also for European consumers.
The boldness with which Americans tirelessly carry their products to
the far corners of the earth, unafraid of foul weather and sometimes
not stopping at a port of call for months at a time; the almost constant
participation in the undertaking itself; the comparatively low shipping
charges; and the desire to outdo the English, all combine to make
Americans the best, most active, and cheapest of shippers. The Americans spare neither labor, health, nor life to ship and sell goods overseas for a few pennies less than the English do. To maintain their
markets is the aim of the Americans, and they will achieve it. Although all the sea-trading nations of the world do business with New
York, most of the shipping is done by the Americans themselves.

The active participation of the North American states in foreign
trade is necessarily reflected in shipbuilding. If the Union cannot
boast of its naval fleet (even the government is little concerned about
it in peacetime), still the merchant fleet is vast and in time of war it
is ready to serve the state. The American navy, however, is insignificant compared to the English navy. Moreover it is scattered about
various stations in all the world's oceans and only a small squadron is
at the disposal of the federal government. By its location, however,
North America is a sea state and in the event of a dispute with another
power it would insist first of all on an expansion of the navy. But in
peacetime Americans do not understand the purpose of supporting a
huge defense capability when there is no need for it.

The speed with which boats are built in America is incredible and
if, as in other kinds of work, the Americans are far from that finished
quality that distinguishes the work of the English, the riches of the
various forests, nonetheless, make possible amazingly luxurious trim-
mings. Americans are also little concerned about durability. Capital
must return quickly and the faster a ship is replaced by a new one,
the greater is the profit to the shipbuilders, to the owners of the forests and wharves, and to others. Meanwhile, however, every new
mechanical technique, every discovery, is taken into account and applied to the matter at hand, so that nowhere do improvements spread
so quickly as in America. This circumstance, along with an innate
American love for activity, is further explained by the large scale
on which goods are produced. Any worker who sees a need for improving one or another part of a machine suggests it to the factory

owner, who in turn provides financial and material resources for experiments. The aid to inventors is not counted in farthings; they are
given assistants and all the coal and wood they need. If the experiment
is unsuccessful, it is not held against the one who made it. On the
other hand if the experiment is crowned with success, the owner
takes the inventor into the company and in due course a patent for
the invention is obtained. Whereas improvements in France are made
almost exclusively by the learned and the members of the Academy,
in America it falls to the lot of anyone who is clever and bright.

Standing as it does in the forefront of American commerce, New
York could not but occupy the place of honor in shipbuilding. There
are several private wharves on the East River, and on one of them,
belonging to Mr. Webb, there is now being built a model steamship
for the Russian navy which will carry the name *General-Admiral*.
According to the experts the dimensions of this screw frigate will
surpass anything ever built in this class (its length is 325 feet, width
55 feet, and depth 36 feet). I will never forget how I was among
those invited to the keel-laying of this enormous steamship, heard a
Russian prayer read on foreign soil by a fellow Russian officer, and
how, along with others, I expressed a wish to see this new warrior in
our waters. This wish should become a reality soon, despite all the
difficulties that have to be overcome in constructing and rigging the
giant. For us it will be eloquent evidence of the degree to which the
power of private enterprise and wealth is developed in America.[1]

[Lakier describes the banking system in the United States in 1857,
when each bank was permitted to issue its own paper money.]

There can be no harm in the existence of paper money so long as
faith in banks continues. Even the state government, which is not per-

---

1. William Henry Webb (1816–99), owner of a large shipyard on
the East River, was one of the great American shipbuilders of his time.
He turned out more than a hundred and fifty vessels, both sail and steam,
wood and iron, merchantmen and warships. Webb conceived the idea of
a powerful steam frigate but was rebuffed at Washington. He then visited
Russia and persisted until he received a $1,125,000 order for the *General-
Admiral*. Besides Lakier, those present at the keel-laying ceremony on
September 21, 1857, were the Russian minister and a number of Russian
officers. When launched one year later, the *General-Admiral* was hailed
as "the largest wooden ship in the world." *Harper's Weekly*, October 2,
1858.

mitted by the American Constitution to issue bills of credit, readily
accepts these notes, and gold and silver money, considered on a par
with paper notes, is necessary only for exchange when traveling to
another state having its own banks. In that case New York assignats
are accepted with some loss: it is presupposed that the assignats must
be returned to the bank that issued them. In general, the better
known a bank is and the more reliable its operations are, the more
readily will people do business with it. And if someone needs hard
currency to pay off accounts abroad, he can usually get it without any
difficulty. But if in the American west, for example, they stop accepting
assignats of even the better banks and start demanding gold and
silver instead; if it becomes necessary to pay five, six, ten, and sometimes a higher percent for having paper money accepted in place of
gold and silver; and if foreign trade requires that excess imports be
paid for in hard currency because the promissory notes of commercial
houses are considered unreliable, then credit can be saved in only one
way: draw out reserves of hard currency from the vaults to satisfy
the demands of depositors, to reduce the charge for changing paper
money into gold and silver, to prove, in other words, that the paper
money is actually worth the value printed on it. Otherwise everyone
rushes to the bank demanding the return of his money. If he gets it,
he no longer puts it in circulation; if he does not get it, he ceases
his activity at least for a time, being in no condition to pay those
whom he owes. If he has a factory, he dismisses the workers and tries
to finish off or curtail trade. Meanwhile the producers of raw materials, the farmers, distrusting circumstances, have stopped loading
the grain that went for the exchange of foreign goods. There is a general depression in trade and industry. Banks lock their doors against
the importunate demands of depositors. The bankruptcy and ruin of
private individuals and commercial houses becomes a common occurrence, one leading to the other. Then there is faith only in hard currency, in the shiny gold dollar. In September 1857 the New York
newspapers reported morning after morning on the fall of the ten
best commercial houses and companies in various parts of North
America, the cessation of activity and general bankruptcy of city and
rural banks. The poverty of workers who lived only by their labor
would have been a misfortune of long duration for America if the
high interest rate paid for hard currency had not drawn gold and
silver from abroad and if California had not supplied New York

with millions of dollars. In mid-December of 1857 all who had been demanding hard cash as the only condition under which they would sell and engage in trade returned to the former order of things and equilibrium was apparently restored.

At the time there were various explanations for an event that will be long remembered not only in America but in Europe as well. They sought for a way to alleviate the misery by limiting the right of bankers to issue paper money insufficiently backed by hard currency. But the reasons for the problem go much deeper; they are to be found in limitless credit, in enterprises begun without a financial base, and in the issuing of a huge amount of various stocks and bonds that were accepted by banks and placed in circulation as if they had some value. Meanwhile the demand for luxury imports from Europe began to grow, and there were too few American raw materials for export. The excess of imports over exports had to be paid for in hard cash, which in turn became insufficient to cover the demands of depositors. Even before the beginning of the so-called financial crisis it was evident from the accounts of the New York banks that nine dollars brought only one dollar in hard cash. Majority opinion, echoes of which were heard in Congress, the state legislatures, and the newspapers, was that there should be a decrease in the number of banks and a reduction in the amount of paper money not properly guaranteed, with a requirement that the reserves of hard cash be equal to at least one-fourth of the assignats issued. In other words, this meant curtailing the private enterprise of a people that knows no limit in its activity. But not three months had passed from the beginning of the crisis and business once again proceeded in orderly fashion. Some had suffered, others had gained, and banking principles in essence remained unchanged.[2]

With all of that, Americans were not dejected, and affirmed over and over again that they were far from being bankrupt, that their common property was more than sufficient as a guarantee for those with whom they were doing business, just as in the nation as a whole property far exceeds the figure for bonds.

In any case, New Yorkers are right in maintaining that they are a long way from general bankruptcy and are in a position to pay off

2. Lakier's description of the financial panic of 1857 is generally accurate.

their obligations. As for property taxes, it is natural that with the growth of the city, the laying out of new streets, lighting them with gas and paving them, supplying water, erecting new buildings for needed charities, poorhouses, and hospitals, and the strengthening and improving of the police organization, expenses for city govern-ment are bound to increase But at least the people can enjoy the bene-fits their money makes possible: free schools open to every city-dweller for the education of his children; clean, lighted streets; and running water and gas everywhere.

II

Every American city, however small it may be, is concerned about two matters regarding the health and well-being of its residents: that clean fresh water be provided everywhere and that streets and houses be lighted with gas. For New York, with its vast area and population, these requirements are all the more urgent. Furthermore, despite the fact that parks and squares already exist in various sections of the city and that entire streets are planted with sycamores and other trees, a central park became a necessity for the recreation and convenience of the inhabitants in the city's distant parts. More than five million dollars have been allocated for its construction and this one sum is enough to demonstrate the size this park will be. Americans say there will be nothing like it in any capital of the world. Its seven hundred acres will include the most varied paths, a botanical garden, and a place for training troops and militia. It is two and a half miles long and more than two-thirds of a mile wide. But the principal treasure of this park is a reservoir supplying water to all of New York, even its most distant parts. The reservoir is open to visitors. One can only marvel at the mass of clear bright water that man has managed to gather within stone walls for the use of city inhabitants.

Millions of dollars are necessary for such an undertaking and taxes on property and income are the sole source of funds. If the city ad-ministration authorizes a loan to be made, the payments on capital and interest come out of the same source.

[Lakier describes the functions and organization of the New York police. He notes that for national defense there is only a small standing army of less than eighteen thousand but a large civilian militia of nearly two and a half million. "In such a way," he comments, "the democratic Americans reconcile their dislike for an idle, expensive

standing army in peacetime with the need for protection in case of
enemy invasion."]

Civic spirit is even more clearly manifested in mutual self-help in
the event of fire. What in other countries is done by hired people, in
America is carried out by the citizens themselves. An alarm bell atop
the town hall has only to clang one, two, three, up to eight times, and
everyone who is assigned to one of the eight fire districts into which
the city is divided runs to a fire equipment shed (these sheds house
fifty-one fire engine companies) and grabs some light gear. One company after another quickly appears at the fire. Hoses are connected
to the water reservoirs that stand at every crossroads, and the Americans, sparing neither strength nor time nor health nor even life, throw
themselves into saving someone else's property. A great many spec-
tators attracted to the spectacle also help pump water. A private matter is transformed into a public concern and the fire often yields to
the pressure of the persistent Americans. Fires are quite frequent in
American cities, for in distant parts the buildings are still made of
wood. Hence a great deal of attention has been given to perfecting
fire-fighting machines. The requirements are lightness and easy movement. As soon as a fire-fighting company obtains improved equipment
or when the anniversary of its founding comes, it takes advantage of
the occasion to dress up in red fire-jackets, to take hoses, hooks, ladders, and buckets, and to parade down Broadway past the decorated
balconies and houses to the accompaniment of music, fireworks, and
happy, thankful shouts from the people. The evening then ends with a
public banquet (these processions always take place in the evening
when the workers, who are the firemen, are free from their daytime
jobs). Every city has its firemen's holiday (in New York it is June
14) on which firemen from everywhere gather together. Railroad
companies reduce their prices for firemen, the city assumes a holiday
mood, and thousands of firemen from various sections of the Union
take part in a merry procession. However, companies of firemen not
infrequently parade on other days and on nearly every holiday both
they and the militia take part in the celebrations.

The duty of everyone to run to a fire is incomprehensible to a European. But in this lies the difference between American society and ours,
that no one can, no one must, and no one wants to refuse labor for the
common good. Labor is respected in all its aspects and forms and only
idleness and parasitism are condemned by public opinion. I cannot

but add that the equipment of the fire companies (one must not call them commands) is notable for its smart appearance, and at the New York Crystal Palace Exhibition [opened in 1853] I saw models of fire-fighting equipment that were indeed luxurious and dashing. Only reluctantly will Americans move away from this kind of fire-fighting system. Otherwise steam equipment, which was invented in Cincinnati, Ohio, and operates incomparably better and more powerfully than human hands, would have long since been introduced. But then horses would be necessary, and all the poetry of the firemen's camaraderie and of their parades would vanish.[3] There is no other way to explain why a really outstanding invention has not taken hold in a country that lovingly applies steam to all parts of the economy and to all work.

III

We ought now to cross over from the city to Blackwell's Island and Randall's Island to see how the millions in city taxes are used for the care of the poor and the orphaned and for the correction of wrongdoers. But first we must take a look at the courts of New York State. The basic system is generally the same as for the Union and the separate states, that is, circuit judges, oral legal proceedings open to the public, and the presence of lawyers and juries. These ancient popular institutions of the Anglo-Saxons were brought to the New World unchanged, along with statutes that were, properly speaking, remnants of feudal and Roman times.

On the other hand Americans can point with pride to the fact that each state of the Union has published and added its own statutes to the system. In this sense the New World is far ahead of England where, in the opinion of the most experienced jurists, the law is a mystery to both the people and the judges. The English, while putting a curb on arbitrary rule, respect written as well as common law as authoritative. But the halls of Parliament have more than once reverberated with loud and just complaints that the chaos of laws is unworthy of a country and a people who claim to be in the forefront

3. Unlike the hand-pulled fire-fighting equipment in New York, the steam engines introduced in Cincinnati for pumping water were drawn by horses. For Lakier's description of steam fire-fighting equipment in Cincinnati, see pp. 153–54.

of world civilization; that of fifty thousand statutes entered on the statute books, literally tens of thousands have been cancelled or replaced; that lawyers are like priests, introducing others to the secrets of their art for payment; and so on. In this respect the situation in the United States is more advantageous; indeed it would be unnatural if the people did not know their own laws, since everyone is called upon to serve as a juror and anyone can be elected to judicial office.

Judges in New York are elected for limited terms from among those who know how to win the favor of the voters. The disadvantages of such a system are clear: playing up to the people, especially in matters where the whole community or city is involved, in order to stay in favor; pandering to the powerful; being too lenient toward common failings, such as bankruptcy; and frequently an ignorance of the laws —were it not for lawyers, a judge from another city would not always be able to get to the truth. But that is not to say that a lawyer is always courteous to a judge. An attorney seems to sense that he is indispensable to a judge, and he restrains himself as little in court as in any other place. His speech is loud and sharp and sometimes might even be considered insulting to the judge.

American legal procedure has many aspects worthy of detailed study and, where possible, of application. Its foundation is English, but, in adopting it, those writing the Constitution were able to benefit from the advantages of the youthful, unconstrained history of the state: what could not have been introduced in England, even when recognized as advantageous and necessary, was introduced on the new continent without great difficulty. The cheapness, simplicity, and quickness of the procedures are enviable blessings, for which one can readily forego historical anachronisms and institutions valued merely because they are old. In this regard, one must give America its due and point to the following, additional advantage: each state has its own legislation, and innovation is not hindered by having to consider the profit to, or the opinion of, a neighboring state. If the innovation turns out to be bad, the means will be found to substitute a more suitable one. If there is a flaw in this procedure, it results from the fact that judges are popularly elected and that an eight-year term is too limited for so important an office as a judgeship.[4] This circum-

4. An eight-year term for New York State Supreme Court judges was adopted in 1846.

stance may partly explain the complaints of Americans that crimes about which there can be no doubt sometimes go unpunished, as well as complaints that judges are not always indifferent to money and bribes. Americans see the way to combat this evil, which so directly cancels the benefits expected from the court system, in electing people who are trained for the office of judge and in making the term of office as long as possible. A life term through elections, however, is impossible and would even be more dangerous, for then there would be no way to remove a person who is perhaps honest, but incompetent and lacking in energy.

IV

Closely associated with criminal procedures is the prison system. With legislation that does not permit exile and does not recognize corporal punishment, a great deal of attention is always given to prisons.[5] And so it should be. In meting out punishment the state does not seek revenge by means of damp, stifling rooms and putrid food; it only deprives the guilty of the chance to harm someone. On the other hand the state cannot allow a convicted criminal to have more material comforts in prison than has the person who lives in freedom and earns his own keep. In addition the people must be certain that at no future time will a former prisoner disturb the peace. The question of the prison system is not a new one, and America can take pride in its prisons no less than in its schools. Other countries have also benefited from the experiments made across the ocean. Examples of such experiments are the prisons and workhouses of New York, which in turn are explained by the city's large number of poor and unfortunates, the abundance of crime, and consequently the frequent use of prison confinement. It is remarkable that in very serious crimes, where sacred feelings of honor have been impudently offended or violated, or where the guilt of a person who has committed several crimes is at last demonstrated, the people seem not to want to wait for a regular trial, as if fearing the evidence will not be found sufficient, and they take the law into their own hands. Not infrequently a criminal is shunted from prison to prison to conceal his place of confinement from the public and, it is hoped, keep him from being lynched; the same

5. Exile to Siberia was a common form of punishment in nineteenth-century Russia, as was corporal punishment.

danger, however, is present on the day of the trial. There have been instances when whites who pursued runaway Negroes into free states fell victim to their own cupidity at the hands of defenders of freedom.

Every police court has its prison or, more correctly, jail, where those arrested wait for twenty-four hours for their preliminary verdict, so to speak—for a decision whether they will be turned over to criminal court or set free. But the most remarkable and architecturally unique jail is located downtown and is called the Tombs.[6] On a great square expanse stands a building constructed of dark gray granite quarried in the state of Maine. Massive columns support the portico leading to the courts. Beyond that is a special interior court enclosed by a thick granite wall in which rather high slanting apertures have been made to admit light and air; there are no windows. Access is easy for prisoners and for witnesses, and, as with all institutions in America, jails are open for anyone to visit, especially foreigners. There is a free flow of air since the cell doors opening onto the corridor are latticed, and those who have had the misfortune to be put here can await their fate without detriment to their health. There is a cell for each person; youngsters are separated from adults; no one is forced to work, because prior to conviction no one is presumed guilty and everyone is permitted to have whatever conveniences he can obtain.

However to gain a full appreciation of how cleverly the American derives benefits from the criminals he feeds and whose manpower he utilizes, as well as to gain an understanding of how far his deep feeling of responsibility in caring for the poor and unfortunate extends—a feeling that is in contrast to his reticence and cold exterior—one must proceed to Blackwell's Island and nearby Randall's Island, both of which are located in the East River. In all parts of the city there are charitable institutions, asylums for orphans and the poor, for whites and blacks, for the sick and the idle. But the two islands named above are designated only for care and correction, and it is most gratifying to visit them.

Having obtained a pass in the workhouse office in New York without any difficulty or questions, I had to cross the entire city before I

6. A new city prison was completed in 1838, which the Common Council named "The Tombs" because in appearance the building resembled an ancient Egyptian tomb. Charles Sutton, *The New York Tombs: Its Secrets and Its Mysteries* (New York: United States Publishing Company, 1874), p. 48.

reached the East River. A whole series of prisons and correctional institutions stood just on the opposite shore, but I had to wait for a special boat from the island before crossing over. This boat belongs to the prison administration, and after an official makes certain that you have permission to visit the island, you are carried across the river without charge.

It would be difficult to choose a better place for institutions of this kind. From afar the island has the appearance of a garden in which there are huge buildings. Its location is such that, if guards are not totally superfluous, then fewer of them are needed than would be the case under other circumstances. Moreover the air is always fresh, so that while improving the morality of criminals or supporting the poor and the unemployed through charity, the government does not ruin the health of those confined.

The institutions on Blackwell's Island are arranged in the following fashion: at one end of the island are a penitentiary and a hospital; in the middle is an almshouse, behind which stands a workhouse; at the other end of the island is a lunatic asylum. There are no other inhabitants here except those belonging to these institutions. Blackwell's Island and Randall's Island, and the buildings on them, are managed by ten directors who together constitute a special department. According to their report for 1857 it appears that eight thousand people of both sexes and various ages were charitably supported by the city and that taxes for their maintenance came to $843,600. It goes without saying that those being supported in these institutions are distributed according to age, sex, and degree of crime, and that the poor and unemployed are completely separated from the criminals.

I began my survey with the prison. It is designed for those convicted of crimes and misdemeanors who have been sentenced for up to two years. Here, too, the Auburn system is preferred to the so-called Pennsylvania system, which requires that even long-term prisoners constantly work and live alone, seeing and communicating with no one except the warden, the minister or pastor, and a few selected visitors. All prisoners are obligated to work. According to the generally accepted rule in America, production is not run by the prison itself but by contractors who hire the labor of prisoners, show them how to perform the task, and furnish the materials. They thus improve the skills of individuals who often become scoundrels through lack of training. The goods produced by the hired labor belong to the manufacturer. The demand for prison labor is commensurate with the demand for production, and it may be remarked that the commercial crisis of 1857 resulted in a slackening of prison activity. I came to hear about this constantly from the supervisors of the institutions and to see for myself that the prison stores were overstocked with furniture, boots, locks, felt hats, and other similar goods. And because of the lack of sales the contractor closed the factory as it were, that is, he refused to hire prison labor. At that point the prisoners turned to domestic work, building various kinds of equipment for the prison and digging ditches. In general a large part of the prison has been built by the prisoners themselves, mainly a huge court enclosed with high walls. But the inmates are not taken out of the prison and its shops. Otherwise many guards would be needed, and, for all the supervision, escapes would take place more frequently. On the contrary, no guards are to be seen at all now and escapes seldom occur, compared at least to the number of prisoners.

There are 500 cells for men and 240 for women in the two separate buildings of the New York penitentiary on Blackwell's Island. The sexes are kept completely apart. Prisoners convicted for misdemeanors are kept distinct in terms of dress and location of cell from those convicted for felonies. The former wear blue uniforms and the latter wear striped uniforms of dark blue and white. Prisoners are required to work in the small shops during the day. Given the huge commerce of New York, a little extra production could not be harmful to free labor. But since labor in America is considered a person's most important right, to compel work as punishment would be degrading to free and honest labor, and the competition, at least, between these two kinds of work would be harmful. As a result, the trades chosen for prisoners are either those with which free workers have nothing to do, or those that duplicate imported products, or those where the demand for the product is so great that free workers cannot satisfy it.

Prisoners start work at six in the morning, each in his shop. Breakfast, lunch, and dinner are in a general dining hall where each has his place on a bench and there are tin utensils on the table. Morning breakfast consists of coffee and bread; lunch at twelve is soup, meat, vegetables, and bread; at six in the evening the prisoners are given boiled corn or some other boiled vegetable. In the steam kitchen, whose tidiness would do honor not only to a criminal, but to any institution, one could see how the American, an enemy of petty miserliness, does not begrudge necessities. When I tasted the soft white bread, I asked the officer guiding me around the dungeon whether the portion was large enough for the prisoner-workers. The answer I expected was that it was forbidden to give more than an authorized amount. But what I heard was quite different: "If they don't have enough, we give them more." The honesty and conscientiousness of those in charge of the prison serve as a guarantee that nothing will go to waste, and one can see from reports that taxes collected for the support of prisons are not even all spent. At night everyone proceeds to his narrow cell, which is aired out during the day when the prisoner is at work. There is gas in the corridors and prisoners can read and write by its light. The doors are locked but everything going on in the cell can be seen through the lattice. A night guard stays in the corridor to prevent escapes, because shackles and chains are never put on the hands and feet of the criminals. Punishment consists of confinement in a dark cell for days on end, reduced portions, and cold showers on the bare back and neck of the offender. On Sundays there are church services which the prisoners also attend in silence.

The second institution on Blackwell's Island is the municipal almshouse. It houses up to two thousand men and women who, because of old age or weakness, are incapable of working enough to support themselves or who earned less for their work than was necessary to sustain themselves and their families. All these old men and women are kept at the expense of the city; they have clean lodgings, with beds placed in spacious rooms (halls). The senile and those unsuited for work have no responsibilities; they can stroll and warm themselves in the sun but may not leave the section of the island reserved for them. No supervision or constraint is to be seen and only with the greatest difficulty was I able to find a supervisor or watchman. The healthier women work for the institution, cooking, sewing, and washing. There are three large rooms for infants in the almshouse as well as a hospital. But this aid, which is generously provided to anyone who comes to the almshouse, turns out to be inadequate for a city in which so many new arrivals in the population have no relatives who could support them. Hence relief is also provided outside the institution. At the end of 1857, when the commercial crisis had left many without work, the number of poor who received help at the almshouse reached 2,300.

Work becomes compulsory when drunkenness, vagrancy, or begging are the reasons for being sentenced to the workhouse on Blackwell's Island (the sentence, incidentally, is never for more than a year). This institution, which is unique in size if not in purpose, is so constructed that four wings extend out from the center. Each wing has three stories and can house 600 people, so that in all there are 2,400 idlers who must be given work and sustenance. When I was there it was not yet finished, but one could see in what had already been completed the future benefit of this kind of institution. The purpose of the workhouse, aside from punishment, is good, that is, to train the inmates for work and to give them at least some safeguard against indigence and perhaps more serious crime in their first days of freedom. Part of the wages earned remains for the inmate's use and is given to him when he leaves the institution. Will these workshops and those yet to be built really always be full of people? I asked the superintendent taking me around the building. Of all the institutions that already exist in New York, were there really so few for training and charitable care? Of course there are too few, was his reply. But do not the multitude of institutions where people are cared for, made warm and fed, themselves promote the development of poverty and the spread of vice? An American, of course, will not go to an almshouse of his own free will; he will always manage to figure something out and make a dollar; but a large part of the population on Blackwell's Island is Irish and German, helpless people who crossed the sea in search of dollars only to find here the same poverty that gave them no rest in the Old World. The layout of the institution benefited from previous experience. Steam is used in the kitchen and in heating, rails have been laid in all the corridors for the distribution of food to the different floors, and attention has also been given to the airing of the rooms. I must confess that however sad it was to go from one prison to another and see vice and crime everywhere, I was consoled by the thought that the poor and the unfortunate are not forgotten, that everything humanly possible is done to suppress evil propensities in the young, to help people voluntarily choose the right path, and to lift up through work and meditation those who have fallen.

The main concern in America in housing convicts is that the different age groups not be mixed. The young are carefully separated from adults so that vice will not be freely spread, particularly in a place where vice is being punished. The young criminals of New York are even moved to another island, Randall's Island. There are two institutions on the latter: one is a nursery for the care of helpless children who have lost their parents, and the other is a House of Refuge, for criminals who need to be reformed through discipline and work. To the House of Refuge are sent, by court order, children from ages six to sixteen who have been found guilty of stealing, lying, and vagrancy. They remain until age twenty-one, at which time they are released if prior to this age they have not been placed somewhere else; if the boys, for example, have not been hired to work on farms or in factories, and the girls have not become domestics in homes. To assure that the noble goal of this institution is actually achieved, there is a special organization, the Society for the Reformation of Juvenile Delinquents, which counts among its members many philanthropic ladies.

In approaching the home for juvenile delinquents one cannot immediately guess the function of the building: one might more easily take it for the home of a rich person than for a prison. It is a long, two-story building with a columned portico in front and a small cupola on top. I entered a bright clean lobby where I found an office with a busy young lady, who was evidently making up lists for the children. She received me gently and politely and then turned me over to the supervisor. After discovering that I was Russian, the latter tried to impress me not with the splendor and magnificence of the structure but with the actual benefits that the people anticipate from the institution. The layout of the building was rather simple: the large central hall formed a semicircle around a courtyard; and from it, like the spokes of a wheel, issued four long, two-storied wings. The cells were in the wings along both sides of the first floor and were separated from each other by thick walls. Opposite the door of each cell was a window that admitted clean fresh air. On the second floor were the classrooms. Four hours a day were devoted to lessons and additional time was set aside for work which here, too, was hired out to manufacturers from the city. In the workshops, which are separate from the building which houses the classrooms and sleeping quarters, I met shoemakers, bootmakers, and carpenters, and one could see white and black youngsters happily hammering nails in shoes, weaving wicker seats for chairs, sewing, planing wood, and forging iron. In this way the youngster himself pays for his keep, with little cost to the state. Having become accustomed to labor and work, he returns to society a useful citizen and becomes a part of the community. Fortunate is the youngster who, having committed an illegal act, lands in an institution where he can be reformed before vice has taken root and results in more serious crimes, for which he would then have to pay with a long-term prison sentence.

It is intended that another refuge will be built on Randall's Island for girls guilty of fraud, theft, and vagrancy. Meanwhile they are housed in one wing of the boys' institution. They sew linens and dresses in exchange for shoes and furniture supplied by the other half of the institution. The rest of the time is devoted to classroom lessons. Totally wayward girls can be transformed into housemaids and good wives and mothers. All this is achieved through resources furnished by the citizens themselves and without unduly burdening the state and society.

The goal of this institution is a great one and the results gained by society are most beneficial. From the time of its founding to the end of 1856 care was extended to 6,884 children and in 1856 alone to 858. Most of them were Irish and one-fifth of the total were from New York City. The study of the Holy Scriptures, daily prayer, reading lessons (a good half of those sent to the institution are illiterate), arithmetic, and productive work can to some degree positively change the nature of children. And as is evident from the opinions of employers and farmers who have hired these minors, that goal is actually being realized. They are pleased with these workers, who under other circumstances could expect only poverty and prison. The institution corresponds with employers and keeps track of the foster children even after they have left the refuge. In 1856 145 white and 13 colored youngsters capable of doing farm work were sent to farmers. Other children who worked in the institution brought in an income of $13,414.

In the orphanage, which was also hospitable and just as readily opened its doors to a foreigner, I found children in a broad courtyard overlooking the East River. They were running, skipping about, and playing, and there was one supervisor for the whole group. As everywhere in America, children are left completely free. The sun had begun to set when I left the distant island and hurried to return to the city. But the lusty cries of the orphan children were with me for a long time, children who have forgotten that strangers have taken the place of those dearest and tenderest beings, their parents. One really has no desire to leave any assistance or money behind: no one requests it or feels a need for it. But blessed be the Lord and those who are fulfilling His holy commandments!

However it would be unfair to limit our discussion of New York's orphan asylums to the one on Randall's Island. In the city itself there are orphan asylums under various names, including special asylums for the blind, the deaf, and dumb, the colored, and even the insane (the Bloomingdale Asylum for the Insane). A great many of them have been created by societies and are supported by private means; they benefit a large city where so many of the population are without refuge. It would be difficult, incidentally, to find a city in America where private and public charity was not concerned with the care of those unfortunates who lack the physical and moral means to support themselves. Of course New York makes a showy display of its charitable institutions, including one that I have not yet spoken of, the lunatic asylum on Blackwell's Island. During the past year there were 627 unfortunates of both sexes in the asylum; in caring for them the attempt is made to apply the same principles of freedom that exist for the other charitable institutions. During the day the sick are accommodated in large halls and if the weather does not permit strolling outdoors in the garden, it can be done in an enclosed gallery built for this purpose around the whole asylum. The sleeping quarters are bright and roomy and usually accommodate two people. In several rooms the walls are covered with drawings, done by the occupants themselves, or are pasted over with pictures. My guide was a young doctor who was liked by the sick people entrusted to his care. He talked with each one, a second violin, so to speak, to the inmate's insanity. In order to show me what kinds of things drive an American out of his mind more quickly than anything else, the doctor took me to a man who seemed to be perfectly healthy. He sat absorbed in some kind of computations, drawing them up and making corrections. The doctor introduced me as a traveler from Russia, whereupon the man offered me his hand and began to demonstrate the possibility of crossing the Atlantic Ocean in twenty-four hours and, with the aid of this secret, seizing control of England, Cuba, and so on. Another patient talked on and on about dollars, dreaming of riches; he had gone out of his mind because he had been ruined.

In addition to fresh air, strolls, gentleness, and tolerance, those in charge make use of studies in natural history. Stuffed animals, fish, and rocks of interest to the sick are displayed in bookcases. Isolation from the others, a reduction in food portions, or withholding permission to spend time at a favorite occupation serve as punishment for the disobedient. And however strange it is to see cold showers applied in extreme cases, the doctor explained to me that the fits of madness abate under the impact of cold water. This method is considered extreme but at least it is not irritating, as are straitjackets, chains, and similar means of constraint which torment the unfortunates by leaving them immobile. Whether doctors should be denied the opportunity to use cold water as treatment is a question for physicians to decide. In any case experiments in America cannot be disregarded by those charged with restoring the health of the sick.

V

Several weeks are hardly enough to become well acquainted with life in New York. It is indisputably the best specimen of a purely American city with all its good and evil qualities, regardless of what the Puritan Yankees say about it. But why is it, I thought, as I bid farewell to New York, that while much in individual Americans is not personally pleasing and offends our senses, yet from a distance one looks at these lively, clever, practical people and begins to have a reverential attitude for their boldness, their activity, and their realistic views of things? One may not love certain particulars in America, but one cannot help loving America as a whole or being amazed at what it has that Europe cannot measure up to—a people who know how to govern themselves and institutions that, unaided, give a person as much happiness and well-being as he can accommodate. But one must leave on Europe's doorstep many beliefs and distinctions which are not appreciated in the New World with its common equality; a foreigner who does not understand and cannot respect the concepts and new attitudes of a country that does not recognize caste and feudal distinctions may disapprove of America. But when your elbows no longer hurt from the blows of Americans on the run, and when you are no longer seated at the dinner table next to an American in a hurry, it is another matter. Then you love and marvel at him!

ʃ

Up the Hudson

[Lakier decided to leave New York City by steamboat and go up the Hudson River. One of his first stops was Sing Sing.]

I

The Sing Sing prison courtyard was readily visible from the ship. Sailing by, one might have thought it was a steampowered cotton-spinning factory or something of that sort. Not far from the shore stands a huge five-story building with its smoke-stack for the steam plant; one hears the rumble of wheels and machinery and sees activity in a courtyard unfenced either on the land side or the river side. And yet the prison, one of the largest in New York State, is designed for the most hardened criminals. I left the ship and approached without difficulty. I had no pass or other permit but I was already so used to easy access to institutions in America that I did not worry about a slip of paper that might be demanded of an inquirer. Americans reason that if something is good, let everyone use it; if something is bad, it should be abandoned. Since they are fully convinced that everything is good, there is open access to everything. Walking along the path, I came across a sentry box manned by a guard who saw to it that none of the prisoners took it into his head to take advantage of the river's proximity and the trustfulness of Americans. I looked at the "anthill" in which the inhabitants of the dungeon were bustling about, and truly I did not believe my eyes.

A detachment of armed soldiers stood at the entrance to the prison. Having no walls, Sing Sing had to be surrounded with sentry boxes and an armed guard was put at the gate. Presumably escapes could occur frequently, but such is not the case. How did the Americans manage to build such an institution? After paying a quarter at the entrance (a quarter of a dollar or thirty silver kopeks) and getting a guide, I went with him first to the shops. American prisons are organized on a commercial basis, a rule that is followed inflexibly, no matter how they might have been established, whether according to the Pennsylvania system with its permanent separation of men, or according to the Auburn system in which the convicts work together and are separated only at night.[1] In either case, the criminals' strength and activity should not be wasted, and the burden of maintaining them should not fall on innocent citizens. This reasoning is perfectly just and of course occurs to anyone who has seen the empty passing of time in the prisons of other countries. But Americans have managed to make the work of criminals productive for the criminals themselves, diverting them from the intolerable boredom of inactivity, training them in work useful for other citizens, and removing them from the ranks of parasites. Finally, they have managed to make the work of criminals profitable for the productivity of the country, compelling them to produce whatever is generally needed and required. Let us begin with the fact that the prisoners themselves build the prison, the stores, the shops and machines, and that they dig the canals. Hence with the large quantity of stone that abounds in the northern part of the Union, the building of a prison turns out to be inexpensive for the government. In addition, the general rule is followed that prisoners are not assigned to work outside the institution. Each person's labor is evaluated and the contractor sets a specific wage (usually forty to forty-five cents, that is, fifty to fifty-seven silver kopeks a day) to be paid for the work, provides the material and the supervisors, and takes care of selling the finished products. One circumstance might spoil this business: work is the privilege of honest citizens in America, consequently punishment should be precisely the opposite, namely, enforced idleness. Does involuntary labor therefore have the right to compete with voluntary labor? In order to avoid so disadvantageous a clash and one to which the working class might be especially sensitive,

1. Sing Sing, begun in 1825, was the most frequently visited prison of the Auburn class. The Pennsylvania system was begun at Cherry Hill near Philadelphia in 1829. In the 1830s various European governments sent investigators to study the new-style American prisons. The first and most famous of these investigators were Gustave Auguste de Beaumont and Alexis de Tocqueville, who came in 1831. By 1851 England, Belgium, Sweden, Norway, and Holland had partially adopted either the Auburn or Pennsylvania model. McKelvey, *American Prisons,* pp. 14, 26. See also above, pp. 91–93, and below, pp. 122–28.

the kinds of production chosen for prisoners are either those that would in no way hurt private activity, as for example the manufacture of articles imported from abroad such as felt hats and carpets, or those items produced by free labor that do not get to market in sufficient quantities and for which there is still a demand, as for example various-sized barrels for transporting flour, potatoes, sugar, and the like. The entire institution can accommodate a thousand men. During my visit I personally saw no fewer than nine hundred and all of them were working, except for some who were sick. Silence is the prescribed rule and they try to observe it, but as long as one is in the company of other men he does not die of madness and boredom. That is why the prisoners await Sunday with horror, for they must spend the whole day alone in their cells and are allowed out only for church. By the warden's own admission, Monday is a veritable holiday for the convicts.

This is how the day is divided: morning breakfast of coffee and bread followed by work in the shops; after his tasks are finished a prisoner can rest, and I noted several workers with books; at twelve o'clock there is a lunch of soup, meat, and vegetables; all eat together in a huge dining hall where each has his own place and tin utensils. The kitchen is steam-operated and the portions are generous; after lunch there is again work followed by dinner at five or six in the evening. After that a roll call of the prisoners is made and each one is placed in a cell that has not the smallest opening into that of his neighbor. The latticed door of the cell faces the corridor so that the night guard can monitor the conduct of the inmates. The small room gets its air and light from the corridor. All precautions are taken to prevent nighttime escapes, with greatest attention being paid to the lock that with a single bolt secures up to fifty cells in a row.

I did not see anyone with chains on his feet; they would interfere with work. Punishment consists of confinement in a dark room and reduced rations; corporal punishment is replaced by cold showers, which the convicts especially fear.

Two hours were hardly enough for a detailed inspection of the shops, cells, kitchen, and dining hall, or to become acquainted with the administrative system of the institution. Women are separated from the men. There is a smaller institution for the women, similar not to a factory but rather to the private home of a well-to-do person. However the administrative system is the same as for the men. The

women work together, do washing and ironing for the institution as
well as sewing; they finish items made by the men, sewing linings into
hats, shoes, and the like. There are several beds for children born of
pregnant prisoners in the institution.

II

I waited for the railroad train and rode to the station at Garrison,
where one could cross the river to West Point. The evening sun was
already gilding the mountain tops, and as twilight descended from the
heavens one's imagination was involuntarily carried back to the time
of the Europeans' first arrival here, when the amazed and perplexed
Indians who had been hunting in the fields saw the uninvited guests for
the first time, never suspecting that these new friends would in time
seize the best lands and drive the Indians far to the west, to the
prairies and cold forests. Only the formidable, majestic cliffs have
remained unaltered; the people, and even nature, have changed. The
names of places have changed too; they are derived from the personal
names of estate owners or from the names of forts erected during the
War of Independence. The vast ruins of these forts are easily seen
even from the steamboat; they remind one of the old medieval castles
along the Rhine at Bingen and at several places on the Danube. Of
course, the Hudson has a different history and different monuments,
but the general coloring of these American highlands is the same.

West Point is one of the favorite places for summer residences of
wealthy New York families. Cozzens' Hotel, situated in a picturesque
spot with grounds extending down to the river, is always full in summer, and even the cottages scattered around the hotel are put into
use.[2] As the summer heat had passed, the hotel guests had disappeared.
I did not find many belated travelers at the hotel; it was somewhat
strange going to the huge dining room and not seeing hundreds of
hungry Americans with their pale, dressed-up ladies, and not seeing
the crowding and the general rushing about.

The following morning the weather could not have been more
favorable for strolling to the Military Academy. The road ran along

2. Built in 1849 just south of West Point and overlooking the Hudson,
it became a popular summer vacation spot for the nouveau riche of the
Lower Hudson who sought to escape the heat of New York City. Letter
from Michael J. McAfee, Museum Curator, West Point Museum, December 29, 1976.

a high bank in sight of the Hudson, past charming cottages whose owners were living quietly and peacefully with the honorable title of gentleman farmers, and past gardens where youngsters were frolicking about. The buildings of the Military Academy soon appeared on a promontory jutting out into the Hudson. One of them had a blue cupola which could have been taken for the cupola of a church, had I not known that in America churches are not erected in the buildings of the academic institutions themselves, nor in that style besides. The cupola belonged to the observatory, and the same building housed the library. I addressed myself to the sentry standing at the door, a sight so untypical in America, and was startled by the reply that one could not enter the library without permission. From his accent I knew he was not an American, though his very reply, the only one of its kind during my entire stay in North America, sufficed to tell me so. "Was für ein Landesmann sind Sie?" I whispered a little more pleasantly in the ears of the stern sentry. Whereupon he explained to me that he was a Prussian, that most of the soldiers and noncommissioned officers training the cadets in combat and riding, as well as the musicians and drummers, were Germans. But to the question of whether I could see the institution he gave the same negative reply. I saw that from a Prussian even in American service little was to be gotten, so I turned to an officer walking by. "Everything is open!" was his answer and with the greatest courtesy he took me into the building and turned me over to a guide.

I already knew that the institution was founded in 1802, that its purpose was to supply the Union army with officers, that it was supported with federal funds, and that like the Naval Academy at Annapolis in the state of Maryland, the West Point Military Academy was also the only one of its kind. But my eyes had somehow grown unaccustomed to military uniforms and glittering epaulettes, which one sees neither on the street nor in society, and I looked with curiosity upon military braid and buttons I had not seen for such a long time.[3]

3. As a Russian bureaucrat in the Ministry of Justice for more than ten years, Lakier had long been accustomed to "military uniforms and glittering epaulettes." During the reign of Nicholas I (1825–55), the wearing of uniforms became a distinctive feature of Russian officialdom. In addition to the military, every rank in the civil bureaucracy, from minister on down, had its own special uniform. Richard Pipes, *Russia Under the Old Regime* (New York: Scribner's, 1974), p. 286.

There were about 225 youths aged sixteen to twenty-two in training. They are supported by the Union and are appointed as officers
in the army (by army is meant the regular army; there can be no
presidential guard); they study primarily military science, mathematics, chemistry, drawing, and so forth. Auditoriums and museums
are located in various spacious structures. Among the trophies taken
by past graduates of the Academy is a collection of Mexican banners
and cannon captured in the last war with Mexico.[4] In demeanor the
young men were courteous and attentive, and it was evident from
everything I saw that these grown-up youths are conscious of their
personal worth and therefore do not insult people of their own kind.

At midday I even had the chance to be at the riding exercises of
these future leaders and heroes of America. The main requirement in
the training of these young people, however, is a knowledge of the
sciences. It is interesting that for the 225 cadets there are forty-two
professors and assistant professors, of whom seven are for mathematics
alone. French and Spanish are taught in addition to English. The
instruction of the young people rests on those same principles of
freedom as those for American education in general. The military
man does not forget that he is a citizen like everyone else and has civic
duties the same as others.

A part of the three thousand acres of the Military Academy is occupied by buildings, a parade ground, and a monument to Kosciuszko,[5]
one of the defenders of American independence; part of it is rented
out and serves as one of the main sources of support for the Academy,
to which Congress rather sparingly assigns $70,000.

The heights over the site of the Military Academy are ravishingly
beautiful: on a bright day the mountain tops of New England are
visible as is a wide panorama of the Hudson. Since the river is narrow
at this point and the area is especially suitable for strategic defense,
the Americans depended on the fortifications here during the War
of Independence. Forts Putnam, Clinton, Webb, and Willys were
established here; from their present ruins it is impossible to deduce
anything of their former sturdiness.

4. 1846–48.
5. Tadeusz Kosciuszko (1746–1817) was a Polish patriot who from
1776 to 1783 served with distinction as a colonel in the Continental Army.
In 1783 Congress raised him to brigadier general.

After crossing the Hudson on a steam ferry, I had to go several miles by railroad to New Hamburg, near which was Clinton Point. From there I traveled with our honorable consul to his summer home in a light American "buggy," similar to our high-wheeled cabriolet.[6] On the way he told me about his neighbors. Among them was the veteran American writer, Washington Irving, who lived year round in his Sunnyside cottage. In a foreign country, meeting with a compatriot who speaks the mother tongue and who is interested in the same matters that occupy everyone's attention in Russia is to meet with a friend or relative, especially when an intelligent and pleasant lady enlivens the evening conversation. Stories about Washington and his contemporary Clinton, who in his day was governor of New York and owned the property where our consul now lived, added interest to the evening conversations by the fireplace.[7] American families who have been to Europe live in their own way outside the cities, and this is even more true of foreigners; the English style of life, with all its comforts and luxuries and all its distinctions and liveries prevails here, far from the public's censure of this violation of democratic equality in social life.

The grounds at Clinton Point extend down to the Hudson, from which they are separated only by the railroad tracks. The constant activity on the river, with the steamboats and sailing ships scurrying back and forth, as well as the railroad trains, made for a lively scene in which one felt close to everything, despite the separation. One could live here absolutely as if in an English castle, although the situation is different. Farmers cultivate their land, are called gentlemen, take quiet pleasure in their gains, manage their own affairs, and exert an influence on voters during elections and in the selection of officials. They are a kind of *pomeshchik* [Russian noble landowner] who usually got their start with the simplest and cheapest kinds of work, with petty trade. Although they are unacquainted with real gentlemen, the owners of summer homes, these gentlemen farmers are respected people. Their children are educated in a township school, and one should

6. The Russian consul general in New York was I. K. Notbeck, who had a country home at Clinton Point, near New Hamburg. Lakier had an invitation to visit him.

7. George Clinton (1739–1812) served as governor of New York for seven terms, from 1777 to 1795 and from 1801 to 1804. He is considered the "father" of the state.

hear the lovely choir of these children's voices at Sunday services in the Anglican church! The fresh air is not without influence on the girls: preserving the same determination and courage that gives them their independence, they are prettier here and, in spite of an innate desire to be liked, are dressed more simply. The eye feasts with pleasure upon the contentment and prosperity as it involuntarily rests upon still another gray little house with green shutters.

I was halfway on the road between New York and Albany, the capital of New York State, and in a few hours was already there. The Empire State, that is New York, has for its capital not the city bearing the same name but Albany, which is inferior to it in everything, in the advantages of location, in population, and in commercial activity. This is how it is in all the states, with one city being the main center for private enterprise and another one for the government, so that the influx of foreigners does not interfere with business and the mob does not have any influence on government operations. In addition it is considered essential that the place designated for the legislative assembly of the state be at about the center and not on the border, as is nearly always the case with commercial cities. Albany, although quiet and sparsely populated compared to New York, is rather noisy for the capital of an American state. For one thing the navigability of the Hudson ends here, and for another this is where the Hudson joins with the canal that runs all across New York State to Lake Erie.[8] Consequently this is the main commercial route from the west and a gathering point for immigrants. At the same time this is the starting place of another canal that runs north and connects the Hudson with the St. Lawrence River via Lake Champlain; it is called the Champlain Canal. A huge boat basin (4,300 feet long) has been built in the river to accommodate ships coming from the canals. From here goods are dispersed to all corners of the Union and, via New York, abroad.

From the time of its first settlement Albany was of great significance. As is well known, New York, originally New Amsterdam, was founded by the Dutch; Hudson, the navigator, first discovered the river that bears his name. In order to protect navigation along this main artery, the Dutch East India Company, in whose service Hudson was employed, founded Fort Orange, which eventually grew into the

8. The Erie Canal was completed in 1825.

present-day city of Albany. Despite the fact that from 1664 this entire part of the country was in the hands first of the English and now
the Americans, families speaking seventeenth-century Dutch have
survived down to the present day. All along the Hudson one hears
names that are obviously of Dutch origin. Many place names, for example, end in "kill" (German *Quelle*), meaning "source" (Catskill,
Normanskill, Fishkill).

As with all the other state capitals, present-day Albany has a domed
capitol building for the state senate and legislative assembly. It also
has a university, an academy, a number of primary and middle
schools, quite extensive collections of books in the fields of natural
history, geology, and agriculture, an orphan asylum and other charitable institutions. The officials of the state government live here. Not
only does each state have its own government, administering affairs
according to its own best interests and abilities, but each city is in
charge of its own finances and collects taxes from the very same
citizens. What Americans fear most of all is a joint state-city government whose decisions would be untimely for one or the other.

Just as the Hudson is still wide, deep, and lively at Albany, it is
quiet, narrow, and shallow at Troy, several miles upriver from the
New York State capital. Even further up the river the Mohawk pours
in its waters, and forms, together with the main source, the Hudson.
The transition from a wide deep river capable of carrying naval craft
to a small stream is startling. Not without reason were there scholars
in America who supported Hudson's views that the sea gulf ran up
to Troy and only there did the rivers empty into it. However that
might be, the Americans dug a canal to bypass the unnavigable river
and named the heights above the city of Troy Mounts Ida and Olym-
pus, in memory of ancient Troy.

Giving names to newly created towns in America is done in a
rather unusual way. To name a town after an individual would
mean that he was considered the owner or founder. Americans do
not want to allow this and do so only in exceptional cases. Hence in
the Alleghenies, for example, there is the town of Golitsyn, founded
by one of our Golitsyn princes.[9] But for the most part the names of
towns explain the place of origin of the first settlers. The prefix "New"
is virtually inescapable in distinguishing a new town from the old

9. See pp. 137–38.

city, and it is understandable why the same names are repeated in
various parts of the Union: the whole geography of the Ancient World
is here. Russia has made its contribution no less than other countries.
One could count some twenty Petersburgs, Moscows, and Warsaws,[10]
but "New" was not added because their founders were not from the
old cities; they named the settlements that way because they had to
have some kind of name. Names were also taken from ancient geography, so that the states have their Troys, Alexandrias, Memphises,
Capris, and so forth. The names of Washington, Jefferson, and other
glorious sons of America are also frequently repeated. The difficulty
encountered in naming towns can be easily explained if one takes
into account the number of populated points throughout the Union
that are constantly being generated from one log cabin or another;
other houses gradually join it until the population finally reaches that
of a full township, which is in a position to have its own officials, its
own school, its own churches, and its own council. The township then
tries to discuss what name to give to the future town. There is a lot
of noisy debating and wrangling, and finally a decision is made in
favor of a new name or an old one, depending on who gains the
upper hand.

The railroad runs through Saratoga, which with its mineral springs
serves as a gathering spot for high society in the summer but was
now completely empty; then on to Whitehall where the train gives
way to the steamboat. The railroad and steamboat companies have
established a mutual relationship with one another. Immediately upon
the train's arrival the passengers change over, while baggage and
freight are transferred to huge, mobile, enclosed bins (so-called cars)
that are sent to an assigned place alongside the ship. It is exactly the
same in crossing large rivers, over which they have not yet built or
simply have not wanted to build bridges. Baggage and freight, and
sometimes the railroad cars themselves, are carried across the river.
On the other side a new locomotive is hooked up, and the train once
again moves along solid ground with its freight and passengers. Thus
there are no stops for bridges, and to use a steamboat for this purpose
is not expensive since it simultaneously serves as a ferry.

10. Lakier's Russian readers knew that Warsaw was a Polish city,
which became part of the Russian Empire in 1795 as a result of the Third
Partition of Poland.

A white steamboat, similar to all the others and used for sailing on rivers and lakes, carried us over Lake Champlain, the rocker arm of the engine working above deck between the funnels. There was the same comfort as on other steamboats, the same abundance of space for strolling and resting, the same washstands, and the same shops. It seemed to me that the Americans, who for other reasons had not had time to shave and comb their hair on the land route, purposely traveled on this restful steamboat in order to take care of some of their everyday necessities. Quite unexpectedly there was a predominance of French-speaking passengers on the steamboat. I had not seen a Catholic abbot for a long time, but there was one on board, adding a dash of color to the gathering of Americans. Among the servants, and even the sailors, were Frenchmen, or, as they are called here, Canadians. In the evening the Canadians struck up a song on the deck and the tune clearly revealed its French origin. When I asked one of the older men among the singers whether he had been here long, he replied that he was born in Canada and that his parents spoke no English at all; he understood a little, although for business it would have been advantageous to know more. It was the same here as everywhere: the Frenchman does not readily learn a foreign language. Whether this is because his native tongue is widely spoken everywhere or, on the contrary, has been widely spread by those who speak only French, I do not know. In any case a Frenchman never renounces his nationality and in this sense provides a sharp contrast to the German, who is content wherever he has taken shelter. In America the German calls himself an American, as in Russia he calls himself a Russian. He changes his language and notes the favorite expressions of the Americans. The second generation forgets the mother tongue and is very likely to take offense if reminded of old Braunschweiger or some principality where its predecessors were born and lived.

6

Buffalo,
Philadelphia, Baltimore

I

From Niagara my route lay through the middle states of the North American Union. The first remarkable point where I wanted to stop was Buffalo on Lake Erie, the main city in the western half of New York State. There are railroad lines in various directions out of Buffalo; some go east all the way to New York, others go south and west. Moreover, Buffalo is tied to New York and New England by canals. Obviously this circumstance could not but have an effect on the flourishing of trade in Buffalo. And its location, beyond the rapids and falls of Niagara, is exceptional. It is here that the convoys coming by lake from the distant states in the west must necessarily stop, and here that bread grains are unloaded and ground. The city benefited from the confluence of peoples and in a short time its growth reached extraordinary proportions. Not too long ago, there were still impassable forests here, and the first log cabin was put up no earlier than 1801. From that time on Buffalo grew from a small village and town into a city with a hundred thousand inhabitants. Today it is a great commercial and trade center whose annual turnover reaches hundreds of millions of dollars.

Of course it cannot be said that the government provided any protection or conferred any special rights and privileges on this town. Quite the contrary. Like all other populated places, a small town comes into existence, builds itself up, and manages its own affairs. At first it is simply part of the county in which it is created, but as it grows in importance and size it seeks to become a county seat. The newly arrived population begins to manage its own public affairs; it has its own courts and schools, and organizes them in accordance with its own judgment. The state government and legislature turn their attention to a rising city only when the latter manifests its prosperity. In this respect the choice of place for settlement is of utmost importance, but no less important than location is the fact that a private individual does not create a town with a specific goal in mind: a settled place is left to follow its own course of development. On the way from Niagara to Buffalo we had evidence of how important this principle is in the history of American cities. A Major Noah had taken it into his head to gather Jews from all over the world and establish the city of Ararat on Grand Island in the Niagara River, which connects Lake Erie and Lake Ontario.[1] But the city to which they directed their efforts declined at the same time that Buffalo prospered and grew. The practical Americans point to these ruins as evidence that no one individual alone can truly know what is best for society.[2]

Our trip was not long. We were soon at the source of the Niagara at Lake Erie on the Canadian side. Fort Erie was there and directly across was the commercial city of Buffalo. The train had hardly stopped when stagecoach agents and drivers appeared with various kinds of offers, praising hotels and private lodgings and pulling off the baggage. Despite the fact that snow was falling in huge, thick flakes and a sharp wind from the lake had been mournfully howling during the entire journey from the Falls to Buffalo, stagecoaches were nonetheless dashing around the city and people were hurrying and scurrying about. The broad avenue along which I rode to the hotel

1. Mordecai Manuel Noah (1785–1851), an American of Portuguese Jewish descent, was a politician, journalist, playwright, and philanthropist. Although born in Philadelphia, he made New York City his home in 1816, after having served as U.S. consul in Tunis. In 1825 he tried to establish a Jewish colony, which he named "Ararat," on Grand Island in the Niagara River. Jews in Europe and America failed to support the project and it was abandoned. *The Jewish Encyclopedia,* vol. 9, pp. 323–24.

2. This may be a subtle allusion to Peter the Great's stubborn determination to found St. Petersburg (present-day Leningrad) in 1703 at the mouth of the Neva River, on the eastern end of the Gulf of Finland, despite the fact that the marshlands and the severe northern climate made the location impractical. Peter's city was constructed at the sacrifice of thousands of lives, to say nothing of the huge cost in treasure.

was lined with tall five-story stone buildings. There were signs, shops, and auctions everywhere, exactly as in other large American cities. The hotel where I stayed made the same impression.

Is this then the replica of a prototype? No! The layout, buildings, and institutions of the city took that form and not some other only because it could not have done otherwise. When a town is still only getting started, broad avenues are laid out and the future city is spread out over a vast, almost measureless expanse, for millions of inhabitants are counted on. No section or street is given preference over another; all streets are equally wide and long, all intersect at right angles. But the people themselves will determine what street is most convenient and of course the one leading to the wharves, the port, or the stock exchange will soon be covered with large palatial-style buildings, glittering stores, shops, and huge hotels. On another, less convenient street, however, the log cabins hastily thrown together by the first settlers will long continue to stand until there appears on the street some stone building furnished with shops, stores, and signs, until the rich, or more accurately, the newly rich, begin to settle on the secondary side streets because there is no more space on the main one. In this way every city develops its own Broadway, and the other streets are settled only in the course of time. It has always seemed to me that even the cities in America bear the stamp of a common American equality. Birth does not confer any advantages, either to a street, a class of people, or a private individual. But since absolute equality is impossible and inconceivable anywhere on this earthly globe, distinctions certainly do develop. Thus there are favorite, populous streets with beautiful buildings just as there are families that have become wealthy and esteemed, and people who have become famous. The way to this desired end is open to all. There are no obstacles and hindrances, and one can be confident that at some time those who have remained in the shadows will have their turn.

Buffalo already has its Broadway with its palatial buildings, but farther off to one side there are still whole streets of log cabins, those original homes inhabited by working people and recent immigrants. However, various commercial institutions have already opened here and, although they are still in their infancy, there is no doubt that they will have a brilliant future. It will be interesting to see these places in about ten or twenty years. A child generally grows faster than an adult and there are years when growth ceases. What happens to people also happens to American cities and their populations.

All of Buffalo leads directly to the wharves to which the city owes its prosperity. Lake Erie freezes over rather early, and the cold weather had already made itself felt. It was to this circumstance I attributed the large number of white barges and steamboats that were crowded together at Buffalo. I remained convinced of this until I visited a steam-powered grain mill to acquaint myself with its operation. The owner explained to me that commercial activity in the present year had been insignificant compared to what it was earlier, before the impact of the commercial crisis.[3] At that time the western grain-producing states trustingly shipped their huge cargoes to New York, and from there the grain was sent to all ports of the world. But now that overseas trade had fallen or significantly declined, business at an intermediate point such as Buffalo had of necessity dropped too. What must have been the situation previously, before this commercial slow-down, if even now no water was visible behind the barges and steam-boats? The vessels were putting in to shore or announcing that they were departing, some for Detroit at the other end of Lake Erie, others for Chicago or Milwaukee on Lake Michigan and other points ashore. Meanwhile the shore is covered with huge steam-powered mills, and grain brought from the western states is ground into flour and loaded onto barges in small barrels for shipment to New York and Europe, as well as for storage in huge multistoried wooden buildings along the banks of the canal. The grain is raised to the upper stories by means of a steam engine. When it is necessary to load it on a ship for shipment to ports, it is lowered along an inclined plane. There is no need for thousands of stevedores or for sacks and wheelbarrows; steam replaces all these contrivances and expensive muscle power. It is enough that man takes the trouble to control a power whose significance he understands and values, and which he applies to business. One can say without exaggeration that a sailing ship is unloaded and the cargo stored and loaded on barges for shipment by canal—without the aid of human hands. It is the same with timber: there are steam-powered sawmills along the shore of the lake where timber arriving from the wilds of the Far West is sawn into boards. These are

3. The financial panic that began in August 1857.

then made into the sides, bottoms, and hoops for the small barrels in
which flour is shipped. They are made quickly, cheaply, and in enormous quantities.

II

Snow and bad weather still pursued me for hours on end from Buffalo
to the interior of Pennsylvania. It could now positively be said that the
so-called Indian summer I was so recently still enjoying in Canada
had come to an end. I thought that an early winter had begun in the
latter half of October. Iron stoves had been placed in the railroad
cars; they were kept constantly hot from early morning until late in
the evening. The cars were stifling, but the American puts his long
legs on the iron just as he does on marble, in order to find a resting
spot for his lithe body. Furs and woolen blankets made their appearance, but fellow travelers predicted that all we had to do was just
get through the Alleghenies and closer to Philadelphia in order once
again to enjoy the warmth of autumn or even the remnants of summer.

The railroad runs through towering forests in New York State just
as it does on the other side of the lake in Canada. But the leaves
of these tall trees had already fallen and it was sad to look at the
giants which only a half-century ago had served as a refuge for the
Indian hunting wild animals. Only recently, my neighbor was telling
me, bears, bobcats, and even panthers were caught here, but now the
white population has pushed out both the Indians and the animals
that get in the way of civilization. In any case one could not but agree
that the country through which the railroad was laid is "new country,"
as the Americans say. Only here and there did the white log cabins of
settlers show up, for not everywhere has the axe that fells trees left
its trace. But judging from the fact that until quite recently there were
no inhabitants here at all, it is impossible not to predict a flourishing
future for this "new country." Moreover there are rich deposits of
coal and iron here, and this region of America promises to supply
both to the whole Union. Up to the present time coal has not yet
rivaled timber, of which there is such a quantity here that it is cheaper
to use it for railroad locomotives, steamboats, factories, and mills.
Until recently it was more advantageous even for oceangoing steamships to use coal brought from England than to have it mined here.
But when railroads were built throughout the entire Allegheny country
and were linked up with those leading to Philadelphia and New

York, there was a great change in what had been the situation just a few years earlier.

After hours of riding through flat plains, we saw the first rises of the Alleghenies that cover the southern part of New York State. They could be called mountains, but the Americans speak of them as hills.

For the most part the train headed through the valleys, and where it could not escape the inclines, the cars were pulled to the top by means of chains attached to several engines positioned in various places on the mountain. To our great delight we found ourselves in forested valleys, with enormous oaks, elms, and sycamores in full greenery; not infrequently we crossed streams, mountain waterfalls, lakes, and precipices beyond which clearings were visible. The scenes changed continually and the Americans were constantly exclaiming "very fine!" Among the various beauties of nature in the wild was Mauch Chunk,[4] for which the train was heading. This town, the center of the coal country, is located on the banks of a small, tumultuous river, at a place where the river bursts through a mountain ridge. This is one of the wildest and most picturesque spots in the Alleghenies. The mounts rise up to a thousand feet, and it is here that the famous Summit Hill is located, on which rails to the coal fields have also been laid.[5] A better place could not have been chosen for familiarizing oneself with the method for mining coal.

All the while that we were traveling through the Alleghenies there were enormous piles of coal scattered about the surface of the ground alongside the tracks. According to the American sitting next to me, who knew the business, the coal is to a large extent mixed with iron ore; the main advantage stems from the fact that the layers of coal lie close to the surface and close to rivers, so that the mining of fuel and iron presents no great difficulty or problem. These gifts of nature comprise the true wealth of this part of the country, and thousands of people are employed here, some mining coal, others smelting iron, and still others manufacturing rails, wheels, and engines for the railroads. The predominant type of coal in the northern outcroppings of the Alleghenies is anthracite, and the brilliance of its fragments is the reason why the American poeticizes his benefactor and calls it

4. Now called Jim Thorpe, Pennsylvania.
5. Summit Hill derives its name from being atop Sharp Mountain in the heart of the anthracite district. The elevation is fifteen hundred feet.

the "black diamond." In truth anthracite is worthy of comparison with precious stones, and however much they at first objected to it in America, preferring English coal, they finally recognized the advantages of anthracite. Since it gives off no smoke and leaves no soot, it does not poison the air and is not so intolerable and injurious to breathing as in the smoke-filled factory towns of England. The use of anthracite is now widespread in Pennsylvania and the mining of it increases every year. Simultaneously there has been a growth in the value of land rich in anthracite, and the population is becoming more dense.

I was interested in going down into one of the coal mines, and with so many of them in the area there was no difficulty in satisfying my wish. Incidentally, there are places where the veins of coal lie so close to the surface that it is sufficient to scrape off the top cover of grass and thin layer of earth-crust to be able to dig out the coal with tools similar to our crowbars. But where the vein lies deeper it is necessary to descend into the earth and work underground.

Geological studies conducted in the Alleghenies have led to the conclusion that these mountains are interlaced, to what extent is unknown, with huge layers of anthracite ranging in width from twenty to thirty and in some places sixty feet. After digging down to these layers, man tries to extract and bring up into God's world what has lain concealed for centuries on end. Steam is again put into service, and steam engines, utilizing the very same coal that is being mined, lighten man's labor and enrich him.

They dressed me from head to foot in miners' clothes and took me down into the underground world. In the excavation of a mountain, this cavity is the first mine. Its depth varies, depending on how far from the surface the layers of anthracite are. When the working of the coal begins, it is taken to the surface from this first mine, and then the digging branches off into the vein itself. The corridors are at first narrow, then gradually widen as the coal is broken off, and only the supporting pillars of coal are left. When you enter a corridor and fleetingly glimpse the miners' lamps in the distance, they seem like fantastic underground creatures. The dark places between the columns where the coal had already been excavated, leaving enormous unpolished caryatids to support the ceiling, reminded me of the inner recesses of pyramids and the remains of ancient temples whose former greatness is preserved only in the fragments of columns. But in place of death and stillness there was life and activity in the mine. Everything was business and work.

The broken-up coal is rolled down inclined planes from corridors in the vein to a common passageway. There mules harnessed to wheelbarrows move the coal along rails. Because of the weight, a steam engine is again necessary to pull it to the surface, and haul it from the mountain so that it can be delivered to the railroads, rivers, and canals by which it is distributed to various parts of the Union and points beyond. When all the coal is at last removed from a designated section of land, they set to work on the pillars. Tens of feet in girth and height, they can still yield several thousand tons of material, and they become superfluous once the mine has been worked and there is no need to fear the collapse of the covering, that is the earthcrust. First the coal pillars are buttressed with wooden props, and then as much of the mineral as possible is removed while there is no danger of a cave-in. Then the mine is abandoned, usually in the fall or winter when accumulated moisture and masses of snow burden the land surface to the extent that, not getting enough support from below, it collapses. And then here and there through the holes of the collapsed mine an untouched pillar of coal, like the charred smoke stack of a plant, will long be visible, or the remnants of a vein not worked to the end will glitter in the sun.

The workers engaged in this heavy dirty work are, for the most part, Welsh, Irish, and German. Youngsters are employed to load the coal in wheelbarrows and pick out stones and other extraneous matter. Wage rates are usually a dollar a day and sometimes even more. However much it appears that work in the coal mines is contrary to the American idea of common equality, in essence it does not violate that idea. "Is the work hard?" I asked a miner who was diligently using a crowbar by the light of a dim little lamp. "Yes!" he replied, "but I have only recently come to America (he was a German). My contract with the owner will soon be ended and then I will not come underground any more; I will go west where, in fact, I was going when I stopped here." Asking the question of others elicited the same response with some variations: the same hopes for an independent, self-supporting life working on a farm of one's own. The job was no more than a transient situation to enable one to gain a foothold. Given the workers' penchant for hard work, this dream will certainly be realized. There also lies concealed in it the principle of American equality; I will work, says a poor man, until I get rich. And he really works and saves part of his wages, and in the end finds an opportunity to secure his future.

No one has tried to calculate how much coal lies hidden in the Alleghenies because the extent of the coal seams is unknown. But according to studies that have already been made, the figures are enormous. If there is everywhere else the same wealth in the "black diamond" as there is in these fields, then one cannot foresee the exhaustion of a treasure that will surely elevate and enrich the whole region.

From Mauch Chunk one can see how the mountains slope toward the Atlantic Ocean. The eastern half of Pennsylvania begins here, and we had barely gone a few miles when huge fields planted with corn began to appear. Sturdily built, fenced-in farms were visible here and there, as well as other evidences of settled life, such as kitchen gardens. Generally not noticeable were those anxious activities to which one gets accustomed in the newly settled areas. The homes no longer had the aspect of American log cabins, painted white as if to serve as guideposts in the forest where they were built. The difference was so striking that I could not help but be curious and asked my neighbor whose farms these were that the train was racing past. My assumption that the architectural style and mode of life expressed a character different from the American was confirmed by the reply that these people were German, or as they are called here, "Dutch," from "Deutsch," which is what the Germans called themselves after migrating to America. Although he praised these Germans for their industry and love of order, the American could not forgive them for their adopting few American customs, not preserving the Sabbath with Anglo-Saxon strictness, always opposing temperance societies, and loving mainly their settled way of life. Once he has chosen a place to live, a German does not change it without good reason: he is wedded to his farm and passes it on to his descendants, refusing to scorn the old in pursuit of the new, which—because it is unknown—may seem more profitable and more attractive. Just as in Europe, the German here loves his family circle and values his peace and quiet. Life without a permanent dwelling-place and life in hotels, which Americans are so fond of, is simply not part of the German temperament, and he remains true to his past. It is precisely on Sundays that he likes to dispel the boredom of daily life in the Alleghenies with rounds of beer and conversation, just as he did in Old Germany.

Only in one respect did the Germans betray themselves—in language. This is again a characteristic feature in Germans, and it distinguishes them not only in Russia but anywhere else they happen to be.[6] In America, and all the more in Pennsylvania where the Germans are a good half of the population, an outrageous mixture of German and English has developed. The words *vell* ("well") and *nou* ("now"), badly pronounced and incessantly repeated, serve as a veil with which the Germans vainly try to cover their non-American origins, as if they were ashamed of remaining Germans in America. German endings are added to English words: out of "stop" they took it into their heads to make "stopiren," pronouncing it "shtopiren," and instead of *nein* they always say "no." It is remarkable that one encounters the same Germanized forms of English words in all states having German populations, as if the Germans of Cincinnati, distant Wisconsin, and Philadelphia had made an agreement amongst themselves. Nevertheless the Pennsylvania settlers call their language Pennsylvonian, that is, Pennsylvanian, or Low Dutch, and sometimes Forest German (*Buschdeutsch*). Be that as it may, a Pennsylvania German is difficult to understand: even if he begins in German, he will mix it up with so many English words, forming them after his own fashion, that you absolutely do not know in what language he is speaking, though you listen and a large number of the words sound familiar. But little by little you become accustomed to this mixed-up Pennsylvania dialect, and you learn to make out the root of a given word. One might mention that the predominance of the German language and national character inevitably resulted in the fact that even the Americans of Pennsylvania adopted into their language some German words, though the number is insignificant.

6. In Lakier's day there were two major groups of German settlers in Russia, one in the Volga region and the other in South Russia. Both had been invited by Catherine II in the late eighteenth century to colonize new lands and were lured by the offer of free land, religious freedom, self-government, exemption from military service, postponement of taxes, and interest-free loans for building farmhouses and stables. Forming compact settlements and retaining their own language, they were free peasants in a country of serfs. Walter Kolarz, *Russia and Her Colonies* (New York: Praeger, 1952), pp. 67–76.

III

Philadelphia at last began to come into view before us. On the left was
something like a Greek temple, except that it was not erected in honor
of Zeus, as in ancient Athens, but for education. It was Girard College.[7] Farther ahead there was something like a medieval castle with
jagged walls and embrasures. Yet it was not the castle of some feudal
baron; although the form was the same, the content was altogether
different—this was the Pennsylvania Prison. With the engine bell
ringing and scattering people, the train came rushing into the depot
(as Americans call the railroad station), which was virtually in the
center of town.

Although located on the edge of the huge state of Pennsylvania,
Philadelphia for the most part is a commercial and industrial city,
while the governmental center of the state is in quiet Harrisburg.
Nevertheless Americans do not forget the past history of the city, its
peaceable founder, or the profound significance that this city of Quakers has in the history of the American Union. It is remarkable that the
gentle character of those "friends" of peace and harmony and haters of
war and discord was reflected even in the history of the city, which
does not bear the name of brotherly love in vain. Just as William Penn
obtained land from the Indians for his followers through peaceful
agreement, and just as his relations with the settlers to whom he ceded
lands in the New World were peaceable,[8] the same characteristic
manifested itself in the later history of Philadelphia: even its participation in the North American war for freedom and independence was
inspired primarily by the hope that the war would result in a properly
established union and a peaceful constitution.

Present-day Pennsylvania was settled long ago by immigrants from
Europe, and however much the Quakers of Penn's day were mixed
with other nationalities who poured into the original stream, the
Quaker element has remained predominant. In the streets, omnibuses,
and trains one continually encounters the Quakers' ever-present black
wool hats, their long, peculiarly cut black frock-coats, and the old-

7. Founded in 1848 as a school for educating poor white orphan boys.
8. In the various treaties that he concluded with the Indians, Penn
(1644–1718) made every effort to satisfy them in his negotiations for
their lands. He attracted large numbers of settlers through very liberal
terms for the purchase or rental of land.

style attire of their wives and daughters; moreover, the predominant
type of face remains one constantly sunk in serious thought. The same
imprint has been preserved in the city itself and the life-style of its
inhabitants. Start to speak with a Quaker: his reply is polite, short, and
quiet, with a soft voice and no gestures. You quickly understand that
silence and reflection are pleasanter for him than speaking of things
that have little or no significance. But sometimes a Quaker can be
roused to conversation and it pays to get him started on the history
of his sect and its teachings. Then he readily goes into details about his
thoughts.

[Lakier quotes at length a statement of Quaker principles given
him by a Philadelphia Quaker to whom he had a letter of introduction.]

If Philadelphia had remained the property only of the Quakers,
there is no doubt that, given the principles by which they are guided,
the city down to the present day would have had the very same
boundaries and population as in Penn's time. But its advantageous
location, the haven and vocations open to all poor and oppressed
people regardless of creed and belief, and the political equality, all
imparted new life to the city and gave it a more active direction. Ships
and steamboats have appeared on the Delaware not only for internal
trade but for trade with other countries as well; companies using steam
power have taken advantage of the proximity of the Alleghenies and
the sea. Indeed, when you sail along the Delaware and see the shore
through the smoke and soot and hear the whine and rumble of machines, you cannot imagine the eternal stillness and quiet you meet on
the streets. Just as in Penn's time when the Germans particularly loved
Philadelphia and Pennsylvania and chose it for their abode, they subsequently also preferred this quiet refuge where they found their native
tongue and native customs, whereas in the other states they would have
had to accustom themselves to American habits. But here, as everywhere else, trade and industry became the Yankee's domain. It is
particularly startling to a foreigner to see in the same city two completely different populations living side by side and not interfering
with each other: one is anxious, active, and commercial while the other
is quiet, pensive, and agricultural.

It took great effort on my part to track down the elm tree under
which the father of American Quakers concluded the treaty with the
Indians that ceded him the lands, and even more the house where

Penn lived during his first stay in America (Penn Cottage). The Union of North American States cannot boast of relics from the ancient past: not having a history, America obviously cannot have monuments to it. But America does not value even those it has, especially if they are older than the War of Independence and the adoption of the federal Constitution. Whereas Penn's house is in ruins and virtually no one knows it, the room where the first defenders of American independence met and drafted the federal Constitution is preserved as sacred. This State House or Independence Hall remains the center of Philadelphia down to the present day. Despite all the changes and additions to this building, the room where the principles of American independence were worked out has been kept sacred and inviolate. Everything is in its original place. . . . Americans love to visit this room, which is associated with so many memories of the past and so many hopes for the future.

IV

If the court system in Philadelphia offers little that is unique in comparison with the systems of other states, the prisons of the capital of Pennsylvania, on the other hand, deserve special attention.[9] The prison system itself is even called the Pennsylvania system, and the term is applied to several prisons in Europe. It was therefore particularly interesting to investigate this system of confinement in the very place where it was created and widely introduced.[10]

Love for mankind, which constitutes the true dogma in Quaker teachings, found broad application in the system of confinement for those suffering from vice. As early as 1786 the evils of the then-existing prisons called forth a society of right-thinking people who set themselves the task of assuaging the grievous situation.[11] They deliberated a long time, however, about how best to combine punishment with reform of the criminal; finally in 1822 they reached the conclusion that this goal could be achieved only through totally separating the prisoners from each other and requiring them to work. Constant solitude,

9. The state capital was Harrisburg, which Lakier refers to as "the governmental center." See p. 120.

10. See chap. 5, n. 1.

11. Formed by Quakers and friends, it was named the Philadelphia Society for Alleviating the Miseries of Public Prisons. McKelvey, *American Prisons,* p. 7.

they said, would do the most to promote full repentance and reform while at the same time the labor of a healthy man would not be lost. Today there are two prisons for the whole state of Pennsylvania; the one for the eastern half is in Philadelphia, and the other for the western judicial district is in Pittsburgh on the Ohio. Both are organized on the same principles. I headed for the Philadelphia prison with a visitor's permit, let me say in passing, given me by the mayor of the city without any difficulty. Besides "State Penitentiary," it is also called "Cherry Hill State Prison," derived from the former name of the location.

About eleven acres are enclosed by thirty-foot-high stone walls. As with feudal castles in Germany, there are towers in the corners of the walls and over the entrance to the courtyard within which the prison is located. But beyond that there are no indications of what the walls and building are designated for. A knock on the gates brought a guard who meekly unlocked them. Given his old age and lameness not everyone would have entrusted him with the guarding even of a private home. Having looked at the visitor's permit, he took me to the central building and from there one of the supervisors guided me through various sections of the prison.

Seven long corridors fan out to various sections from the central building, like spokes from the hub of a wheel. By remaining in the middle of the prison the supervisors can keep order in the entire building. Dead silence reigns in the prison; everyone is behind locks and must work. The number under which a prisoner is registered in the prison log is displayed in the cell, along with the work to be done, when it was assigned, when it must be finished, and how much has been done and handed over. In this way the supervisor has no need to talk with the prisoner every time to find out what work the prisoner has and when he is entitled to rest. There are openings in the cell doors through which food is passed at specified hours, in the same manner and the same portions as at other prisons.

There are five hundred cells in all seven corridors. Once having entered a cell, a convict does not leave it until the prison term is completed, he is pardoned, the penalty is changed, or death puts an end to human justice. Since the cells are designed not only for night but for work during the day as well, and consequently for living, they are more spacious than those in the Auburn prison system. For the most part the cells are eleven feet nine inches long and seven feet six inches wide; each also has a small plot of ground, fifteen feet long and eight feet wide, enclosed by thick stone walls. There are also double-size cells for work requiring complicated tools. Each prisoner is allowed to make up his own mind on how best to utilize his plot: one plants trees, another grows flowers, and a third cultivates grape vines and treats himself to grapes. But fresh air and rest can be enjoyed only when the work or daily task has been completed. Every cell is a complete unit: it is heated by steam from a common source, is lighted by gas, and is supplied with water through a faucet. Only prisoners incapable of other kinds of work are used for cultivating the kitchen gardens laid out in the prison yard between the separate corridors. Of course even in the garden everyone works separately and the main concern of the guards is that the silence not be broken. Failure to observe this rule brings the strictest punishment.

According to the rules of the Philadelphia prison, when a person sentenced to imprisonment first enters he is taken by two stone-faced attendants to the baths and after washing is dressed in convict clothes. If he is illiterate and has no trade, he is taught reading, writing, and a craft which he uses during imprisonment. There is a religious teacher at the prison charged with the edification and instruction of the convicts. Services are held on Sundays and each one hears the word of God from his own cell. In addition, the doors of the cells are opened for every Christian ecclesiastic, regardless of sect: he can visit the prisoners, preach to them, and instruct them. Conversation with the prisoners is permitted when the warden grants permission to enter one or another cell. I was accorded similar trust, and having learned that two Russians (from Poland) were in the prison, I asked to be taken to one of them. I found him at work, sewing boots. He understood Russian very little, and found it easier to speak German.[12]

12. The prisoner was very likely a Pole. Poland's political independence ceased in 1795 when the country was partitioned for the third and last time by Russia, Prussia, and Austria. Russia absorbed the bulk of Poland's territory and its people, who politically became members of the Russian Empire. But the Poles retained a strong sense of national consciousness and clung tenaciously to their culture and language. Few Poles, especially of the lower classes, had the desire, need, or opportunity to learn Russian. American officials made little distinction between ethnic and political identification and arbitrarily designated anyone from the Russian Empire as "Russian."

His pale face showed long suffering and he complained about a pain in his chest. Having already spent more than a year here for theft, he spoke with gratitude about the gentle and conscientious treatment by the guards and those in charge of the prison; and said that all he wished for was more exercise and fresh air. He still had more than a year, however, to drag out the same insipid life in boredom and solitude. It was obvious that all his affection was centered on the little garden, which the cell door led to, just as, in happier times, it would be transferred to a wife and children. After coming to America with the goal of improving his condition, the prisoner did not immediately find an occupation for himself. He ran through what he had brought with him from Europe, ended up destitute and in poverty, and found himself in prison. But when I asked whether his work caused him difficulty, he launched upon a panegyric and repeated more than once that without it he would be miserable, and that the boot he was sewing was his only friend and neighbor, that without it he would not know what to do with himself in his boredom and would long since have lost his life or his mind. "Luckily," he said, "I have no family and I left no one destitute or in shame and in need of care outside the prison doors." In the words of the prisoner there was already a tear of repentance and regret over the past.

Virtually the same story, the warden told me, could be heard from any other prisoner. And that, he kept repeating, was the good they wanted to achieve with the Pennsylvania prison system. To my question about the total number of prisoners, my guide gave me a report for the year 1857. From that it was evident that 146 people were admitted to the prison during the year. Of those, 127 were white (118 men, 9 women) and 19 were colored (17 men, 2 women). In addition to natives of Pennsylvania, the prison contained people from nearly all the states in the Union who had committed a crime in the eastern half of Pennsylvania. In addition, there were people who came from various countries in Europe: Ireland and Germany had fourteen representatives and Russia two. It is interesting that illiteracy did not have as much influence on crime as did the lack of a trade and especially drunkenness. Of the 146 individuals whose crimes sent them to prison, 108 knew how to read and write and 17 only how to read; only 1 was well educated and 20 were totally illiterate. Meanwhile 108 individuals were without a trade and 18 had one but had left it, leaving only 20 with an occupation. A good half were charged with theft and larceny.

Altogether there were 423 people in prison in January 1857. From the time it first opened on October 25, 1829, the Pennsylvania prison has had 3,505 people. Of those, 234 died, 9 entered lunatic asylums, and 8 committed suicide. Two have died in the past year and there was one suicide.

These figures, said the warden, serve as a strong refutation of those who dispute the benefit of solitary confinement by claiming that it leads to insanity and suicide. Frankly speaking, he continued, I am surprised that attempts upon one's life occur less frequently than might be expected, since prisoners are given sharp tools for work and eating. It means a person gradually adjusts to perpetual seclusion; in general, despair mainly takes hold of those who have recently been put in prison and have not had time to make the necessary adjustments. The blessing of life is dear to man and the gentle treatment of the prisoners by the guards and prison heads aids that innate feeling. Furthermore, working in the garden is a diversion for the prisoners, as are discussions with teachers and ministers and even the obligatory work, and when the work is finished they can read books they themselves select from a catalogue each one has of the prison library. There is a Bible in each cell in the prisoner's language, and in addition the library contains selected discussions and stories of an edifying nature. It is comforting to read in the librarian's report that in one year 11,919 books were charged out to the cells.

After having inspected the cells, the kitchen, and the prison equipment, I had to admit that those in charge had done all they could to improve the life of the convicts and ease their hard lot. But it cannot be said that the upkeep of the prison cost citizens dearly in the taxes collected for public institutions. Here too work is farmed out to industrialists and has brought in $17,918 a year. Since the entire maintenance cost for prisoners came to $24,034, the deficit was only $6,116, if one does not count the salaries for the small number of prison authorities (twelve in all), the cost of keeping the building in good condition, and other minor expenses, all of which came to $16,028.

The advantages of the Pennsylvania prison system are numerous: if one is interested in the moral reform of criminals during their imprisonment, it can be achieved here most quickly of all. I am quite ready to do justice to the principle at the base of this system, all the more so since the judge who keeps in mind the severity of such imprisonment may impose a less extreme sentence. Thus, while in the

Auburn system I met prisoners serving twenty-five-year and even life sentences, in the Philadelphia system a large number of criminals are sentenced to confinement for one year, and even for the most serious of crimes the terms do not exceed twelve years. In a whole year such a penalty was inflicted only on one person. Clearly one month of such isolation more than compares with a year of confinement in other prisons. The law's intent, however, is to punish only guilt, whereas incarceration in the Pennsylvania prison undermines a person's health and weakens him, and he grows unaccustomed to life and people, just as a person living in a cellar or cave for an extended period of time is cut off from God's light and goes blind as soon as a ray of light that is beneficial to any other person begins to play on his eyes. Supervision in the Auburn prison system prevents communication between criminals in the workshops, and at night the prisoners are separated from one another, so there is no need to fear the development of vice and its attendant evils. But a man is not meant to be buried alive; by working with others, as he does in the Auburn system, he is not removed from the realm he was in before his fall and to which he must return upon the expiration of his term of punishment. The Pennsylvania system may be granted an advantage as a method of confinement before trial, and just recently it was applied to the Paris Mazas prison, which is designed precisely for the confinement of criminals prior to conviction.[13] But for prisons whose principal purpose is punishment, one cannot but give preference to the Auburn system. This accords with the view of most people who have seen prisons based on both systems, and it is difficult to quarrel with that opinion.[14]

It is not worth refuting again the point often made in defense of the Pennsylvania system, namely, that prison escapes are impossible. Neither in the Auburn nor Pennsylvania system are convicts put in chains and shackles, and it might be thought that in prisons based on the

13. The Mazas prison was opened in Paris in 1850 as a new-model prison with twelve hundred individual cells.

14. To Gustave de Beaumont and Alexis de Tocqueville, the two types of American prisons were simply variations of the same system. The basic purpose was confinement in solitude, for which one used walls and the other rigorous discipline. They concluded that "the Philadelphia system produces a deeper effect on the soul of the convict . . . while Auburn . . . is more conformable to the habits of men in society." Quoted in McKelvey, *American Prisons,* p. 26.

former system, especially in view of the small number of guards, escapes occur frequently. Not at all. During the day when all are together at work and when the jailers have an interest in seeing to it
that there are no idlers and even more, no absentees, it would be difficult for anyone to escape over the walls that almost always enclose
the work yard, even if there are only a few guards and no natural
obstacles, such as the cliffs and the Hudson River at Sing Sing Prison.
According to the report I mentioned earlier, ever since the Philadelphia prison was founded, only one person has escaped from it. But
in other prisons, too, the number of escapees has not been large in
comparison to the total number of those confined.

The Philadelphia prison can also be faulted for the fact that those
who are not quite of adult age, although separated in accordance with
the general rule, are also left alone to their own repentance. Besides
weakening themselves through immoral acts—an ineradicable evil in
all prisons—young criminals, one fears, will not in any way be reformed as a result of this solitary confinement. The undesirable consequences of such a system, however, are partly eliminated by a special
institution which has as its goal the employing, teaching, and reforming of young boys and girls who are idle, or ignorant, or who have
shown a tendency for evil ways. A House of Refuge for black and
white children, similar to the one in New York, has been established
in Philadelphia. Boys under twenty-one and girls under eighteen are
sent here by sentence of the state criminal courts, or by city officials
where there are complaints of depravity by parents, guardians, or close
relatives and where there is evidence that those responsible for the
minors cannot maintain proper control or supervision. I found a
total of 630 persons in this institution. Activities among them are
segregated according to age and sex, and as in all American reform
institutions, the inmates' work is sold to industrialists. In addition to
eight hours of work per day, four hours are devoted to schooling.

V

Whatever differences there may be among the states in their schools,
on which the citizens concentrate their attention, they all have as a
common goal the formation of good citizens. Hence for all the diversity of principles upon which the school systems are based, education
remains practical and has none of the exclusive classical tendencies
that characterize schools in England. I repeat, the American is con-

vinced that only free general public education can have a beneficial influence on the well-being of the nation; it is that to which he feels he owes his present rapid prosperity. Quite apart from the donations every American willingly makes for a good cause, United States history is replete with people such as Smithson, Astor, and Girard who are remembered for the fortunes they made and the assigning of them to social and educational institutions.[15] If the first used the surpluses of his huge fortune for establishing the Smithsonian Institution in Washington and the second for a public library in New York, the third devoted his wealth to founding a school for male orphans in Philadelphia.

Girard in his will left $2 million to the institution, which was to admit [white male] orphans aged six to ten. They were to remain until their fourteenth or eighteenth year and receive a practical education, after which they would devote themselves to some useful and productive business, agriculture, trade, or art.

Girard College is on a somewhat elevated spot and is visible from afar. It is an excellent example of a Greek marble temple and were it not such a pity that millions were spent on the colonnade and portico, were it not for the fact that every column represents the sighs and tears of those orphans who will not get an education because of the money thrown away on ornamentation, the Greek Corinthian-style temple would be appropriate. Today one necessarily sees in this extravagance the vanity, if not of the testator, then of the executors of his will, and it is painful that, in light of so noble a goal, one is reminded of so unpraiseworthy a deed. But one is all the more willing to push this thought aside in that one of the main points in the will plainly says that the children must be brought up with the very best moral principles so that they will carry away with them a warm feeling for their fellow men and a deep love for truth, temperance, and work.

Not so easily explained is another requirement of the founder of the college, namely that no minister of whatever faith is to enter the

15. James Smithson (1765–1829) was a British chemist and mineralogist who left $550,000 to the United States for the founding of a scientific institution. John Jacob Astor (1763–1848) was a German immigrant who made a fortune in the fur trade and left $400,000 for the founding of a public library in New York City. Stephen Girard (1750–1831) was a French immigrant who became a successful merchant in Philadelphia.

college or any of the grounds belonging to it, neither for preaching, teaching, or even simply visiting. It was explained to me that this is why to enter the institution one is required to have a pass from one of the college directors. The supervisor who took me around the institution said that nowhere has the field been left so wide open for sects and the diffusion of the most varied and arbitrary teachings as in America. The testator, in excluding men of the cloth so strictly from even entering the institution, wanted to guard against harmful influences on the young hearts of the helpless orphans for whom the school acted as parent and guardian. Nevertheless the orphans did not remain without moral training: teachers and supervisors became their mentors. Nor was the institution noticeably suffering from the exclusion of missionaries and preachers of different faiths.

[Lakier describes a variety of philanthropic educational institutions, scholarly societies, and public libraries in Philadelphia, and comments that "with such auxiliary resources for the schools, it is not surprising that everyone understands his responsibilities as a citizen, and that the desire for education is not limited to a select few." He observes that Philadelphia has a smaller proportion of poor than does New York, and that the title "city of brotherly love" is fully justified by the large and numerous charitable institutions. Philadelphia, he says, is "lush with gardens" but also has "the most modern improvements in city management and services," including running water and gas-lit streets.]

VI

In bidding farewell to Philadelphia I carried away an even warmer feeling of respect for its founder, William Penn, than I had when I arrived, my only acquaintance with him having been through history. If the nobility and greatness of his soul were not adequately appreciated by the immigrants whose benefactor he was, it has become much clearer now when one can see the happy results of his ideas and activities. The industriousness of Pennsylvanians is exemplary, and they have an especially great love for agriculture. The fields on both sides of the road running along the shore of the Delaware to Baltimore comprise an unbroken chain of clean, well-laid-out farms and gardens; the contrast is all the more startling, then, when one crosses the southern border of Pennsylvania into the state of Maryland.

In looking at a map of the United States one cannot but be surprised that the borders between the separate states appear as straight lines. For the most part the states are rectangles measured off by the human hand, unless there is a large river which could not but be accepted as a natural boundary. Nonetheless, in crossing this border, this imaginary line between two states, one sees other concepts, a different method of cultivating the soil, a different economy, and different people. Maryland provides striking evidence of this. Pennsylvania is the last of the free states in the northeast. To the south of it is a whole series of slave states. Needless to say, the Quakers were always enemies of slavery and with all the means at their disposal worked to abolish this ulcer oppressing America. The southern border of Pennsylvania, the so-called Mason and Dixon line laid down in 1767, separates the free from the slave states. There was a time, one Quaker told me, when a slave who crossed this border became free, and the philanthropic Friends guided Negroes to free soil through secret routes and tunnels. Nothing was easier than to dispossess the Maryland planters in this way of their property. Only after a long struggle did the states hating slavery have to concede that a slaveowner had the right to pursue his runaway slaves and demand through the courts that they be returned from wherever they might be found.[16]

But the Pennsylvania border serves as the boundary limit of slavery not only in name; indeed, the influence of another principle is profoundly reflected in the Maryland population and its way of life. It is worth crossing the Susquehanna River in order to understand a phenomenon that is not at all unique to this part of the Union, but in fact is repeated all over the country. Instead of small parcels of land into which a farmer puts his whole soul, land which he cultivates for himself in the most careful, painstaking way, there are huge plantations where a manor house towers above cabins that house Negroes. The land is tilled in a haphazard way; the fields planted in corn or tobacco are intermixed with lands still untouched or abandoned. Since the big landowners could have their fields worked by slaves, there was no possibility for free workers to settle next to them. The direct consequence was a generally insignificant increase in population. It could not be otherwise. The restraints imposed by cheap slave labor on the activity of a free worker who might want to bring his labor and skills

16. Lakier is referring to the Fugitive Slave Law passed by Congress in 1850.

here are such that the immigrant prefers the far-off plains of Wisconsin
and Iowa to the rich soil of Maryland. And in the former he has to
cultivate amidst danger from Indians and wild animals and be a long
way from any society, though, of course, at the same time he encounters no hindrances from it.

"You can see," said a young man from Pennsylvania who was traveling with me, "that we are no longer in our blessed state. Equality
ceases here. The black offering us apples is selling them for the profit
of his master. What would simply be done by a youngster of ten in our
state, is here assigned to a grown Negro, and he is little concerned
whether he sells all the apples or not. Ultimately the profits and the
losses fall to his master, and the Negro is indifferent to both one and
the other. He would be even more indifferent if he did not know that
he would be beaten and punished in the event he returned home with
the fruit he was supposed to sell, for then he would no longer be sent
to the railroad station and would be deprived of the possibility of getting off the hated plantation again. Why the local planters do not
realize they are obviously losing from slave labor, I do not understand," said the Pennsylvanian, "but the record is clear and some day
slavery will be ended. But when this hoped-for time will come I cannot predict."

There is no bridge across the wide Susquehanna. The waiting
steamboat ferried the passengers across the river and deposited them
on the other side, where a train and locomotive were waiting. A few
cars were designated for blacks, and they had to have some evidence
with them, such as a passport, that they were allowed to travel, that
they were not runaways, and had their masters' permission to be
absent. Only in exceptional cases could they be together with whites,
as in the caring for or nursing of a white baby. Otherwise they
were immediately moved to another car for the colored. "Let's go into
the Negro cars," my companion said to me, "and you will see how
they travel. The train is going through completely desolate places, so
there is nothing to admire along the way."

American railway cars are arranged in such a way that a passageway
is left in the middle and one can walk through the whole series of cars
along this aisle. Having come to the Negroes I was prepared to witness
a sad scene of people brokenhearted over their desperate situation. But
what did I see? The black faces of the sons of Africa were far brighter
than the pensive, somber faces of their masters. One of them was tell-

ing a funny story, and the white teeth of the Negro men and women were visible in all their brilliance. The listeners were chewing tobacco as well as any other Americans, and the men were paying court to their black women. I was convinced that the compliments lavished in the stifling, low-class, filthy cars where the slaves rode for half-fare on hard benches were in no way worse than those that Americans whispered to ladies dressed in silk and sitting on velvet in the luxuriously decorated cars, where this harmless activity was sweetly named "flirtation." Men are everywhere the same, and I am certain that while admiring the black fleshy cheeks of the Negro woman, while gazing at the yellow-tinged whites of her eyes and at the woolly head of her companion, the Negro man wonders with amazement what his lean master has found in the frail, pale-faced American woman. Perhaps he is even more amazed that she cares to respond to the compliments of her lean, carelessly dressed companion, who has been snatched away from his business and is venting on his lady the long silences of his office.

"Only one thing is bad here," I said to my friend, "the unpleasant odor in these stifling cars." "Yes, it's the smell of codfish, which follows the blacks everywhere, especially in the local hot climate when they pay little attention to cleanliness. For whites the odor is unbearable and it impregnates the railroad cars, even the ships, in which blacks are transported. The Negro does not mind it at all; gaiety is innate in him. Habit has accustomed him to slavery and, although I am an enemy of slavery, I think our imagination pictures the suffering of Negroes in blacker colors than is actually the case. If an idea is evil, its consequences are evil."

In any case I was glad when we returned to our seats. Several times the train had to cut across coves formed by Chesapeake Bay. The rails were laid across piles sunk in the ocean floor, with a broad expanse of water on both sides of the tracks. Upon hearing the train's clatter, flocks of birds rose from the surface of the water and my neighbor named for me the various species of wildfowl found along the entire Chesapeake Bay coast in almost countless numbers. He strongly urged me to go hunting some time on the islands scattered about the bay, promising me a rich bag.

At last there was Baltimore, the most industrialized city in the state, although it was not the capital. That honor belonged to Annapolis, but the commercial center was named for one of the principal founders of Maryland, Lord Baltimore.[17] The train, dispersing people with its bell, rode far into the city and came to rest at the depot. However the tracks extended farther, along the most crowded streets; only, instead of steam engines, horses were harnessed to the cars, and they pulled them right up to the wharf formed by the branches of the Patapsco River, which empties into Chesapeake Bay. All of Baltimore is oriented around this wharf, and all commercial activity is concentrated there. One continually finds Negroes on the broad streets, many of them dressed in rags, poor and begging alms. However, Baltimore is the liveliest city in Maryland and owes its prosperity to advantageous location and proximity to the sea. While the population of the state as a whole increased so insignificantly, the city of Baltimore grew quite rapidly and almost alone took part in the population increase. In 1790 the entire population of Baltimore was 13,503 and since then has grown to 200,000. Although the population of the state had not doubled in this same period, that of the city increased more than fifteen times. Clearly the great tobacco plantations, cultivated by slaves, did not have the adverse influence on city-dwellers that it did on the rural population.

Baltimore with its buildings resembles any other large American city. Public institutions are huge and there is a significant number of them. As everywhere else, there are numerous columns and buildings in the style of Greek temples. But it is remarkable that the original Catholic character Maryland had at the time of its founding has been preserved down to the present time. Currently Catholics constitute the predominant part of the population. Their churches are distinguished by glittering wealth and architecture, and the high cupola of the cathedral is visible from afar. The interior of the latter is adorned with two superb paintings: one, the removal of Christ's body from the cross, was a gift of French King Louis XVI; the other, a portrait of St. Louis burying his soldiers and officers in sight of Tunis, was sent by King Charles X.

Nor are education and philanthropy forgotten in Baltimore, as they are not anywhere in the Union. Located in the city is the University of Maryland. Nuns of various Catholic orders staff hospitals and orphan

17. George Calvert (1580–1632), whose charter for the province of Maryland was granted in 1632.

asylums, and schools for Catholic children have also been established here.

A trip on Chesapeake Bay deeply interested me. If wildfowl were served for dinner at the hotel, everyone felt obliged to remark that it was the best specialty from the waters washing Maryland's shores; if I strolled along a basin that penetrated into the city and that was filled with sailing vessels and steamships, at the slightest rustle flocks of birds flew up and cried out. I decided to go by water to Annapolis, partly to satisfy my curiosity as to why there were so many wildfowl, and partly to look at one of the oldest cities in the United States, if there is something "old" in America. Chesapeake Bay, with the rivers emptying into it, is the route from Baltimore to the ocean, so there was no difficulty in finding a means of transportation. The bay penetrates inland for two hundred miles, is four miles wide at its upper end and forty miles wide at its mouth. But the principal uniqueness of this sea route is that on both sides there are countless coves that are quite deep, with numerous islands in them. Rivers and streams empty into these coves, the shores are covered with green trees and the islands are overgrown with grass. Here are the haunts for the waterfowl that attract hundreds of hunters. There are many wild ducks, but especially renowned is the canvasback, a species which is only found here and is the favorite for hunting. The American traveling with me on the steamship, a sometime hunter, could not find words enough with which to extol the delicacy of the meat of this highly prized wild duck, and more than once pointed out whole flocks of them to me, naming the islands and coves as we passed them by. There are times of the year when all the men from the neighboring towns around the inlets go off hunting. After several days they return with a rich bag. The wild ducks are packed in small barrels, and the main depot for them is Norfolk, Virginia, at the mouth of Chesapeake Bay. From there they are shipped to all parts of the United States.

7

The Ohio Valley
Pittsburgh and Cincinnati

I

Since I was so close to the city of Washington in the District of Columbia (Americans never fail to add this designation since tens of cities in the Union are named after the great man), I could not bypass the governmental city although I knew that December was still far off and that Congress was not yet in session. Nevertheless I was afraid I would not get there another time. The president too was not in town and Washington, with its broad avenues and huge buildings, its magnificent Capitol and monuments, was absolutely dead. The streets and hotels were virtually empty, the heat had driven the diplomatic corps to the seashore, and it is no exaggeration to say that the city which two months later struck me as lively and interesting in the highest degree, resembled a desert. Where only recently large numbers of people had been living, there were now deserted mansions, an exhortation to the next generation, as it were, that nothing on earth was lasting. I am glad I was able to visit there another time and could be persuaded that the desolation was only temporary. Otherwise I would have carried away a false and unfavorable notion of Washington. Later on I will describe my impressions of the city.

According to the plan I had outlined when I began my journeying around America, I was to go back north, traverse the states of Maryland and Pennsylvania, make for the southern end of the Alleghenies, cross them, and then visit the central states of the Union along the Ohio. It goes without saying that this route, too, presented no difficulties: the railroad was at the service of travelers. While returning from a slave state to Pennsylvania, I had a chance to confirm the impression that struck me earlier, on the way from Philadelphia to Baltimore. The plantations lying here and there were cultivated in the same haphazard fashion, whereas beyond them were the settlers' farms only

recently come into being, with their small household operations and
their herds, pastures, and fields. The train made several stops amidst
the rich lush forests to let off or take on a single farmer, or deliver a
package of household utensils sent to him from a nearby town. A
minute for the stop, the engine whistle blew, and once again the cars
began to tear along: the deed was done, and the farmer would not
have to go to the train station or send one of his expensive laborers. The
conductor never hesitates to stop the train at an unscheduled place, as
if he were merely stopping a public carriage or some stagecoach, for
he remembers that transportation routes exist for those who need them
and that it is precisely because they can count on conveniences being
made available by these routes that people have decided to penetrate
into the distant wilderness and cultivate it by the sweat of their brows.

As we gradually wound our way through the Alleghenies, they rose
higher and higher, running parallel to the ocean as they did at the
northern end and dividing the waters that fell from the eastern and
western slopes. In crossing the mountains one never tired of the ex-
traordinarily picturesque valleys and the scenes of eternal snows, cliffs,
and uninhabited wilderness. Here, as in the northern half of the Alleghenies, Americans are not deterred by natural obstacles. At a fright-
ful cost of two and one-half million silver rubles[1] they built at
different intervals a total of thirty-six miles of portage railroads. These
are constructed in such a fashion that ten locomotives, set up at different places on the mountain, pull the train up the mountain and keep it
from rolling down the other side too quickly. Altogether these climbs
and descents account for 2,570 miles. On one of the heights where
tracks have been laid I came across the Russian name of Gallitzin
among the settlements that owe their origin and well-being to coal
mining. I found no explanation of the name in the guidebook, nor
could my neighbor give me a positive answer when I told him why I
was interested. The American's curiosity was aroused no less than
mine. He remembered that there was an inhabitant from the town in
our car, a Catholic priest, and went to ask him whether the population
was Russian. The American, referring to me as "a Russian gentleman,"
repeated my question to him. It turned out that while not a single
Russian was now living in the town, it preserved the name of Gallitzin
in memory of its founder, Prince Dmitri Golitsyn, who came here in

1. About $1.92 million.

1795 as a Catholic missionary to preach the word of God to Irish and German settlers scattered in various towns of the Alleghenies. Since a title of nobility was quite out of place among plain workers in a country of equality, the missionary adopted the family name of Smith, a name which one encounters very often in England and America. He remained in these mountains for forty-one years and died not long ago, in 1840. I remember him well, concluded the priest, and there are many people in town who are grateful to him.[2]

For me this explanation was enough and the name of the town made sense. The priest, who was also going to Pittsburgh, had not yet finished his lengthy praise for the courage and selflessness of the Russian missionary when the train entered a long tunnel cut through the Alleghenies for more than a verst[3] and suddenly before us appeared Pittsburgh with its countless tall chimneys from plants and factories. In England at least one knows what awaits each person who has just arrived in a great commercial and industrial city, beginning with London and ending with Glasgow and Edinburgh. In America one can only speak of the degree of dense smoke in the atmosphere, of the black and unhealthy faces of the workers, and of the houses covered with soot. In England one can get used to the eternal fumes and smoke and not get depressed, but in America, after the fresh mountain air of the Alleghenies and the virgin forests of Pennsylvania, one is far more sensitive to that kind of dismal atmosphere.

Pittsburgh is a "very smoky town," my neighbor told me, just as the English say of Manchester, Leeds, and Birmingham. It is well that there are many Negroes here; by comparison the white faces of the Europeans are bright but otherwise would appear to be smoke-colored.

That the city is dull and boring to a foreigner is understandable. From morning till evening the Americans in this manufacturing cen-

2. Demetrius Augustine Gallitzin (1770–1840) was the son of Prince D. A. Golitsyn and a member of one of Russia's illustrious noble families. He came to the United States at the age of twenty-two under the name of Demetrius Smith, entered a Catholic seminary in Baltimore, and became a missionary. In 1799 he founded the settlement of Loretto, some two hundred miles from Philadelphia, where he spent the rest of his life in missionary work. Gallitzin became an American citizen in 1802, thereby renouncing a great fortune and a princely title. He never returned to Russia. *Dictionary of American Biography,* vol. 7, pp. 113–14.

3. Thirty-five hundred feet.

ter are busy with accounts and reckonings, and everyone who can is glad to escape from the stifling smoke of the city. The wealthy and well-to-do who have stores and shops in Pittsburgh prefer to live in the suburbs, especially in Allegheny City located on the other side of the Allegheny River and linked to Pittsburgh by several bridges. There are whole rows of bright residences and villas of industrialists in Allegheny City. Across the Monongahela, on the other hand, are the richest coal mines and plants. The mineral is virtually on the surface, and with the river having formed its channel among the mine fields, the mining and delivery of coal is extremely cheap here, despite the high wages of $1 to $1.25 paid to workers. Not only is iron from mines in the Alleghenies shipped here, but so is iron from the mountains of Missouri and even copper from the Upper Lakes region, despite the distance of the latter and the difficulties and costs of transportation.

According to American calculations, the coal area of the southern slopes of the Alleghenies, which embraces Pennsylvania, Ohio, Maryland, Virginia, Kentucky, Tennessee, and Alabama, contains 65,000 square miles, and if the anthracite fields of the northern Alleghenies are included, 130,000 square miles. That total area is twelve times larger than the coal zone for all of Europe and thirty-five times greater than the area occupied by the coal fields of England, Scotland, and Ireland. Before the beginning of the present century no coal, or almost none, was mined here. In 1768 the descendants of Penn obtained the entire area of present-day southern Pennsylvania from the Indians for ten thousand dollars. And now more than a million tons of coal a year are required in Pittsburgh alone, and how much is sent to various parts of the Union!

Besides for iron and iron products of various sizes and purposes, such as rails and machines, Pittsburgh is renowned for its glass factories. These factories manufacture primarily plain and inexpensive glass which is then shipped to the remote regions of the Union, especially to the newly created states in the West. These factories are also concentrated on the Monongahela in the Pittsburgh suburb of Birmingham. Another suburb is located lower down on the Ohio from Pittsburgh and also bears the name of an English industrial town, Manchester.

It is no wonder that for a long time Pittsburgh enjoyed the title of Queen City of the West. In moving on toward the Mississippi the immigrants followed the Ohio and in turn bestowed the title upon Cincinnati and St. Louis. And if it is Cincinnati that really deserves this title by virtue of its central location, Pittsburgh will always remain a point of departure for the westward movement of settlers. It is here especially that there begin those states the Americans call new or western. And just as civilization moved from east to west on the Ohio, so may a traveler follow the same route from a state only recently formed and a city only recently populated to states and cities still in embryo, and then cross the Mississippi into lands where the Indians still hold sway and where their activities are limited solely to hunting buffalo, fishing, and warring amongst themselves. If it is a valid supposition that the Indians came to America across the Bering Strait and reached the Atlantic coast by following the Ohio, doubtless it was along that same route that they were driven back from the lands which the whites occupied.

One of the flat-bottomed multidecked steamboats that was tied up at Pittsburgh, unloading and loading cargo and taking on passengers, had a huge sign inviting people on board who wished to travel down the Ohio to Cincinnati and to the Mississippi, and announcing that it would depart at precisely the appointed hour the following morning. I headed for the steamboat to look it over and see whether it could be trusted: one so often hears about accidents on river steamboats. The captain assured me that the steamboat was new, that it was first-rate and surpassed the others, and that, as for departure time, it would leave at the appointed hour. Knowing how business is conducted in other countries, I obtained a ticket and the next morning hurried to board the steamboat, fearful of being late. But there were not yet any signs of movement, no preparations had been made, they had not yet thought about getting up steam, and one might have thought that it was not the right steamboat. Seeing that it was the same *Morningstar,* I went looking for the captain. "Are we getting under way soon?" "Right away," and this reply was repeated with different variations until the next morning. The matter was very simply explained: an American does not want to lose the least bit of profit and will make every effort to take on as many passengers and as much cargo as he can; since ours was the only steamboat departing for Cincinnati that day, our captain was waiting for more "booty." What did it matter to him that those who might be in a hurry were displeased with this policy, for he would please himself and those who were late. And indeed the number of people increased little by little, with everyone considering it his duty to bargain to make the trip a bit cheaper and to send his cargo more profitably. Threats to leave the ship would not have led anywhere: the captain knew there was no other way to travel, and only when he was convinced that another steamboat was making ready to go did he raise steam and depart. On the other hand one lives on the steamboat and has free room and board for the extra day because of the fare paid for the trip. One might think that the captain or company would sustain a loss, but the American knows his profit and does not throw a dollar away if he is not convinced it will return to him a hundredfold.

"You will meet not a single sailing ship now along the entire Ohio and Mississippi, except perhaps for some negligible shipping of products from one plantation to another." So said an American going to Louisville, condemned like me to waiting, though he bore the delay patiently, without the slightest murmur, as if it were something legal or at least customary. All the movement along these waterways is by steamboats, which are counted in the thousands.[4]

Despite the dangers of navigating these changeable rivers and despite the constant encounters with other steamboats, the captain never refused to sail at night, however dark and black it might be, just so long as there was no fog. True, a lantern is hung between the two tall stacks, but if that somewhat reduced the danger of collision, there was still the possibility of getting off course. To give the pilot a fixed point by which to steer, a black ball hangs from a mast on the bow. It is reflected against the sky on even the darkest night and, by having it in front of him, the pilot can make for some object with which he is familiar. He has every right to call his guide the "Night Hawk."

The trouble comes when another steamboat wants to pass: the captain never refuses a race with a rival. Those on the bridge do all they can to maintain high speed because winning the race means enhancing the reputation of the steamboat and getting as a reward, not deer antlers or a horseshoe, but extra income in cash dollars. Everyone

4. Steamboating on the Mississippi and its tributaries reached its peak in the 1850s, when speed, service, and splendor attained their highest levels. But even in this decade of glory the decline of steamboating on the western rivers was foreshadowed by the rapid growth of railroads. Louis C. Hunter, *Steamboats on the Western Rivers: An Economic and Technological History* (New York: Octagon Books, 1969), chap. 12.

knows which boat enjoys the prestige of victory, which in turn serves as a recommendation for choosing it. The whole steamboat—all its parts down to the minutest detail—is planned for the kind of river it has to sail on. Hence not all steamboats are capable of going from Pittsburgh to the mouth of the Ohio or are in condition to sail the Mississippi. Not every pilot who knows the upper Mississippi perfectly can take a steamboat down its lower course, and vice versa. Experienced master pilots are therefore expensive and their work is compensated rather generously.

I must confess I had lost hope of ever departing from Pittsburgh: it seemed so long while waiting and counting the time and seeing yourself suddenly and needlessly confined to one place. To persuade people of an imminent departure—which there was not the slightest thought of doing—the crew got up steam several times and rang the bell, all of which was designed to hasten stragglers. In a day I managed to get used to these sly tricks that true Americans pay no attention to at all. Hence the next morning when smoke rose from the funnels, I looked at it rather indifferently. Unlike my traveling companion, I could neither justify nor excuse the captain and his tricks, and I was extremely glad when at last the long-expected moment came and the wheel of the steamboat began to turn.

"Praise be to God," I said to my acquaintance as we finally got under way. "I hope we will be in Cincinnati in two or three days."

"Maybe," he replied, "but don't count on it for sure; the river is low and there is very little water. If this were the month of May or the end of November, it would be another matter. But right now the river is the least accommodating. Some days ago a steamboat like ours broke its wheel and got stuck in the sand in sight of Pittsburgh and it is still sitting there crippled."

But our pilot was extremely careful and the steamboat wound along the river, sometimes keeping to the middle of the turbid, yellow, muddy Ohio, sometimes veering to the left or right. How and why he changed direction only he knew. He had his signs: either the surface of the river was smooth or the waves struck the sand and left a wake; sometimes a sounding-lead was thrown over the side and the speed was reduced in order to pass a shallow place. Once we had to help another steamboat that had gotten stuck in sand, for however much the forward spars held it off and the wheels frothed the water, it remained stationary. But the combined power of our ship and theirs pulled the latter free. Steamboats constantly render such service to one another, however much they may be rivals. In time of trouble it is all forgotten; Americans rally to one another's aid with their steamboats and with their combined power do what they could not do separately. An accounting may be made later, but the service is done free of charge, as between brothers.

II

There is more steamboat traffic on the Ohio than on all the other rivers flowing westward from the Alleghenies. This part of the country has several well-populated industrial and commercial cities along the shores of the river, to say nothing of the mineral wealth of the land to which the cities owe their rapid growth. But quite aside from that, the river rightly deserves the name *Ouo,* which means "beautiful river" in the Indian language, or as the French say down to the present day, *la belle rivière*, so picturesque and green are its shores. True, there are no huge rocky precipices and gorges along its course, but on the other hand the shores are not barren and uninhabited. On the contrary, the hills covered with forests and greenery are for the most part cultivated. Towns have already sprung up and developed at the mouths of small rivers emptying into the Ohio, as well as along the last rich outcroppings of coal in the Allegheny chain, and they have their own steamboats to carry on trade.

The first stop-off point for our steamer was the city of Wheeling on the south bank of the Ohio in the state of Virginia. This most important area is a narrow strip of Virginia contiguous to Ohio where a great deal of capital is concentrated for trade with Pittsburgh. The first and so far the only bridge (another is being built at Cincinnati) crossing the Ohio is located here, uniting the free state of Ohio with the slave state of Virginia. I think the desire to impede easy communication between them was one of the main reasons for the drawn out and heated dispute about whether or not to build the bridge. The continental party, so to speak, saw the advantage of an uninterrupted continuation of the northern chain of railroads to the South and passionately defended their interests. On the other hand the party of the steamboat companies, especially those in Pittsburgh, tried to prove that the bridge would mean interfering with free navigation on common routes like the Ohio, and that for them navigation would either have to begin at Wheeling or they would have to rebuild all their steamboats, which would not be able to pass under the bridge with their tall funnels at high tide. There were numerous defenders on both sides; more than once the dispute left the realm of brochures and journalistic battles and erupted in fights and violence. It was decided to allow the Supreme Court in Washington to review the case: the bridge was declared a public nuisance and the Wheelingites had to cease the construction already begun. But they did not despair and the Virginia representatives raised the question in Congress, demonstrating the necessity of a bridge for proper transportation of the mails, especially in winter when the Ohio froze over and the mails could not be transported by steam ferry as in summer. Congress could not but agree with this argument for the public's benefit and thus authorized construction of the bridge. It was suspended by cables at such a height that steamboats could freely pass under it. But it did not last long, for a storm blew it down in 1854. Last year a new and stronger suspension bridge was constructed.

Beyond Wheeling the river continues to divide Ohio first from Virginia and then from Kentucky. The general rule in the Union is that all states north of the Ohio must be free and all states south of it remain slave until they wish to do without Negro labor. It was remarkable that what I noticed in crossing from Pennsylvania to Maryland repeated itself here. Whereas on the northern side of the Ohio bright clean farms and flourishing little towns with active, industrious populations were visible, the southern side of the same beneficial river turned out to be somewhat desolate; people live somewhere or other, but it is as if they were purposely moved away from the shore so as not to see the other side and get any ideas about freedom's happy consequences. On occasion, as if by accident, a log cabin thrown together by the original builders came into view, only emphasizing the emptiness and offering a striking contrast to the opposite shore where even nature was more beautiful.

But if that difference is now understood (and we need not tarry here to justify the common and widely accepted rule that large estates cannot prosper as quickly as small farms cultivated by their owners), then a question arises which is not so easy to resolve: why is it that for several thousand years, according to our reckoning, the wandering hordes of Indians preferred to settle north of the Ohio and along its tributaries, and did not go south? At any rate the most significant of their burial grounds are found on the northern side of the river. They have a remarkable resemblance to the burial grounds in southern Russia: the same regular conical mounds and the same earthen wall around them. Today they are overgrown with trees and grass, and Americans rack their brains as to why the Indians built these burial mounds. It is difficult to believe they wanted to perpetuate a memorial to themselves. That concept was too sophisticated for a nomadic people who lived from day to day and did not do anything remarkable. Were they strongholds and forts, places from which to observe enemy movements? Or tombs for heroes? The problem is as little solved here as in our country, and Americans are even less concerned about it because they take pride in the newness of their country and do not pursue archaeological research and excavations. However they suspect them to be tombs for entire tribes who were at odds with and destroyed one another in war. This supposition is all the more probable in that the burial mounds are rather closely grouped together, and sometimes several small ones are gathered beside a large one, as in a cemetery. Americans are so convinced of the validity of this supposition that they call the most important burial ground, measuring seventy feet in height, not a "mound," as they call others of a similar kind, but the great "Grave Creek." It was quite visible from the steamboat and its conical top was clearly silhouetted among the seven other small ones, forming Seven Mound City. In time many things may be anticipated that will bear on the history of the Indians—perhaps the remains of clothing, tools, and vessels. Perhaps, too, their comparison with those that have turned up in our own burial mounds and the tombs of western Europe will explain the origin and subsequent history of these mysterious people.[5]

5. Grave Creek Mound is at Moundsville, West Virginia, in the upper Ohio Valley. It originally measured 69 feet in height and 295 feet in diameter at the base, and represents one of the largest known mounds of the Adena people. The latter were a major Indian group who had "attained to the highest cultural achievements north of Mexico during the first millennium before Christ." Their heartland was the Ohio Valley. Excavations of the Grave Creek Mound have turned up shell beads, copper bracelets, and fragments of mica. William A. Ritchie and Don W. Dragoo, *The Eastern Dispersal of the Adena,* New York State Museum and Science Service Bulletin No. 379 (Albany, N.Y.: State Education Department, March 1960), pp. 5–11. Thousands of mounds dating from the Scythian period of the sixth to the third century B.C. are scattered through

I was extremely interested in these burial mounds but no matter whom I asked about their significance, no one could give me an explanation. Even the captain himself, who had been sailing by them for several years already, had little interest in them. Nowhere perhaps are people generally so well and widely informed about what is new and current as in the United States, but the past, which provides no direct and essential benefit, seems to be of no concern to them. There will come a time when even for a young nation the past will be important and they will turn to their history, or rather to the history of the country they so recently and quickly occupied and cultivated. The captain, however, listened with curiosity to the stories of our burial mounds and stone images. Unfortunately I could tell him little that was certain and positive. Laughing to myself, I recalled how when I was traveling around the southern district of Kharkov Province a little old peasant very coolly remarked that those stone images were simply ancient landmarks or the boundary stones of private landholdings. For his part the American told me that near the town of Marietta, Ohio, he at one time saw a great mound surrounded by a vast earthen wall but that it had not been investigated.

III

Meanwhile we stopped at Portsmouth, which is several hours' journey from Cincinnati, the Queen City of the West. For an American, the Promised Land, which he longs for in his dreams, thoughts, and hopes, is the Far West and he spares nothing in order to settle there. "Is there really so little room in Pennsylvania? Are the old, settled, and secure states really so heavily populated that they are already crowded? Why drag wife, children, and household effects, God knows where, to a town just sprung up, not knowing what awaits you there, what kind of climate it has, whether you will find there the conveniences to which man is accustomed?" I asked this of an immigrant who was traveling with his whole family to Kansas. I was

---

the vast steppe zone of southern Russia. Excavations have revealed that most of them are burial sites of common warriors; some are the graves of Scythian kings and are extremely rich in gold and jewelry. George Vernadsky, *Ancient Russia* (New Haven, Conn.: Yale University Press, 1943), p. 44. No connection has ever been established between the Adena and the Scythians.

probably thinking that he was a poor fellow, who was unlucky in the Old World and in the New and who wanted to try his luck once more. This urge to move, as the pioneers themselves call it, is not at all understandable to a European. The immigrant's old mother and his young wife apparently agreed with me and did not know why or where the restless head of the family was dragging them, but obviously this topic was not new for him and he defended himself cleverly and boldly; he demonstrated that with the money he earned in Pennsylvania he could buy ten times more land in the West, be a rich farmer, and always have security for himself and his family. He quoted figures on the price of land and produce, and cited the possibilities for trade and industry. One had to conclude that the thought of transferring his activity to a new region was not a whim that had occurred only yesterday. Anyway, Americans have always acted this way, and even before them the English. Was it not really they who populated the present areas, after having cleared out the virgin fields with great effort and constantly having had to fight off Indians? True, after them came the Germans and the Irish, but without the Americans these people could have done nothing, just as now all rapid improvements issue from them [the Americans]. They are always at the head of the forward movement and this eternal "Go ahead!" is repeating itself even now, only farther on. "There is nothing remarkable now in getting as far as Cincinnati: any youngster can do it when there are steamboats and railroads. No! We will try our luck in the Far West, and wait: in some twenty years Cincinnati will no longer be the Queen City; our capital will rise up, and I think," concluded the immigrant, "that it will be in Kansas."

Let him have his say, and he would surely name even the future city where in time great buildings, banks, stores, and factories would be built. . . . The American is really like that: full of courage, he strides forth boldly, and he will reach his goal without fail. He knows this well and that is why there are no limits to his enterprise; and he loves his dream as if it were actuality, because he is convinced of its realization. I became used to the boundless praise which the American lavishes upon his own people, to such an extent that he finds nothing to add about another nation, and I rested content with the hope that he would at last find what he was looking for.

From the first days of my sojourn in the United States I heard much about Cincinnati as a model of the true American western city;

on the steamboat itself so much was repeatedly told me about the wonders that awaited me that I was already somewhat impatient and lamented that the steamboat proceeded slowly for fear of running aground. This is a realm of pure equality, said one, here everyone still works and wants to labor until he becomes wealthy; here there are none of those merchant princes who live off the labors of their neighbors, said another; there is still a wide open road for everyone; and so on. What a wonderful city I was going to, I thought. It must really be America in its original condition, and I joyously looked forward to reaching the Promised Land. In reality the Ohio near Cincinnati was crowded for three full miles with exactly the same kind of steamboats I had seen in Pittsburgh. Their smokestacks, without exaggeration, seemed like a black, charred forest and I wished for the sake of diversity that there were just one white sail. The river bank bustled with activity, with carrying to and from the steamboats, loading, unloading, selling, buying. Our steamboat just barely found space for itself, tied up to the shore, that is, the levee, and via a small plank we were able to go ashore at Cincinnati. Over the city lay a cloud of smoke as sooty and black, if not so dense, as the one over Pittsburgh.

The first thing I came across on solid ground was a huge sow with a full litter of suckling pigs. It was obvious that she did not come here by chance but was accustomed to being here. At least no one drove her away; on the contrary, everyone went around her, and coming up into the city I encountered with every step the same species of animal in the most crowded streets. Were this in another city which was not called "queen," it would be a different matter: I knew that the pig was the indispensable companion of the immigrant heading west, where in the virgin forests food and open space were readily available for it. For the first settlers in these forests, pigs were of course indispensable, but now. . . . Well now they are even more useful than they were earlier; Cincinnati is the world's greatest slaughtering center for pigs, and since the pork trade earns several million dollars for Cincinnati, such social protection for the source of wealth is pardonable.

While I stood somewhat dumbfounded before the audacious creature which, as it were, demanded for itself a place befitting its significance, a tall, powerful Negro loaded up with my baggage. Following behind him, I went up into town. We walked along Broadway:

it is a rare town that does not have its own wide street (quite simply, that is what Broadway means). We walked on stone sidewalks, along a beautiful roadway, past huge five-story houses which lined the street, past splendid stores. One could imagine that this city was at least several centuries old. Perhaps there was only one such street, but we turned into another one just like it and there stood a magnificent hotel. And what a marvel it was! Well really, one has to believe in the magic wonder of America, for after all, it was only at the end of the last century that the first pioneers arrived here from New England. They had to build Fort Washington in 1789 for protection against the Indians. In 1800 there was a total of 750 people here and now in the same region they number up to 200,000, and this tremendous increase in population, along with the growth of the city, took place in something like fifty years.

"Have you had a good look at the town?" asked a new acquaintance, to whom I had a letter of introduction. When I replied in the negative, he proposed to show it to me in all its beauty from one of the neighboring hills, the so-called Mount Adams. "There are still several hours till sunset so we'll be able to climb the hill without difficulty and visit my old friend, the biggest winemaker in this area." It was an excellent proposal for a stroll, and I shook my guide's hand and thanked him most sincerely. "If I come to Russia you will do the same for me, won't you?" Of course, but I do not know whether I could put our cities to the test of praising all improvements with the same degree of enthusiasm that Americans praise theirs. If we passed by an iron foundry producing smokestacks for steamboats (and the entire shore of the Ohio, down to its last hillock, is covered with such factories), he without fail stopped in to show me the steamhammer or the enormous wheel which drove hundreds of others; he explained to me that all necessities for settlers in the western part of America are made here, beginning with small locks, hooks, and all kinds of bolts, up to steamboats themselves which carry these goods to the remote wilderness and even uninhabited forests. That is why there is such monotony in the original dwellings; despite the fact that a cabin is just put together with logs, the door without fail has a white glass handle and a good lock, and they are exactly the same at each house. Even the houses themselves are built right here and my acquaintance suggested that we drop in on a manufacturer of them. He lived almost on our way.

And quite soon there appeared before us a six-story building with a tall smokestack. This was a factory that produced walls, doors, and frames for immigrant houses which were sent mainly to Kansas and Nebraska, and that is why they are called "Kansas and Nebraska portable cottages." The sizes and prices of the portable cottages are of course not the same, depending as they do upon the needs of the immigrant, that is, whether he is single or has a family and what his occupation might be. There are cottages for $100 for single people and for families they come with several rooms for $200 and $250. All the component parts are packed in crates, which are also manufactured here, and are sent out on order. Should the immigrant arrive at his new place in the morning, his house is ready by evening with no trouble. And the need for these convenient dwellings is so great that more than two thousand a year are bought. These kinds of houses are immediately available for sale and several were displayed outdoors as models.[6]

But inside the walls one had to think about furniture, chairs, and beds for the house, and again steam made it possible to reduce the amount and price of labor. With woodworking machines powered by steam engines instead of hands, the wood was cut, planed, and worked to give it the desired shape of component parts which, already marked with numbers, were fitted together quite without need of any special skill, so that from these parts were assembled the chairs, beds, and in general the furniture needed by the settlers. Every item is so constructed that it can be transported easily and cheaply, without being damaged or soiled: in short, to a certain extent comfort is made available to everyone. But for the settler furniture is hardly enough: he must have tools for domestic chores as well as various agricultural implements. Cincinnati takes care of these needs, too. Thanks to this foresight the immigrant can provide himself with all necessities for something like three or four hundred dollars. Land he will get either for nothing or will acquire for an insignificant sum, and afterward how he will rush to this long-wished-for West with all the passion of his dreams!

While chatting about these conveniences we came upon a narrow

6. Charles Cist, *Sketches and Statistics of Cincinnati in 1859* (Cincinnati: 1859), pp. 236–37, describes such a manufacturer of prefabricated dwelling units.

little stream which meandered almost parallel to the Miami Canal. This was the so-called Deer Creek and I could not but express surprise at the sight of the bloody or, more accurately, the opal-like color of the water which was sharply distinguished from the yellow water of the Ohio.

"What do you think that is?" my companion asked me. I did not know what to answer. Right here was the main slaughtering center for pigs; here they were salted, packed, and shipped to various states and even more to Europe. Up to 500,000 pigs are processed yearly in this pork business, and considering all the ham, sausage, and salt pork, this activity produces more than six million dollars for Cincinnati. In the whole world there are no comparable slaughterhouses for pigs, and torrents of blood poured into the small stream near which we stood. The remains of suet and suchlike are not wasted; they are made into lard-oil and used in candleworks. It is clear from all this why the pig enjoys such respect and freedom in Cincinnati.

Finally, after crossing the canal we began to climb a hill past a reservoir from which water, flowing from the Little Miami, is distributed to the entire city. On top of the hill is an observatory. From here there was a magnificent view of the farthest reaches of the Ohio, of the fleet of steamboats which had docked at Cincinnati, of the hills on the opposite Kentucky side, and of the clearly defined ridges on which the city was spread out. I could not get my fill of admiring this wonderful panorama of a living, active city. Below the mount a noisy railroad train sped along, steamboats plied the Ohio, and the scene became even more picturesque when in the bright, starry sky the moon appeared, and the opposite Kentucky shore was shrouded in mysterious semidarkness.

[On the Ohio side of the river] the hillsides sloping to the south were covered with vineyards and fruit orchards, and the greater part of them belonged to the winemaker Longworth.[7] He became famous here for cultivating Catawba grapes. There is not the slightest doubt that these grape vines always grew wild in the American woods and that the Indians who roamed here long ago prized them; one can find

7. Nicholas Longworth (1783–1863) was a Cincinnati lawyer, millionaire, and patron of the arts, who was also one of the ablest horticulturists America ever produced. Through his experiments Longworth made the growing of native Catawba grapes a commercial success and in 1828 produced a marketable wine.

them even now in the Canadian woods and in faraway Missouri. But only in recent times has wine been made from them, and in this respect the name of Longworth occupies first place. In his cellar we tasted "sparkling Catawba" in the family of champagnes, which is mostly distributed in the United States. It appeared to me too heady, but due to good winemaking the taste of the grape was well preserved. Besides sparkling wines, he produced dry, unsweetened wines of various kinds and brands. Attempts were made to transplant French vines here but they degenerated and did not yield good fruit, much less good wine. Little by little the use of grape wine will spread here, and along with beer, will force out strong drinks, whiskey and brandy, against which a campaign has been mounted by the temperance party. It was a pleasure to see in the chambers of the famous winemaker, who unfortunately was not at home, that he knew how to apply his fortune to the arts. He has a rich collection of paintings by American artists and a lovely marble bust by the sculptor Powers, in whom America takes pride no less than in Crawford, who so recently passed away in the prime of life.[8] Powers, who is greatly indebted to the patronage and assistance of Longworth, they say, has for a long time been living in Italy, and his statues *Fisher-Boy, The Greek Slave, America,* and *California* are considered to be among the best works of sculpture.

The gas lamps on the broad streets of Cincinnati had long been lit and stores and homes flooded with light when, tired, we returned to the city. Gas is everywhere and although there are many candle and stearin works in Cincinnati, virtually no one uses their products. Illumination with gas is so cheap and popular that in the stores it is left on all night long until morning, for a thief will not steal into a lighted room where the watchman will immediately see him from the street, and if the robber were to turn off the gas, it would be even worse for him. Neither shutters nor bolts are needed and a store owner can protect his property at small expense. In other lands they do just the opposite: they turn off the light and protect themselves against thieves with heavy iron bolts and shutters. Which is better? Whatever the answer, the novelty of invention remains in Cincinnati.

8. Hiram Powers (1805–73) was a Cincinnati sculptor who expatriated to Italy in 1837 and spent the rest of his life in Florence. Thomas Crawford (1814–57) was a New-York-born sculptor whose best-known creation is the statue *Liberty* atop the Capitol dome in Washington, D.C.

On the morrow, my obliging guide was telling me, you will see the municipal courts and public institutions. I took leave of him, but before I reached my hotel room the alarm bell (the signal for fire) began to ring, and in the near distance the sky reddened. Fire in America is not at all an uncommon occurrence but, for all that, it is still an interesting spectacle for a foreigner; no other event makes as clear as does this one the idea of the need for mutual aid. I conquered my weariness and went out into the street to see that instead of light and flimsy fire-extinguishing equipment pulled along by citizens, a steam engine flew by harnessed to four strong horses, the engine belching dense clouds of smoke and leaving a trail of hot embers on the roadway. I did not know what it was. People ran after the machine until it stopped at a factory that was on fire. As soon as the machine stopped, the horses were unharnessed and the hose was connected to the water reservoir; instead of by human hands, the water was pumped by steam. An enormous stream of water soon appeared, far higher than the five-story building, and poured down on the roof of the building, which was engulfed in flames. The stream was so powerful that it brought down windows and walls in its path without help of hooks, ladders, and other fire equipment. Hand tools arrived later and their effect, compared to that of those operated by steam, turned out to be absolutely insignificant. The people did what little they could with the hand tools and the friendship among them was obvious: everyone who was able helped pump water, bustled about, shouted, fussed, and changed places with tired fellow citizens. Meanwhile the steam fire engine huffed and whistled and worked without tiring.

The next day, having asked my guide where the nearest fire house was, I set out for it so that at leisure I could look over the construction of the fire-fighting equipment, find out the manner of operation, cost, the organization of the fire company, and so on. Without ado I walked into the shed where the machine stood. It was the one which had performed the many operations the day before, but everything was already in order: hot water in the steam boiler and firewood in the furnace. With the first sound of the alarm bell the fire in the engine is raised, and by the time the horses are harnessed and the burning structure is reached, the steam is ready and the machine can operate as a pump. Its construction is extremely simple. It is amazing that steam has not long before now been applied to such an important use as the quick extinguishing of fires, particularly in America where they are quite frequent, and that this use of steam is not widespread. Latta,[9] the engineer who built it, told me that in Cincinnati alone, where they were first made, there are ten of them in large and small sizes, the former for ten thousand and the latter for eight thousand dollars each, and that although the city maintains professional fire companies with horses and steam fire-fighting machines instead of volunteer fire brigades, the decrease in fire sheds and number of tools with a resulting economy of property has saved up to fifty thousand dollars a year; this figure, he told me, will increase when the volunteer fire brigades with their toy equipment (that was his phrase) cease to function. In response to my remark that the machine was a bit heavy to move along the road, especially in a city such as Cincinnati where so many streets were rough and uneven, the engineer-inventor called my attention to the new improvement by means of which steam will help turn the wheels and the horses will only steer the engine in its forward motion. The first engine of this kind was built in 1852. Now, besides in Cincinnati, it has been introduced in Boston and New Orleans. Aside from the custom of fighting fires with the personal, mutual aid of citizens, use of the engine is greatly hindered by the rivalry of other manufacturing cities which, not wanting to adopt the invention of another engineer, want to invent their own. The greater number of firemen in Cincinnati are Germans, a lesser number are Irishmen.

Generally in Cincinnati, as in the entire state of Ohio, there are many schools. But why Cincinnati has three medical colleges and one college of dental surgery is difficult to explain. Many doctors are Germans, and it is impossible to walk along the street and not be struck by advertisements that so-and-so treats such-and-such illnesses, that this one or that one makes pills that purify the blood or that quickly and positively save you from virtually any kind of sickness whatever. Meanwhile, apparently, the people are at least healthy and seldom need pills or doctors.

Such are the things to be seen in Cincinnati streets closest to the Ohio. But if one crosses the canal, a quite different part of town reveals itself. It is appropriately called Over-the-Rhine (*Hinter dem Rein*); this is the German quarter and instead of huge five- or six-story

9. Alexander B. Latta (1821–63) was a Cincinnati-based inventor and manufacturer who did pioneer work in the development of the steam fire engine.

buildings with gigantic signs, the streets have small two-story houses intermingled with gardens. This in its own way is just like one of the small German towns with its inhabitants of modest wants, invariable steins of beer, and tobacco pipes. One very often comes across signs reading "Lagerbier," "Tobacconist," "Wine Merchant." In general Americans have left to the Germans the retail trades and minor occupations, which are perfectly compatible with the character of the Germans, who do not look for enterprises in which to make great profits but for those which risk small losses. The American with his daring knows only the first, although sometimes enterprises end up in the second category. But then the Germans have prospered in this place and their number in Cincinnati alone has grown to fifty thousand people. Generally most of them live in the Over-the-Rhine area as neighbors to one another, with the consequence that they have not forgotten their native tongue, constantly speak German, and have their own theater and clubs. They observe Sunday in their own way, not by "dying" the whole day; on the contrary, somewhere or other in a garden they fill their beer steins and listen to music. When I was in the German theater, sitting in the dimly lit hall and looking at the neatly but extremely modestly dressed German girls who went into raptures over everything, and when a little man in an apron offered glasses of beer during the intermissions, I truly wondered whether I were not in a summer theater in some town in Bavaria.

It is not likely that the Germans will ever predominate in America, even in the West. Even with their industriousness, their good qualities and thriftiness, they are not capable of colonizing a new country. They follow, rather, the Americans and wherever there is an American the German must give way, and instinctively he does just that. One can speak only of their numerical predominance, not of their superiority, although even now in the West there are cities and states founded and almost exclusively populated by Germans.

A large part of the German population in Cincinnati is from the southern provinces of Germany. They preserve the memory of their blessed homeland in the name of their Over-the-Rhine district. Indeed the Ohio itself, with its shoreline beauty resulting from the growing of grapes in the surrounding area, has been poetically named the Rhine of America. Catholicism is the religion of most of the Germans who, together with the Irish, built the St. Peter's Cathedral. It is a great building with a beautiful portico and a high cupola; it cost, they say, more than one hundred thousand dollars. In the cathedral itself the altar is all of Carrara marble brought from Genoa; there are many paintings, among them one of St. Peter by Murillo.[10] The organ in the church is huge. In sum, this is the largest Catholic cathedral among those in western American cities. Its size and the richness of its ornamentation become even more striking when compared to the small, plain churches of other faiths, of which there are as many in Cincinnati as in other American cities.

One of the sights in Cincinnati is, or more accurately will be, the [suspension] bridge across the Ohio that will unite Cincinnati with the small town of Covington on the Kentucky side of the Ohio. At the time of my visit only the 230-foot-high towers were built. Between them will be suspended an iron cable which must support the weight of the bridge. They say that the bridge will definitely be finished in three years;[11] and until then, people will cross the river on steam ferries which leave practically every minute. The heavy steamboat traffic is concentrated at Cincinnati, while the shore at Covington is empty, as if the state of Kentucky produced nothing and consumed nothing. All of its trade is concentrated in Cincinnati. Can it be that slavery is the reason for the decay of productive activity in Covington, too?

I liked to ride across to Covington, and after noisy, rich Cincinnati, the little town seemed to me no more than a large village; its streets were unpaved, wooden planks had been laid down in some places, and everything seemed, if not primitive, then in a neglected state. Yet Covington too, like its rich neighbor, trades in pigs and manufactures a great deal of sausage. Hence here, too, the pigs, not caring in the least about people walking by, enjoyed life in the full meaning of the word.

Having learned that a circuit-riding judge was holding sessions in this area, I went looking for the courthouse building. In comparison to the huge structure built for that purpose in Cincinnati, the one here seemed to me poor and insignificant. I attended a trial about a quite unimportant matter concerning some sort of theft. The startling

10. Bartolomé Esteban Murillo (1617–82), famous Spanish artist whose greatest works are his paintings of Madonnas, monks, and saints.

11. Construction of the bridge was interrupted by the Civil War, and it was not completed until 1867.

thing was the simplicity of the court's procedure for the accused who, sitting beside his lawyer, was fondling a baby brought to him by his wife. The father, perhaps having foreseen that they would separate him from his family (as did indeed happen), wanted to embrace his child in the last remaining minutes. But could this not have an influence on the verdict of the jury? This is a natural question, and the lawyer for the accused, arguing before the gentlemen of the jury that the similarity of identity between the person who did the stealing and the person who sat before them was not proven, tried to sway them by dwelling upon the misfortune of the family, which would be left without support. The jurors, not enclosed in a special box as in an English court, sprawled freely about and formed the most varied geometric figures with their long legs; spitting profusely in all directions, they listened attentively to a recounting of the affair. The accused or his lawyer has the right to challenge a prejudiced juror, and the judge is protected by the juror's double oath (administered in both instances without kissing the Bible, something that is continuously done in English courts). The first oath by the juror is that he does not know the person whom he must judge, has heard nothing about the case, and has formed no opinions about it. If he is not rejected as a juror, the town's prosecuting attorney, who defends the general interests of the citizens, says to the clerk: "Take him!" and he is added to the jurors until their number reaches twelve. Then they again, having raised their right hands, swear they will judge the case fairly and bring forth a verdict based on their own best understanding. There was nothing unusual about any of the other proceedings.

In my jaunts across the Ohio to Kentucky I more than once admired Kentucky's low hills covered with grapes and greenery. It was all that same Catawba, and bunches were awaiting the harvest. It is a pity that the famous Weinlese [grape gathering], a poetic time in the southern countries of Europe, is not celebrated as merrily here with song, music, and dance as along the Rhine, or in Hungary or southern France. For the time being winemaking here does not constitute a special field of activity, but in the free [nonslave] area grapes are cultivated with as much love as pigs are raised. Once while admiring a vineyard, I happened upon a cottage; a vicious dog leaped at me and the noise brought out the owner. He did not understand why I had wandered so far, and alone besides. I explained to him as best I could that I was carried away by the natural dense foliage of the oaks, elms, and green vineyards of the place. In the midst of our conversation the farmer's wife came out and in pure Swabian dialect told her husband that he should invite me into the house. When I conversed with the German in his native tongue, his compliments were boundless; he took me tenderly by the arm, repeating, "Marschiren sie doch hinein" [Do come in].

"Have you been here long?" "Are you getting along well?" "Why did you leave your native land?" were the most natural questions. Judging by the clean room, the tidy furniture, the washed and neatly combed children, I was certain I had finally found a family that had no complaints. "We are happy here," my host told me, "we have no fear of the police so long as we behave, and if a man is honest and hardworking, nowhere will he be more content with his lot; there is no power over us, we work hard and take care of ourselves; we go where and when we want to, work at whatever we like, set our own taxes, but . . ." (was it not possible even here to manage without this unfortunate *but?*) "we don't get along with the Americans, with those restless 'know-nothings' who do not tolerate foreigners, or rather those of us who do not recognize slavery and own no Negroes. Were it not for my wife, who does not want to part with the farm, I would have long ago looked for another near Chicago or Milwaukee. Yes, I think if someone can be found who wants to buy my farm, I will sell it and go further west."

"But can one part with such suckling pigs?" intervened the wife, showing me a full litter of her farrow on which she lavished her tenderness. "We'll breed the same kind there and live no worse than we do now. Then at least, the eternal arguments and quarrels with the neighbors—God knows over what—will stop." I, of course, was in no position to persuade the kind farmer of the contrary, and went to see his apple orchard, vineyard, and cornfields. In Germany he would have been considered a wealthy landowner; here a hundred acres is not much at all, especially when the neighboring planter, with Negroes under his control, has an enormous estate. "I have laborers, too, all Germans, and together with them, I don't fare badly. The river is close by and the market is good."

About three o'clock we returned to the farmer's cottage and found the table already covered with a white tablecloth; the laborers were waiting for the master so they could eat the meal together. I did not decline the place indicated for me and could only marvel at the piles

of roast pork, pork chops, and wild fowl which had been prepared.
Who was to eat this great heap of various greens, potatoes, Jerusalem
artichokes, and corn? Who was to drink the enormous tankards of
beer placed before everyone? But in the end it turned out that nothing
was left over. Americans call laborers their "hands" and between them
and the master there is full equality. God help us if we say they are
servants; no one would stand for that. The meal was finished with
various pies filled with apples, plums, pears, and pumpkin. After
that grapes were served: they were not very large, but they were
sweet and juicy.

My hospitable host insisted that I try Kentucky tobacco. He assured
me that it was in no way inferior to the Virginia brand, that it is
grown by everyone for his own use, and that on the great plantations
in the southern half of Kentucky it is grown for sale and export to
Europe. We smoked cigars and, indeed, they were not bad.

To help me return to Cincinnati, the farmer showed me a road
in the hollow and instructed me to keep to the left. That was the
way I went, but after walking for an hour, by which time I should
have been able to see the river, I was still a long way from it. There
being absolutely no one whom I could ask the way, I checked my
compass and the position of the sun, but still things got no better. I
have probably lost my way, I thought, and will have to spend the
night at some other farm. But luckily for me I met some children
coming from Covington. The oldest of them was hardly twelve; the
others were even younger. "Where does this road go?" I asked the
oldest, and I don't know how "gentleman" escaped from my lips instead of "boy." "To Covington," and I think the title I gave him was
the reason for the sweet smile that accompanied his answer. Had I
called him "boy," it could have turned out differently: louder, more
capricious. As the Americans themselves say, the world does not
produce any youngsters more independent than theirs; the children
and gamins of Paris are gentle lambs compared to these independent
madcaps. In all urban disorders during elections they make more
trouble than everyone else; if there is too little mud, they pelt people
with stones, and they know that everyone will take their side because,
after all, they are children. But my gentleman considered it his duty
to talk it over with his comrades, and during their short "meeting" it
was decided that they would take me to Covington. I was glad of
the company and gave the oldest boy a cigar; he smoked it no worse

than an adult, and he even showed me a wad of the strong dark tobacco which he had gotten in the habit of chewing.

It turned out that these children, who were from a neighboring farm and had been returning from school, were true Kentuckians. Judging by their limbs and muscles, one would say that they promised to become good representatives of their hunter forebears who even now amaze other Americans with their strength, height, and great size. In two years, the youngster told me, he would be fully grown, would leave school, and go into business on his own. He himself did not yet know what kind, but it really made no difference to him so long as it brought in money, earned profits, and was productive. The youth considered himself prepared for anything necessary to assure his future, and of course, like his forebears, he did not reject becoming a hunter in the woods which Daniel Boone had once roamed after long and bloody strife with the Indians.

On the way the young people made great efforts to brag about their lively horses and huge bulls. In Covington at last, they took me to a sausage factory where the chopping-knife was operated by steam. The boys did not stand on ceremony with the proprietress and picked up whatever they could get their hands on. And she, at heart perhaps not knowing how to escape these uninvited guests, was outwardly affectionate and courteous to them and, as they were leaving, presented each one with something that he particularly liked. It was getting late, and at departure I gave my guides some silver money; they took it with pleasure, as befits true Americans whatever age they might be.

8

Kentucky and Indiana

I

Did I see in Cincinnati that "western man" whom Americans had been dinning into my ears ever since I landed in Boston? What distinguished the inhabitant of the Queen City on the Ohio from the inhabitant of another queen city on the Atlantic coast? Was there not the same eternal race for the dollar here, the same courage, the same passion for anxious, feverish activity, the same wonted obeisance to the golden idol calling for various and constant sacrifices? Be that as it may, the difference is really felt not only in the fact that the city has not yet managed to catch its breath from the latest wave of the magic wand, so to speak, under which it seemed to grow right out of the ground; it is evident not only in the space everyone has at his disposal, but (and this is perhaps the main point) in the fact that the boundaries and distinctions between rich and poor have not yet been delineated. Like a baby lunging forward, the "western man" does not even suspect that there is such a thing as fatigue and that he can encounter obstacles ahead. In his manners, his actions towards others, and even in his dress he is still simpler and younger than his countrymen in the old states. On the way from Covington to Lexington I had occasion to ascertain his searching, at times wearying curiosity. There was no end to questions not about who I was, what my status and position were, but about how people lived in Russia and how the government was organized. I am certain he would have profited more from my company than I from his information about the country through which our train was traveling if I had not asked him, after seeing a revolver in his belt, why it was impossible to manage without firearms here.

He asked with amazement if I were really traveling alone unarmed. He did not want to believe that the revolver I purchased in New York

on the advice of friends seemed too heavy to me and that I was carrying it in my suitcase. Hence I was traveling unarmed and considered
my best protection not to get mixed up in heated arguments and not
to make the acquaintance of people who were not recommended to me.

"Yes, it's different with a foreigner. He doesn't take part in state
and city affairs. He can keep silent where an American must of necessity speak up, defending his personal opinions and their merits. The
slightest offense, disagreement, or caustic remark leads to a fight or
a revolver. When something is to be judged here, we do it ourselves
through lynching. It's quicker and more effective. And not only do
private individuals act that way when their views differ from someone
else's—whether in the street, in a hotel, in the senate, in church, it's
all the same—but even an entire political or religious party defends itself the same way. Some days ago the Negroes on a plantation in Tennessee killed their master, his wife, and his children. Only one daughter managed to escape. Then the Negroes ran away from the plantation. Instead of initiating a court trial, which we know would show no
mercy for slaves, the neighbors of the unfortunate family armed themselves and combed the woods with dogs. After capturing the criminals,
they burned them to death, but not before having tortured them in
ways which you, perhaps, would find too cruel and inhumane."

You have guessed my thoughts. In Europe, yes even, I think, in
the old states of the Union, people behave differently. If the power to
punish criminals is entrusted to a court selected by the citizens themselves, why should one take revenge like a beast? Can society, moreover, endure such a state of affairs? And anyhow there would be no
danger from Negroes on the road from Lexington to Mammoth Cave.

"Oh God, save us from those rascals!" The word "rascals" with
which my companion abused the Negroes and which one hears more
often in the West than one might wish, gave me the courage to ask
whether he had any slaves, although at the very beginning of my
journey through America I was told not to talk about the freedom
of Negroes—about its necessity—in the unfree states as I would in
the free.

My fellow traveler indeed turned out to be a slaveowner and began
to defend himself against attacks which, remembering earlier admoni-
tions, I did not even allow myself to make. He could see or guess my
thoughts from my eyes. A free man himself and defender of free, independent institutions, he spoke about the position of the slaves, about

the gentle treatment by their masters and how that redounded to the benefit of the latter. His defense of the need for slavery was such that I wondered whether I myself was talking with a slave. The poor Negroes were called unthinking animals with no capabilities for improvement and were seriously compared with monkeys. I must confess that the labor of the preacher in the wilderness was in vain. It is difficult, and one does not feel like trying, to dissuade another from believing what ought not to be believed; besides, God forbid that I should object, for the revolver was always ready to revenge any impertinence.

Nevertheless I felt I had the right to ask the Kentuckian what his opinion was of Negro labor. I asked whether slavery did not hinder the full productive capacity of man and whether there was not more advantage to free labor. Since we were riding by empty lands, it was impossible for the Kentuckian not to agree that had those corn and tobacco fields been better cultivated, they would not now be deserted. A counterargument was unavoidable and he found it in the difficulty one has in finding white workers who might want to cultivate such huge sections, and in the cheaper cost of Negro labor. The opposite shore of the Ohio could serve well enough as an answer to that opinion, but it is useless to argue when you know beforehand that you cannot say anything new and that whatever you say will not convince him.

The hundred miles between Covington and Lexington were covered quickly. We seldom stopped; indeed there was nothing to stop for. Lexington itself, although built in an extremely picturesque and lush place, was somewhat deserted with its ten thousand inhabitants, wide streets, several public buildings, and public gardens. At one time the state capitol was here but it has now been transferred to Frankfort. But Lexington lives through the memory of a great citizen of the West, Henry Clay, who was more than once nominated but never elected to the presidency of the United States.[1] He fought strongly against slavery and defended free labor. In accordance with his ideas, Liberia, a colony for emancipated Negroes, was established in Africa. Through his mediation several treaties were concluded with European states. Not far from town there remains as a monument to this statesman the

---

1. Clay (1777–1852) also served as a congressman (1811–25) and senator (1831–42, 1849–52) from Kentucky, as well as secretary of state under John Quincy Adams (1825–29).

place where he lived, Ashland, literally land of ash trees, of which there are a great many here. Leading up to it is a pleasant shady avenue, and as you walk along you imperceptibly come to a charming, modest, two-story little house without any architectural ornamentation. He spent the last years of his life here in solitude, farming, gardening, and cultivating an English park. Up to four hundred acres of ground in this suburban area are planted with various species of grasses, grains, trees, flowers, roses, jasmine, and so on. In other countries and especially in Europe, such a dandified residence, to say nothing of the person to whom it belonged, would be of little curiosity. But in America, where few seek after excessive embellishments, Ashland is a pleasant retreat and one of the favorite spots of Lexingtonians for strolling.

No matter how much I asked how I might go directly from here to Mammoth Cave, I got no sure and positive answer; there was no railroad nor were there regular carriages; the latter, to boot, were not quite safe and were hot and dusty. It was obvious from everything that this was no New York State. Despite the fact that nature has not placed insuperable obstacles in the way of good transportation routes here, the latter serve towns closest to the Ohio. There is still a long way to go before a railroad network crisscrosses the unfree states from end to end as one does in the northern states. If it is thought that the reason for the lack of railroads in Kentucky is due to a small and recent population, it is enough to point out that the other states that have just been created, Wisconsin, Illinois, and Michigan, have rails crossing in all directions. How and why this difference exists is understandable from what I often heard and saw myself in the slave states.

[Lakier decided to go by train to Louisville.]

II

There was a time when people covered the route from Louisville to Mammoth Cave in a mail stage, which was a cramped, uncomfortable, and, especially on a log road, extremely bumpy carriage: every rut took its toll of the unfortunate passenger in jolts and bruises. According to the description of former travelers, the ride was pure torture, especially if it was dusty and the sun was blazing, all of which was made worse by the fact that the road itself was quite uninteresting. Endless forests of oak extended on both sides, and virtually at every turn one came upon pigs rooting in the ground. You were lucky, moreover, if you did not end up with a broken axle or an accident to the wheel. And if you retained from the journey only one conviction, it was that Americans were masters of building railroads and steamboats but that other means of transportation did not exist for them. Nevertheless one could not avoid visiting the gigantic caves; along with Niagara and the Mississippi they are the best examples of the enormity of nature in America.

Today one cannot complain of those inconveniences. The railroad from Louisville to Nashville, Tennessee, although far from completed, runs to within ten miles of Mammoth Cave and drops off at Bell's Tavern those wanting to see the natural wonders. There can be no doubt that this place, named after the eighty-year-old proprietor, Bell, has acquired general renown[2] and will in time be called a town, for one will surely develop here, especially when the railroad no longer stops half-way but crosses the southern states and joins them with the northern and western states. But in the meantime it is nothing more than a tavern, a country hotel. You stop off there of necessity because that is where you have to board the stage and, for a short distance, experience what earlier travelers had to endure for days on end over hundreds of miles. But one can forget the discomfort because waiting for you up ahead is an intricate natural phenomenon that is the only one of its kind.

It turned out there were other nature lovers here besides myself and we decided to ride to Mammoth Cave together on the next day. One of them was an American, a tourist, pale and taciturn in the extreme; he spoke abruptly, made some passing remark about it being a warm evening, and then fell silent. He kept taking a crumpled wad of tobacco out of his pocket. As if by contrast, there was a lively, round-faced German geologist from Erfurt, who began to prove to me that our future fellow traveler had ruined himself with that poisonous plant by having deranged his digestive organs. The geologist was content with that observation, but I wondered whether there might not be something moral at the base of the American's melancholy mood.

2. "Billy" Bell built his tavern nine miles from Mammoth Cave. In pre–Civil War days it was said to be the most popular country inn in the United States and was used by prominent politicians such as Henry Clay for planning campaigns. Helen F. Randolph, *Mammoth Cave and the Cave Region of Kentucky* (Louisville, Ky.: Standard Printing Company, 1924), pp. 57–59.

Were this an Italian or a Spaniard, one might think that silhouetted on his sickly face was the despair of a betrayed lover. But an American scorns such trifles and in his case another question arises: might it be a satiety with life's blessings or an unsuccessful speculation that stamped his face with sorrow and melancholy? For confirmation of my theories I conveyed to the talkative German observations I had carried away from many lunatic asylums in America: that the disquiet of life, the stock-market game, the hundreds of enterprises, stocks and bonds, the lack of family in which the spirit, wearied by life on the outside, might find peace and quiet—those were the things that led to mental disorders and melancholia; that that was why there was much more insanity in the United States than one might imagine among a people who were still fresh, young, and industrious, but perhaps too speculative. But there was no hope of learning the history of the taciturn tobacco-chewer, and gradually changing the subject, the red-cheeked geologist and I began to speak of the cave we were planning to see.

Mr. Bell recommended that we take with us the Negro, Stephen, who had been set free by his master and upon achieving independence anglicized his name.[3] Now he is known to everyone for his knowledge of the caves. He has guided a great many travelers and is in a position to share much that he has heard from others.

The recommendation really justified itself when, after the uncomfortable ten-mile trip in the mail stage, we arrived at the Cave Hotel, close to the cave itself.

At the very entrance to the cave Mister Stephen informed us that with all its windings and twistings the cave occupied an area of about 160 miles and was up to 10 miles long. That much at least had been investigated but it was still far from being all there was to the cave.

My companion's thermometer was continually coming out and he noted down the readings. But even without that there was a palpable

3. Stephen Bishop (1821–57) was a Negro slave who for twenty years worked as a guide and explorer at Mammoth Cave and discovered many new passages. Literate and self-educated, he became well versed in geology and acquired an international reputation as a cave explorer. He was set free in 1856 and died the following year. There is no evidence that he anglicized his name after gaining his freedom. Roger W. Brucker and Richard A. Watson, *The Longest Cave* (New York: Knopf, 1976), pp. 265–73.

difference in the temperature. While on the outside it was stifling hot, in the cave it was quite cool. Without a moment's hesitation our Negro assumed the air of a scholar—he enjoyed the reputation of being a specialist in his field—and explained that the average temperature in the cave was 59° Fahrenheit.

All that shone were the little lamps with which we were each supplied; it was as if God's light had completely disappeared. But our eyes soon got used to the dusk and we stopped groping along. It should be noted that the Echo River, which divides Mammoth Cave in half, undoubtedly connects with the Green River, which runs close to the cave and flows into the Ohio, for the Echo River rises and falls simultaneously with the water level in the main stream; as a result there are days and even weeks when Echo River cannot be crossed. Mister Stephen, serving now as our boatman, told us that there have been occasions when those who crossed to the other side could not return the same way because of a sudden rise in water level; they had to go to another exit, the so-called purgatory, which was troublesome and dangerous.

The little river is not wide, but in the dim lamplight it strikes the eyes rather strangely. When we were in the middle of the river Mister Stephen struck up a song that echoed in the caverns and then died away somewhere in distant rumbles. We stopped the boatman and asked him to sing the same thing again, and there was no end to our delight. Not without reason is the underground river called the Echo River. Had there been Greeks here, or any Eastern people with a lively imagination, what mythological beings would they not have created here; this is where their Acheron and Lethe would have been. Stephen was not a poet: he pulled out a net and began to fish for small fish and crawfish, the remarkable primordial inhabitants of these dark waters; although blind, they are well equipped with organs of touch. The feelers of the crawfish are much longer than usual and the slightest disturbance of the water was enough to deprive Mister Stephen of the chance to catch the desired creatures. He managed, nonetheless, and we acquired some good specimens.

[Altogether Lakier and his companions spent seven hours in the cave which, except for a few features, he found to be tiresome.]

But for the next day Mister Stephen predicted a delight of a different sort. "If," he said, "today's 'big outing' amazed you with the vastness of this natural scene, it does not reveal those details for which

Mammoth Cave is especially famous." A second day's trip was devoted
to surveying them and I must confess it was much more interesting
than the first, primarily because one turns off the main route connect-
ing one section to another and sees the cave's real wonders. That
Methodists preached and held divine services here from time to time
is not at all strange or incomprehensible: given their barrenness and
darkness, the caves themselves must have transported the thoughts of
the pastor and his listeners to those fortunately distant times when the
light of true learning had to be hidden underground. I must admit I re-
gretted that I could not hear a melodious song and a sermon here, as
in the underground temples of the ancient followers of Christ in northern Egypt and the environs of Alexandria. I loved to be transported in
my mind to that far-off epoch and to imagine a primitive Christian
society among deserted, crumbled arches.

We were also deprived of another sight: an underground hospital
for consumptives, which was set up in 1841 by Dr. Mitchell of Glasgow
but which has ceased to exist.[4] The experiment shows that man
snatches at anything to prolong life and that there is no sacrifice he
would not make to preserve it. Relying on the dryness of the air in the
cave and the fact that it is not affected by normal changes in outside
temperature, Mitchell used one of the large spacious caves for a hospital. Several brick cottages covered with a canvas were built in it,
so that even at night the patients could benefit from this air. Except for
their separation from God's world, those confined had at their disposal
all the conveniences of life. There were shops, amusements, entertainment, there were strolls to distant parts of the cave, and music, dances,
and songs filled those mournful, quiet places where bats cluster. Not a
single patient failed to remain in his place of confinement, certain that
God's world and the outside air would destroy the worthy undertaking. But their hopes for relief from their suffering were in vain. Despite

4. The idea of using Mammoth Cave to cure tuberculosis was conceived by Dr. John Croghan, a Louisville physician who bought the cave
in 1839. The first consumptive to live in the cave was William J. Mitchell,
a medical doctor from Glasgow, Kentucky. Mitchell stayed in Mammoth
Cave for one month in 1842 and died six months later. Altogether some
fifteen tubercular patients tried living in the cave in 1842. All died, a
few in the cave, the rest shortly after leaving it. Stanley D. Sides and
Harold Meloy, "The Pursuit of Health in the Mammoth Cave," *Bulletin
of the History of Medicine* 45, no. 4 (July–August, 1971): 370–6.

all the entertainment, the patients began to suffer from melancholy. Their eyes began to ache from the constant burning of the lamps day and night, and the situation could have ended with the same blindness that the fish and crawfish are subject to. Fortunately, the sufferers did not come to that; one after another the patients, and finally the doctor himself, died. A superfluous experiment in medicine and the name "sick room" stand as a memorial to this desperate effort at medical treatment.

It is obvious that, before the vastness and individual beauty of the gigantic cave, the other caverns that abound in this region lose some of their interest for people who are poorly initiated into the secrets of the earth's structure and strata. As for myself, I was satisfied with what I had seen. But the geologist was thinking of staying longer, and Mister Stephen undertook to show him several more nearby caves with their stalactites and mysterious arches and passages. We shook hands and parted. I went back to Louisville and thence to Cairo.

[Lakier takes a mail-steamer down the Ohio from Louisville to Cairo, Illinois. He notes the changing character of the river, bordered by Kentucky on the south, and Indiana and Illinois on the north. Again he comments that "The situation is the same everywhere along the Ohio River: the northern shore is far richer and more variegated than the southern, not because of nature or fertility, but because of the difference in activity between free men and slaves."]

Beginning at the mouth of the Wabash, the picture of the Ohio changes somewhat: the banks become higher and stonier. The cliffs, descending steeply to the river at this point, are called the Battery Rocks. The Ohio flowing by is broader and bordered on both sides by dense wild forests and, as if feeling its impending confluence with the Mississippi, strives to become like it or at least not be left behind. The competition of these two great rivers was and up to now continues to be destructive and dangerous for Cairo, the town established at the point of confluence of two such mighty streams. The history of the town shows that, where calculation and expectation of profit become intertwined, all other considerations seem not to exist. Several German bankers, among whom was Baron Rothschild, were convinced that the place where the Ohio and Mississippi met offered many advantages, advantages not had by any other locality in the entire United States, and they decided to found a settlement here, mainly for Germans. Whether the reason for naming the settlement Cairo was the flatness of the location, or the Mississippi's similarity to the Nile, or simply imagination, makes no difference. The fact of the matter is that the place turned out to be swampy, fever-ridden, and generally unhealthy. The population has already been renewed several times and one can in no way say that it enjoys full health now. It is fortunate that high water on the Ohio does not coincide with high water on the Mississippi, otherwise the force of the waves from both sides would have long since broken off this bit of land with its scanty population and insignificant buildings. Indeed up until recent times Cairo suffered from floods, despite the fact that there is a month's difference between the high water of the two rivers. The inhabitants seemingly grew accustomed to floods and for a long time lived on barges anchored to the shore. There they had their shops, stores, and hotels and the people of Cairo were turning into some sort of amphibians. All this continued up to the time it was decided to build a million-dollar dam for protection, and the town began to move to solid ground without fear.

But none of the settlers wanted to abandon Cairo. They counted on a great future for it, because, since the mouth of the Ohio never freezes, the Mississippi is always open to navigation up to St. Louis, and the big Illinois Railroad goes as far as Cairo and connects it with Lakes Michigan and Erie, and with a chain of northern railroads. Up to the present, in any case, the town's situation is rather pathetic. It is well at least that it can live on dry land and not on the water. If Amsterdam and Rotterdam prospered, why should not Cairo prosper at some time? For their part the settlers see in it a candidate for a future great city of the West.[5]

5. In the 1850s Cairo was "Illinois' great city of prophecy, the speculation of a company of eastern capitalists. Situated at 'the most important confluence of rivers in the world' and at the center of the American republic, at the southern terminus of the Illinois Central, it was expected—as the entrepôt between the northern and southern markets—to . . . [become] a great inland emporium, the largest city in the world. . . . by 1860 the city had an enthusiastic population of 2,188. . . ." Arthur C. Cole, *The Era of the Civil War, 1848–1870,* vol. 3 in *The Centennial History of Illinois* (Chicago: A. C. McClurg and Co., 1922), pp. 7–8.

9

Illinois and Wisconsin

I

At Cairo I took leave of the Ohio and the towns along its shores. This river does for the middle states what the Hudson does for New York or the Mississippi for the southern parts of the Union. I again had the urge to avoid the main route and turned north, so as to become acquainted with Illinois, the Promised Land of the northern states, and its wonder city, Chicago. To be in America and not see this state would mean not to have a true understanding of what man can do with youthful energy, determination, courage, and a thirst for making money. The French were in this same Illinois far earlier than the English, but it may be doubted whether under their continued control the area would have attained its current position and would have gone from 12,000 inhabitants in 1810 to a population of 851,470 in 1850, and almost a million and a half at present. And of course it would not have been possible to cross the whole state by rail. At the present time the Great Illinois Railroad is ready to serve everyone. It runs almost in a straight line from Cairo to Wisconsin in the north, has nine important branch lines to the Mississippi on one side, and on the other has even longer ones linking the railroads of eastern states with Lake Michigan. Whereas in 1851 not a single rail had yet been laid, there are now 2,215 miles of railroad in this new state. They say the railroads have been built badly and carelessly, that accidents occur; but, for all that, there is no other country except America where one could have hoped for so rapid an increase. In 1828 there were three miles of railroad in the entire Union. By 1850 the figure had grown to 7,355 and since then, that is, in some seven years, railroads have quadrupled to no less than 30,000 miles.[1]

1. In 1857 the Russian Empire had less than 800 miles of railroads.

Where did the capital for these huge undertakings come from, since so small a population could not have easily paid for them? Fortunately the question was answered in a brochure provided free by a youngster on the train who earned his living selling newspapers and assorted books for reading during the trip. The brochure announced on the title page that the Illinois Central Railroad Company was offering more than two million acres of wooded and arable land for sale. The booklet consisted of several printed pages and the company offered it free of charge to everyone, counting on its falling into the hands of those who had come here precisely in order to obtain a parcel of land.

To make the company's lands as attractive as possible, their virtues and advantages are described in detail. This includes what their principal products are, what price wood is sold at for use on the wood-burning locomotives, what a good price wheat brings and what it costs to transport it to the distribution point. Due honor is rendered to the Illinois prairies and forests and their natural wealth. It is shown that these lands can be cultivated more cheaply, that the soil is not exhausted, and that because of the rivers and underground springs water is plentiful. And all this is close to Chicago which, our brochure says, is the greatest depot for food grains in the world. No fewer than thirty railroad lines from different parts of the Union converge at Chicago, from which wheat-laden ships sail directly to Liverpool without reloading.

The choice of land is left to the private person, who is guided by his individual inclinations, needs, and tastes. He can give preference to land rich in forests or productive of wheat and corn, or he may choose a section which to a certain extent at least combines various soil qualities. Because of the needs of both the railroads and the settlers, the brochure continues, the demand for mechanics and workers in general is no less than the demand for farmers. Hence the company invites each and all, promising success and prosperity, and pointing out the abundance of forests and minerals as well as the towns and cities that have grown up in so short a time. Included in the brochure are letters from various farmers who have settled on company lands, along with their accounts of how much it costs them to farm the land and what the shipping charges and selling prices are. After reading the brochure one has a true and precise idea of the profits one could and should expect from cultivating one or another section of land. It is easy to understand how such detailed information can induce anyone, even a person who has not yet come to the area, to choose a parcel for himself in the new state. Moreover, the information guides him once he is in the area: I saw that many of my fellow travelers who had come here for land found that the information in the booklet satisfied their expectations.

[Lakier describes the procedure for the sale of public lands, as well as for government land grants to promote railroad construction.]

Thus Congress granted Illinois 2,595,053 acres for 676 miles of railroad, and that generous allotment created a railroad that cuts through the forests in an absolutely straight line and in sight of the growing population. One cannot say the road is solid, on the contrary the train often has to stop or slow down, but everyone remains in place in the cars and there is no fuss or alarm. When the train has stopped, someone may get off to see what has happened, just out of curiosity, and return to report coldbloodedly that the rails are not attached to the ties or do not fit exactly right. Well, be thankful there is a railroad at all and that it's not necessary to jolt along a log road or through mud or over potholes. It is a railroad line, after all, and however bad and less than perfect, it is bound to be beneficial: in time it will bring big revenues and a large population. Only once did the train take alarm when, from a number of half-wild bulls running from the engine whistle to a thicket in the woods, one of them chose our roadbed as its path. However much the conductor blew the whistle, the bull raised his tail and ran headlong in front of the engine. Before the train managed to stop, the merciless cowcatcher, which was absolutely appropriate here, scooped up the unfortunate creature, and the bull fell lifeless between the tracks. It was well that the engineer managed to stop the train. Otherwise it would not have ended without a calamity and we would have learned from experience the virtues and shortcomings of American railroads without embankments and guards. Everyone, needless to say, poured out of the train. But at the same time every American, without distinction, considered it his duty to help the conductor and crew. By common effort they cleared the tracks and the train moved forward again. This little episode led many to recall tales of danger encountered in these empty spaces, not only by surveyors measuring a local region, but also by engineers laying down a railroad line. That they sometimes have to grapple with savage Indians and wild animals goes without saying, but in addition snow

and cold not infrequently cut them off for months at a time from any
other people. Even trains sometimes stop for these same reasons, and
on those occasions one begins to understand the disadvantages of the
haste with which railroads are built and of their simple and cheap
construction.

II

The imagination is so electrified by constant tales of the speed with
which Chicago has prospered (I first heard about the city aboard the
steamship that carried me across the Atlantic) that, if you are approaching the city when you know it only from hearsay, you look for
it but cannot figure out where it is. You ride along some kinds of
islands of streets, barely marked, past barracks, you keep riding and
at last impatiently get off the train to look more closely at this city
and to discover what mighty power is manifested here that so captivates Americans.

Generally a son of the New World is so purposeful that he seldom
or only in passing turns his attention to the beauties of nature. For
him oceans, lakes, and rivers are necessary only for carrying vessels
and cargoes, and forests for building ships and feeding pigs. If a place
is particularly advantageous, he will track it down, extol it, and make
it productive with his activity. Therefore to expect something from
Chicago besides a profitable commercial location would mean to know
Americans little or not at all. But this city does offer many unique
advantages for commerce. On the one side there is Illinois, with its
fertile prairies, and on the other Lake Michigan, its waves ready to
disperse the fruits of human labor to the most distant countries of the
world. There are many similar cities in Europe and even in America.
Why then is Chicago so particularly favored? They destine it for the
metropolis of the West and perhaps the prediction will be borne out.
The restless Americans are constantly moving west, from the old to the
new, and are delighted when at last they stumble upon a place with so
favorable a location. But they do not stay long here either, and move
even farther west in search of a rival to the lucky spot. One cannot
guarantee they will not find it somewhere. Then in some ten or
twenty years people will begin talking about another city. All the
same, the previous lucky city is covered with railroads and the labor is
not lost.

As soon as I got settled in a five-storied anthill of a hotel, the

Tremont House, I set out for a bookstore to buy a guide book with which to acquaint myself with the city. I had found the same kind of booklets in the most insignificant American towns. It was impossible, then, for there not to be a similar guide for Chicago. In giving it to me, the bookseller added, as if showing off the city where he lived and worked, that he was afraid the guide might prove unsatisfactory, although it had been published only two or three months before. At first I thought he was joking, but not at all. He unfolded the map and showed me streets that did not exist when the map was printed, but where now there was a large population. If you ask how it happened, you are told all about the same western miracles, which have become absolutely commonplace as a result of frequent repetition.

From the city's history it appears that in 1830 the place where Chicago now sprawls was still no more than an insignificant Indian trading post. The total population in 1840 was five thousand, in 1850 it grew to thirty thousand, and today it has already reached one hundred sixty thousand with an assured annual increase of fifteen thousand to twenty thousand people. If that holds true, then in about twenty years the population of this area will have grown up as fast as New York's. It is no rarity at all to encounter immigrants in the streets who have just gotten off the steamship, gazing with curiosity upon the city toward which their dreams and hopes have striven. They are mostly German or Irish, with the former being especially numerous. You instantly distinguish them from the foreigners who have already adapted themselves to America; the latter walk without looking around and rush along like any other American.

But where do these new recruits for American civilization settle? Where do they shelter their families? It is winter, there is no time to build a house, indeed there are no means to build with. Hotels obviously are not for them. If you turn away from the big streets, Wabash and Michigan avenues, with their palaces close to the lakeshore and the mouth of the Chicago River, you will see rows of cottages hastily put together with boards. That is where the immigrants live at first, until they either move into the interior of the country as farmers, engineers, and laborers, or they are in a position to move their house to another street, or they can build a new one for themselves. You continually see houses here being moved from one place to another. There is a special class of people for this profession, called housemovers. They lift a house with all its furniture, stove, and utensils from its original place, put it on a kind of sledge, lay rollers underneath, and move it over planks to the new place. The former style of life is in no way disturbed by this move: the owner continues to read his newspaper, to argue, and to carry on his trade. If for some reason it is impossible to complete the move in one day, if, for example, the new dwelling site is too far, or night has fallen, or the ground has softened, the house is stopped in the middle of the street. And if the owner has been engaged in trade, he opens a shop in the new location and carries on his business. I was told more than once that in summertime houses are rolled to the lakeshore in the same manner and those seeking a cooler climate have no need to rent a summer cottage.

One cannot say that the building of the city has already been completed. Quite the contrary, one still hears the pounding of hammers everywhere, although there are many stone buildings. As usual the streets are broad and intersect at right angles, but for the most part they are either totally unpaved or made of logs. Hence when the black earth turns to mud there is no other way to walk except in high boots. Efforts are now being made, however, to build roadways, at least on the main streets, and if everything grows as rapidly as it has up to the present, in about five years the city will have changed in this sense too. I would only wish that the gardens greening every house not be lost to the massive needs of the future population, so that the city will be completely deserving of the title Garden City, by which Americans now dignify it. At present one cannot say positively where the Broadway or main street of Chicago will be. With two branches of the Chicago River emptying into Lake Michigan here, the city is divided into three parts; commerce is concentrated south of the river and the well-to-do people like to settle north of it. Moreover as Lake Michigan recedes from the shore, leaving new spaces for settlement, those will probably become favorites.

The mouths of the Chicago River form basins where the railroads meet the canals to ship out the riches brought here. To permit the passage of barges on the river, the bridges are raised. These stoppages in public traffic are generally not long, but they are repeated often enough to dissatisfy the eternal haste of Americans in various sections of the city. In order to avoid such inconveniences, they have taken it into their heads to dig tunnels under the branches of the river, a project now in progress and for which there is no lack of money. Navigation as well as all the people will gain from the innovation.

However new Chicago may be, it has already managed to satisfy the physical and moral needs of its numerous inhabitants. Gas and running water are found in every solidly constructed house (that is, one that can no longer be moved); they light up and freshen streets and squares and bring health and the comforts of life to the inhabitants.

Of course if the population continues to grow in the future at the same rate it has grown up to the present, the existing number of institutions will prove to be inadequate, despite the fact that they were designed for a hundred thousand inhabitants at a time when the population was only ten thousand. But American enterprise knows no obstacles and there is no looking back—the job will get done.

In satisfying the essential daily needs of its inhabitants, the city did not forget their moral and spiritual needs: churches, schools, and charitable institutions. It is not necessary to describe them for each and every city visited, since it is a well-known fact that there is freedom of worship everywhere in America, that each sect has its own church and teachers and not infrequently its own seminaries and higher schools, and that nowhere does the American betray the common principle of free public education. But it is interesting to see how these same principles have been applied and developed in a city that has only recently sprung up.

Although people have only just come to this area, have barely looked it over and have moved on, the city has already managed to build more than seventy churches of various sects and denominations. Some are in the Gothic, others in the Roman style; they are quite large and expensive, and constructed of a local marble-like stone. When you see all this you begin willy-nilly to believe in the miraculous rise of cities in the magical Far West. There are many Catholics here, as there are generally in all the new western states. The population is Irish and partly German and both groups have their own seminaries. Nevertheless, while every faith has its own institutions, free public education is concentrated in the common or free schools.

New England in general and Boston in particular have not been without influence in the rising American West. Not only have eastern methods of instruction and textbooks been brought here, but directors, teachers, and tutors have also transferred their academic activity from the American Athens. I met these tutors while visiting the schools in Chicago. They are usually twenty-year-old girls and they very cleverly handled young people of nearly the same age. In the presence of these tutor-ladies the independent American boy turns into a lamb. The schools have the same system of teaching as in Boston; the same effort is made to prevent any slackening of attention during lessons. There are the same huge rooms for classes and the same procedures. That there is no distinction here between rich and poor, that a rich man's son sits next to the son of a worker in the rich man's factory or wharf, goes without saying. But Chicago was unique in a way I had not encountered in other cities. What I have in mind is that Negroes receive an education in most of the free states, but they have separate schools. Although their schools have the same system and procedures as do the white schools, there is no desire to mix colored and white in the same building. This is not because Negroes cannot keep pace with white youngsters or are less talented or lazier, but because of an innate American detestation for blacks. In this sense Chicago proved to be a good example of the equality of races, and the children could not have gotten along more peacefully with each other.[2] This notion of equality is transferred from school to life and has beneficial results.

Of special schools, we may note commercial and medical; the city has a public library and publishes several newspapers of various political and religious views. An orphanage has already been built, as well as hospitals and various charitable institutions. In looking at this list one finds it hard to believe that the city has been in existence no more than twenty-odd years and already possesses all the attributes of an old city.

In order to understand how and why the city grew so quickly and attained its present level of prosperity and population, we must turn to the grain trade of Chicago and trace its gradual development. Chicago is no more than a distribution port for bread grains produced in the surrounding countryside, as are Odessa, Berdiansk, and Taganrog for southern Russia. Naturally the supply and distribution of grain

2. The number of Negroes in Chicago grew from 323 in 1850 to 955 in 1860, which was still less than 1 percent of the city's population. Had Lakier visited Chicago in 1863 instead of 1857 he would have been dismayed to learn that the city had abandoned integrated education. In the later year, "at a time when a war was being waged to free Negroes, one or more schools were required to care for colored children who were not to attend schools for white children after such schools were provided." Bessie Louise Pierce, *A History of Chicago,* vol. 2, *From Town to City, 1848–1871* (Chicago: University of Chicago Press, 1940), p. 339.

increased as the means of transportation improved with the growth of canals and railroads. Today, as transportation routes head in this direction from all sections of the country, the distribution of grain from here has increased accordingly. In 1844 no more than 6,320 barrels of flour were shipped by lake; in 1857 the figure was 167,227. Hence in fourteen years it multiplied twenty-five times. In all, more than 18 million bushels of grain were brought to the Chicago market during 1857, including wheat, rye, corn, and oats, and all of this huge mass of grain is going to compete with our wheat in European markets.[3] Given the generally substantial wages in America, the possibility of such a rivalry would be incomprehensible were it not for the fact that plots of land of some one hundred acres are cultivated by individual farmers in excess of their own needs, that work is performed by improved agricultural implements requiring less manual labor and providing greater productivity, and that the supplying of grain to Chicago by railroad and canal and its distribution thence to Europe by steamship reduces the price of grain at both its point of production and point of consumption. Moreover steam has been introduced on a large scale in place of manual labor for seemingly the most insignificant task and further conduces to the same end result: cheapness and surplus.

In Buffalo I had been struck by the huge wooden structures used for grain storage. In Chicago they are even more colossal, usually five stories high. They are arranged by the thousands in groups of four, and in such a way that there is no need to carry sacks of flour from the railway cars to the steamship on the backs of porters or in wheelbarrows. There are simple, uncomplicated steam-driven machines to unload, weigh, and reload the grain. These are elevators. They are built along the lakeshore, with railways coming up alongside them. Huge iron-bound crates are lowered to the full railway cars and, after being loaded, are raised to where enormous wooden scales are located. As soon as the weight of the grain has been determined and noted down, the load either remains in place or, if there is a demand for it, crosses over via an inclined plane to a loading ship. It is then sent to the

3. By the end of the 1850s wheat had become the single most important item exported by Russia to Europe and represented 20 percent of the total value of Russian exports. William L. Blackwell, *The Beginnings of Russian Industrialization, 1800–1860* (Princeton: Princeton University Press, 1968), p. 431.

designated consumer. They convinced me that if need be they can remove a trainload, weigh it, and load it aboard ship in an hour. Of course the initial reason for these innovations was the need to conserve human strength and where possible to substitute steam for manual labor. But at the same time the resulting benefits are of immense proportions.

III

North of Illinois and lying between Lake Michigan and the Mississippi is the state of Wisconsin, which must be ranked as the Promised Land. One of its principal cities, Milwaukee, interested me no less than Chicago because of its rapid rise and commercial growth. It is located on Lake Michigan and several steamboats make daily trips there. Leaving Chicago in the morning, one can be in Milwaukee by evening; the distance is ninety miles. There were very few passengers on the boat. Eternally busy Americans prefer the overnight steamer, although they do not spend the night very restfully and risk not seeing the morning at all in their desire not to lose a single day. Besides, there is a railroad linking the two cities and our steamboat simply did not attract many people. I must confess I thought I was condemning myself to boredom so I bought a morning newspaper. The coastline had nothing promising and the steamboat was precisely the same as those on which I had so often sailed along rivers and lakes. . . . The same despairing thoughts were etched on the face of another passenger who sat down next to me, asked to see my newspaper, and inquired where I was going.

My reply was the start of a long conversation. To begin with, the passenger told me he was a German from Bavaria where he had been a musician. Seeing no way out of the unenviable position he was in, and being persecuted besides for his political views, he sold everything he had and, with tears in his eyes and hope in his heart, emigrated with his wife and children to this distant city. They were among its first inhabitants. "We lived in Milwaukee for several years," he continued, "engaged in trade but were not successful in that either."

"Why?"

"Well, largely because I had no strength to compete effectively against the Americans. As long as they were not in Milwaukee I could earn a decent living; but. . . ."

I interrupted him with a question about the history of the city. He was glad for a chance to recall his personal life and to talk about Milwaukee because he practically grew up with it and was able to follow its growth continuously. Now, perhaps, he could be proud that Milwaukee was in a position to offer Chicago future competition. We spoke in German, sharing mugs of good beer. Altogether the city did not have a long history; in our country it began but yesterday, in 1835, but in the American West that was virtually an entire century.

"When I arrived here in 1840," my fellow-traveler related, "the Potawatomi Indians had already moved away from the shore. The population had not yet reached two thousand people, though a daily paper was already being published. There were some Germans among the immigrants and I decided to open a little shop in a small house. It required part of the capital I had brought with me from Europe. At the start everything went along very well, until the success of the first immigrants attracted large numbers of people, especially Americans from the eastern states. At the time we thought an era of pure happiness had begun for us. The population grew rapidly; it was no less than twenty-one thousand in 1850 and today is already about forty thousand. There was little capital in the area, but there were many people wanting to borrow money to buy land in town or more often farms, and they paid 20 to 25 percent interest. Had I sold my land then I would be a rich man today. But I was doing as well as the others, built a stone house, and developed a large trade. I did not pay attention when a Yankee who settled next to me carried on a better trade by advertising and hawking his wares. It ended up that I was forced to sell him both the house and the shop to pay off a debt. I then went looking for land near Madison, a city that had only just been founded and where the state capital is now located."

To myself I thought: who was to blame and of what was the Yankee guilty, since it was the German who had not calculated very well? I was certain my musician-merchant would not complain that Americans had hindered him in establishing his farm, but again I was wrong.

"In Europe," he continued, "we are enticed by false and flowery descriptions of the western states in America. We think that one has only to come here to make a huge fortune in the very first year. No! Anyone in Europe who is not used to hard agricultural labor, is not young, has a family, and does not have some modest capital at his disposal, had better not waste his money on a voyage. In fact even an established farmer has to change the way he is used to looking at farming: our books and theories are quite worthless here. I know from experience. When I began to look for suitable farmland near Madison, the best sections had already been taken by speculators. They resold them at high prices, claiming that part of the land was fenced, part plowed up, and that a cabin had been put up. Finally we agreed on a price. I provided myself with a whole library of agricultural textbooks, manuals and calendars on what and how to plant, when to plow the ground, what methods to use, and so on. At the time I thought I would far outdo the previous owner. But I struggled and struggled and earned the title of textbook farmer from my neighbors. Then I began to do as the others did. Now things are different. We have a nice farm, quite a few cattle, and lots of land. When you are in Madison," my companion concluded, "stop in to see us."

At least the outcome was comforting and here again I saw a repetition of what both Americans and Germans had been telling me. If the former are courageous and enterprising, the latter are diligent and patient, and what an American abandons because of disappointed expectations, a German will try over and over again ten times and slowly he will come into his own.

We passed the time chatting until the cupola of the Catholic church in Milwaukee came into view. The German wanted to stay in Milwaukee on business all the next day and, taking advantage of his company, I was able to acquaint myself with the city. As we walked along a big street leading to the hotel, my companion greeted nearly everyone he met and it was evident that they all knew him. In passing he showed me the place where his cabin had once stood. Now there was a huge, towering textile mill and a sign with two-foot-high letters which the German from Madison seemed to greet like an old acquaintance. The building, however, proud of its new splendor, stood majestically and did not return the greeting.

But this is not to say that even the main street was completely built up; sometimes between the huge five- and six-story palatial structures there were the original wooden cabins which seemed even smaller and poorer. A great many of the houses were built of ugly, light yellow, straw-colored brick. My guide explained that this was a characteristic of the local clay and that the bricks were so desirable that large quantities were exported to towns lying along the lake and even to the eastern states. Because of the color of the houses, Milwaukee has been nicknamed the cream-colored city.

The street gas lamps were already burning when we entered the hotel. Here my obliging acquaintance left me and, in departing, promised to introduce me to the Musical Society that same evening, if at all possible. Indeed not an hour had gone by when he returned with news that the local Musical Society was giving a concert today and he would introduce me to the masters of ceremonies. He named several German names and on the way told me that even now he still loved to participate in these concerts, whose sole purpose was to foster the love and taste for music that the local German inhabitants had brought with them. But, he said, they could not acquire a taste for American music. For Americans the sound of dollars was pleasanter than the symphonies of Beethoven or the music of Hayden and Glück.

Artists are everywhere the same: they welcome anyone who sympathizes with them and are happy in making others happy. Germans who in the morning were merchants, tailors, and cobblers turned into musicians in the evening. The head master of ceremonies to whom I was introduced said he was glad to have a new listener and spoke about indulgence, love of art, and so on. Somehow among these plain Germans there was a feeling of coziness and an absence of stiffness and tension. The American population of the city was represented by several ladies. The amateur artists performed classical music for the sheer enjoyment of it. My companion was far more at home here than he had been in his shop in Milwaukee or on his farm near Madison. He could not restrain himself, beat time to the music, whispered to me from time to time to listen for this or that motif and its *prachtvoll, wundervoll, wie sanft;* there was no limit to his expressions of enthusiasm. Obviously each has his own virtues: to the German you must grant taste and melody; to the American, activity and courage.

The next morning was to begin with a tour of the city, and with the impression I had of classical music from the evening before, it seemed to me that there was some special quality about the city and its inhabitants. Whether the German majority in the population or its penchant for music actually had an effect upon the Americans, I do not know. It was just that Milwaukee seemed quieter to me than other American cities. My acquaintance held that it was the penchant for music, and he practically began with Orpheus and his exploits to

prove the omnipotence of music. If so, then the Germans might have
been repaid with something a little better for their cultural influence
on the Americans. As it was, the Americans reserved for themselves
the healthiest and most desirable areas on the way to the mountain
bordering Milwaukee on the north; to the Germans they assigned the
low-lying, marshy section. Even the poor Irish settled in the higher
areas of the city. Export trade is concentrated in the hands of Americans and to some degree Irishmen, who have the same loud voices.
They own the numerous steamboats and other ships that fill Milwaukee harbor. Here too the German is either a petty merchant or a
learned musician, doctor, or newspaper publisher. At least a third of
Milwaukee's population is German and the whole state of Wisconsin
can be said to be predominantly German.

I traveled from Milwaukee to Madison, in the interior of Wisconsin, in the company of the farmer. My traveling companion told me he
still came across Indians here and that near Madison he had seen their
wigwams and scattered lodges. He talked as if he sympathized with
the Indians, who were forced to flee before the onslaught of the whites,
and praised the peaceful character of the old chief, Day-Kau-Ray,
leader of the local Winnebago tribe.[4]

For some twenty years whites hardly penetrated the area; then, following the Indian trails, the Europeans moved in. Now they have
widened the old trails, laid rails, selected Madison as the state capital,
erected a capitol building with a high cupola costing more than fifty
thousand dollars, and laid out wide avenues. Although the houses on
the streets are still intermingled with thickets of trees, a university has
been built and an observatory established. It would appear that the
inhabitants need no longer worry that another city in this growing
state will appropriate for itself the honor of having the highest academic institution.

A high gig harnessed to a little steppe horse was waiting for my

4. Day-Kau-Ray (Decora) is the name of a family descended from a
Winnebago woman, Glory of the Morning, and a French officer at Green
Bay, De Corray. They had two sons, both of whom gained prominence and
"chieftainships" in liaison roles between whites and Indians. Both sons
had many descendants, many of whom were also important in treaty rela-
tions with the whites. Lakier does not specify which particular Day-Kau-
Ray is being referred to. Letter from Dr. Nancy O. Lurie, May 6, 1975,
Curator of Anthropology, Milwaukee Public Museum.

German farmer. He could not contain himself telling me how happy his old Lotte would be to see a stranger with whom she could speak German. We did not travel long on the main road, which was in sight of the Indian burial mounds. My farmer absolutely refused to admit that they were the graves of Indian chiefs or of whole tribes. On the contrary, he claimed they were holy places for Indian prayers and sacrifices. As proof he told me that he remembered how the Indians loved to gather on the tops of the mounds for conferences and prayers. But now that the Indians have been driven away by the whites to the far-off forests of the upper Mississippi, they never get back to their old home to clamber up to the summit, smoke their tobacco pipes, and recall the distant past. But then, he said, these curious mounds have been excavated and bones have been found close to the top. I understand it is difficult to determine the significance of the Egyptian pyramids and the original purpose of their builders, but why can't one inquire among contemporary Indians as to why their ancestors built these mounds, or do they themselves no longer remember what was happening here a century ago? Are there no legends or tales? With every passing year there disappears from the face of the earth the remains of what will certainly be precious not only to historians and archaeologists but to every educated person.

The farmer's horse sensed that he was going home, and the farmer himself was occupied far less with the Indians and their burial mounds than with the oak forest through which we were riding. In places it continued without a break, in others there were openings of rich, grass-covered pastures on which cattle were grazing without any tending or supervision. It turned out that they belonged to a neighboring farmer. Cattle stay the year round in the woods, where they multiply, grow freely, and revert to a half-wild state. But in order that the cattle find their way back home, salt is placed in special places. The cattle love to lick salt, and with these salt spots as guides they on occasion return to the farm. Strictly speaking, neither the farmer nor his wife know how many cattle they have. If some are lost to wild animals, it is still more profitable than supporting shepherds and overseers.

Needless to say the road was none too wide, and quite often branches brushed against us. But there was the farm enclosed by a stake fence, with a wooden farmhouse surrounded by a kitchen garden of greens and vegetables. The farmer's two grown sons amicably shook hands with me, the daughter curtsied, and with her husband's prodding the wife uttered a "Willkommen." I recounted for the young people the story of my acquaintance with their father and they promised to show me the farm. Contentment was written on the faces of these pipe-smoking young men who in no way longed to return to Germany. They felt at home here as true farmers and were calculating how things might best be managed, the price at which to sell their corn and wheat, and what the going rate for cattle was. A railroad will be built about two miles from here, they said, and then it will be convenient to sell both timber and grain. But for now they had to take it to Madison, about seven miles away. This family of farmers did not yet have many neighbors. The sections of land were large and had been bought up by speculators who were biding their time in order to sell at a high price. One of the lads asked me whether I would not like to settle somewhere near them. He praised the local land and promised to help get me started with cattle and agricultural tools, and to assist in putting up the house and fences. But I explained I would be more interested in looking over their agricultural tools and the strains of cattle they bred here, and in finding out the price of grain in the local market. Now the farmers were in their element. They related that they had several hundred merino sheep for which the local area is suited. To breed them, as well as strains of various domestic animals, they get European breeding stock from the eastern states. The horses and cattle were out to pasture but there were many hogs and fowl around and the farm was generally well stocked. The farmer's house itself did not remind me of peasant cottages even in the west of Europe. Quite the opposite. The house had a parlor and sitting room with quite comfortable furniture, including a rocking chair which was the favorite of the farmer's wife and daughter. This was the room used for entertaining people; the walls were covered with lithographs and with some portraits of friends and relatives. It also had a library of books on Holy Scripture, including commentaries, guides, poems, and so on. It was a rare farmer who did not have a piano that came out of a steam-operated factory in Cincinnati or Boston and hence did not cost much.

America is particularly proud of its agricultural machines. It was the costliness and sparseness of human labor that impelled farmers toward their invention and universal introduction. All the more so in that huge expanses had to be cultivated and the very quality of the soil was such that it could be freely worked by machines. To make certain of this it sufficed to climb atop a knoll and glance around at the limitless plain that blended into the distant horizon. The large and rather expensive machines that are needed only at certain times, for example, the steam plow and threshing machine, are usually moved around from one farmer to another at a charge mutually agreed upon for the period of use. The proximity of the city, where there are not only mechanics but an entire university and, even more, schools that turn out people trained in the basic principles of mechanics and the skills to handle advanced agricultural machinery, provides the answer as to how it was possible to introduce the use of these machines on a nearly universal scale.

Meanwhile the benefits are tremendous: manual labor is reduced and the decrease in cost of production leads to an increase in the quantity of agricultural products. For example, I saw a threshing machine in an open field threshing grain and pouring it into sacks. In one day that machine with eight horses and six men can harvest up to six hundred bushels of grain.[5] Then, when one farmer has his work completed, the machine is moved to his neighbor, and so forth. How much

5. Steam threshers were not yet widely used in the 1850s. In 1857 the only threshing machine that could separate six hundred bushels of wheat a day, and the one that Lakier probably saw, was powered by a high-speed sweep turned by eight horses. Letter from G. Terry Sharrer, September 18, 1978, Assistant Curator, Division of Extractive Industries, Smithsonian Institution, Washington, D.C. See also Reynold M. Wik, *Steam Power on the American Farm* (Philadelphia: University of Pennsylvania Press, 1953), pp. 18–28. The sweep-powered thresher separated, cleaned, and bagged the grain in one continuous operation. In contrast, a "typical" Russian peasant family in 1860 used a laborious and time-consuming procedure to thresh grain: "[In September] the men complete the sowing of winter wheat and rye and begin to thresh the harvested grain. (If the weather has been dry the sheaves have dried in the field and are ready for threshing. But if it has not, in October and November the Ivanovs have to put them in the upper room of their [drying shed]. They start a fire in the lower room, and the heat, rising through an opening, dries the damp sheaves during the night so they are ready for threshing in the morning.) The Ivanovs have a covered threshing floor. Since they have only three [men] threshers in the family, they form a labor pool with their neighbors. . . . After threshing comes winnowing, which they do with shovels, and cleaning of the grain by sifting." Mary Matossian, "The Peasant Way of Life," in Wayne S. Vucinich, ed., *The Peasant in Nineteenth-Century Russia* (Stanford: Stanford University Press, 1968), p. 38.

time, work, effort, and capital are saved can be appreciated by anyone in Europe who knows anything about agriculture. Because of these machines the price of grain in America is kept low. For example, a 196-pound barrel of flour in Iowa costs roughly from three to three and a half dollars, a bushel of corn thirty cents (about forty silver kopeks), a bushel of potatoes twenty cents (twenty-five silver kopeks).

For dinner at the farm there was a whole display of the greens and vegetables that abound in the area. As for fruit, there were apples and plums. They tried to grow pears, the farmer said, but without success. The farmer's wife was completely satisfied with her present existence and, looking at her husband, said rather decisively that she would not move no matter what the temptations, that she no longer had the strength for a life of gypsy wanderers. Whether the farmer and his two sons agreed with her I do not know. But I must confess I could not understand why one would move from a thriving, well-developed farm, as was this one. But the prospect was alluring and the married couple had doubtless already had more than one discussion about it. The previous owner had moved to the state of Iowa across the Mississippi and perhaps the farmer's wife was afraid of that passion for the *Mover-Leben,* as she put it.

One of the farmer's sons had business in Madison and was driving to the city. I took advantage of this opportunity and the day after my arrival parted with this hospitable family. On the way the conversation somehow got around to what my young companion thought of doing for a living. I hoped to hear him say that he would stay to help his parents. But he was already so imbued with the American spirit that without a moment's hesitation he answered that he wished to try his luck in the new lands of Minnesota, which he heard was an earthly paradise and where there was still lots of unoccupied land. He was trained for hard work, so it did not frighten him in the least, and he was convinced that that was where he would make an independent career for himself. I thought to myself that it is a good thing the world has its limits, for who knows where this common contagion, this indefatigable passion to secure one's future would entice desperate Americans and Americanized Germans!

IV

If the railroad in the upper half of Wisconsin had been completed, it would have been possible to go directly to the Upper Mississippi from

Madison. But to get to the Mississippi one has to go down to northern Illinois again and travel to Galena. The route lies across the plains, sometimes cultivated for miles on end, and there are the same fresh, newly established farms and towns.

Not far from Galena a short spur of the railroad runs to the Mississippi and I joyously looked forward to contemplating this wonder of the world. The idea of it conjured up thoughts of greatness, beauty, and power, but reality, at the very beginning at least, is always less than what one expects. Just as I had stood disappointed for the first few minutes at Niagara Falls, after having imagined so much about them, so I found myself asking, as I crossed the Mississippi on a steam ferry, whether this was really the King of Waters: it was so quiet, so meager in water, so clear. The city of Dubuque rises on the bluff on the other side. Only after I had sailed down the entire length of the Mississippi from St. Paul to New Orleans or even farther, to its delta, was I able to understand the significance, power, and might of this giant.

Until I got to Dubuque, Iowa, I had imagined it as being absolutely primitive and barbaric. But what did I find? Steamboats with the same tall funnels as on the Ohio, a fine hotel, railroads, and the same activity. Although it was undoubtedly less than in Boston or New York, here too people swarmed around, speaking the same English tongue and having the same manners! And Indians can no longer be found here. It is said that while remnants of them can still be seen in Minnesota on the Upper Mississippi, one must hurry because there too they are illegal. They ceded their lands to the United States government, and while they complain of the discomforts and infertility of the wilderness given them in the far north, where they are cramped by the cold and deprivation, it is only in the memories of the elders that they return to the ancient places. Meanwhile across the broad, spacious meadows that once were theirs, the "mover" wanders in an ox-drawn wagon covered with white canvas, a wagon in which he has put his whole family, a few household possessions, and a supply of corn and salt pork. In order to avoid all sorts of future inquiries, he has laconically written on the wagon the name of the territory for which he is headed: Iowa, Nebraska, Minnesota, or Arkansas. A table and chairs are attached to the back of the wagon and behind this moving household a cow and dog plod along. In the evening the family camps by a brook in the woods, if they happen upon one. Thus, in expectation of finding a good place to settle, whole families wander for days and months. . . . Not long ago it was a different story. The Indians were unlimited sovereigns here and to violate their rights would have meant having to deal with enemies, and powerful enemies at that.

Today Dubuque is quite a large town with twelve thousand inhabitants, thanks to the flourishing lead mines. The mining, or at least the existence, of the mineral had long been known to the Indians who lived in the area. Chunks of lead have been found among the bones in the graves of their ancestors. Even now the rich mines extending on both sides of the Mississippi are not worked systematically on a grand scale. They are operated by so-called prospectors, individuals who try to find traces of ore in the ground. These they dig out, giving back to the landowners for whom they prospect an agreed upon portion of what is extracted. It is believed that altogether the lead mines in Iowa occupy an area thirty-two miles long and five miles wide. In any case this is not what attracts immigrants here; rather it is the profitable, fertile condition of this enormous territory. Its rolling prairies, that is, plains alternating with small rises, serve as a lure for industrious people, especially German-Americans who cannot praise the area too much and prefer it over treeless Illinois or distant Minnesota. The towns are called cities right from the start, as if in anticipation of their future significance, and depending upon the taste of their founders, the suffix "city" or "polis" is added to the name.

10

Indians on
the Upper Mississippi

I

In Iowa on the Upper Mississippi I found myself among whites in the very process of creating settlements, among the first people even wanting to settle and set up house. Starting from Boston, New York, and Philadelphia, I had passed through the whole range of civilization, and in going from city to city I was able to observe all stages of human development. To be sure, there was one common idea and one common fundamental that pervaded all levels—autonomy and independent control of personal affairs. This unity smoothed out the differences which otherwise would have manifested themselves more forcefully. But after the cities and towns I had a desire to be in places where there still were Indians, the original inhabitants of America. I wanted to observe their way of life and to verify, as much as that was possible, the reasons for their disappearance from the face of the earth, a phenomenon that Americans, somehow, maintain is a necessity.

At Dubuque I did not have to wait long for the steamboat that sailed to St. Paul on the Upper Mississippi. This time it was almost completely filled with immigrants. They especially prefer to set out in the fall for new regions in Iowa and Minnesota. Everyone figures that he can save more money by acquiring land after the harvest and that he can get the fields plowed by summer. Despite the fact that winter was already knocking on the door, the intrepid immigrants were sailing off to distant places with their wives, their children and all their household possessions. What fowl, what stuff there was on our steamboat! Nearly all the people were German or Irish and despite the fact that they were not very comfortable on the lower deck, close to the engines on one side and on the other to the domestic animals—pigs and cows—that made up part of their new households, and despite the fact that there was nothing to speak of in the way of conveniences and beds for those poor people, it was precisely from that packed deck that the merry songs and cheerful talk were nearly always heard. On the upper deck or in the private salons the tables had hardly been cleared after breakfast or dinner when card games were set up. This activity of idle people continued all day long, with necessary intervals. People were constantly bustling around the playing tables. It was not at all a select group. On the contrary, prices for the voyage were so nominal that no one would grudge the few dollars it cost to be in a first-class cabin and to enjoy a good table. There was an awful mixture of classes and levels of education in first class. Hence a large number of the passengers kept silent, not knowing what to talk about or with whom. The ladies were separated by draperies from the other mortals and seldom came out. Here and there groups formed. The steamboat captain was obliging enough to acquaint me with an American government agent who was bringing annual payments to the Indians for lands they had ceded to the federal government. The agent was a mestizo, half-Indian and half-white. It was partly evident in his face, with its white color, angular shape, and black, bristly, straight hair. He spoke English and the language of the Dakotas, and was the intermediary between them and the United States. He was carrying with him a quantity of blankets, provisions, saws, axes, and agricultural tools.

Did the Indians benefit from the trouble the federal government went to for them? Why was the race dying off and vanishing? These were the questions I posed to the agent since I wanted to find out what principles underlay Indian policy and whether Indians could be expected to benefit from that policy.

"I can speak of the tribes I know," the agent answered, "because I myself am one of them by origin and because I have been dealing with them for fully ten years. Although they no longer belong here and have been allotted different and more distant hunting grounds, nevertheless since the Dakotas, Chippewas, and Winnebago behave peacefully and do not wage war on the whites, the government does not disturb them. Of course the government would grant them even more privileges if it were not afraid of the harmful influence of whites."

This position was not quite clear to me and I asked the agent to explain.

"The American government has the noblest of goals with respect to the Indians. In no way does it want their extermination; on the other hand, neither does it want the white population to suffer from Indian raids and the Indian notion of unlimited domains. The government's thinking is that the Indians can be accustomed to the idea of landed property with defined boundaries only when they are actually allotted small, measured sections of land marked off by boundaries. But the federal government does not want to deprive them of their former domains without compensation. On the contrary, it enters into a treaty with the chief of a tribe whose lands have or can become necessary for colonization. The government pays him a fixed sum arrived at by mutual agreement and facilitates the migration and resettlement of the tribe in a new area. Moreover, foreseeing that the Indians might squander the money, fall into poverty, and be a burden upon the government and neighboring states, and that poverty might lead them into crime, the government pays them in part a lump sum of cash to enable them to move to the new territories, set up their farms, and provide themselves with agricultural tools, and it also makes annual payments of either money or clothing, provisions, arms, and so on. For example, two treaties were concluded with the Dakotas in 1852. One half of these people sold twenty-one million acres west of the Upper Mississippi for $305,000 in cash; in addition, the government was obligated for fifty years to pay them $68,000 annually in money and goods. In a treaty concluded with the other half of the Dakotas, the Indians gave up their land to the whites and received from the government a payment of $250,000 and a promise of $58,000 in annual payments for the same fifty years. The government then divided up the land into sections and put them up for public sale to settlers. For the Indians, whole territories were set aside somewhere further on; there the Redskins can hunt their wild buffalo, which are now also moving farther and farther west. But as long as the white population is not large and the Indians conduct themselves peacefully, the government looks tolerantly upon the fact that several tribes still remain on their original lands."

To my question of whether it might not be better to let the Indians remain in association with whites, whose example might have an influence on their activity, diligence, and economy, the agent replied by defending the customary United States policy of segregating Indians. He argued for ways to prevent any further mixing so as to

save the last remnants of Indians, and to spare the government from
the criticism that it allowed through negligence, or even worse, de-
liberately planned, the extermination of the Redskins. The white exploits the advantage he has over the Indian, so that the latter is always in his debt, and of the hundreds of millions of dollars the
United States has paid the Indians for their lands, hardly anything
is left. If it were not for the yearly provisions, they would be completely helpless and ruined. The Indians do not know how to deal with
large sums of money, and for every little thing that strikes their eye—
a bugle, paint, rouge, or a knife—they give all they have or all that
is asked of them. White traders take advantage of this and, worst of
all, they sell the Indians hard liquor and by that means dominate
them completely. This is strictly forbidden by law and by compassion
for fellow human beings, but what is not done for the sake of profit!

"Whites have always behaved this way and one has only to see
what claims fur traders raise against the Indians when the latter receive money for their lands. A large part of this money passes to non-
Indians. The Indians do not know what needs they may have in
migrating hundreds of miles. And the care taken by the government
in setting aside money for it cannot rectify the evil, let alone eliminate
it. There is a special Indian Bureau in the Department of the Interior
in Washington and a special superintendent is put in charge of each
of the three great Indian regions; he has special agents who live
near the Indians and who work with one or more smaller tribes.
We," said the agent, "are strictly intermediaries between the government and the Indians; we transmit the needs and requirements
of the Indians to the government and we protect them against injury
from the whites. But we do not interfere in the internal government
of the tribes. Each is left completely on its own and the federal government conducts business only with the chiefs or sachems, who
know and deal with their own people. Each tribe is autonomous and
is organized according to its origins and individual language. But in
terms of government they all have the same purely patriarchal clans,
as do other primitive peoples. In addition, the tribes are divided up
into several subtribes and clans, and each has its own petty chief.
The chiefs all meet together on important matters concerning the
whole tribe and their decision is binding upon every member. For
less significant affairs, the head of the clan and family sits in judgment on the conduct of his relatives and also has the duty to investi-

gate disputes arising between them. Individual landed property does
not exist among the Indians: each tribe owns the land it occupies.
Everyone hunts and fishes as he wishes and only the members of other
tribes are excluded. Of course such notions cannot properly promote
the productive cultivation of land. The government's purpose in limiting the Indians' domains, acquainting them with agricultural tools,
and educating them to the extent that that is possible, is to let them
savor the advantages of true enlightenment and a settled way of life.
The government is also setting up schools for future generations.

"Meantime travelers and missionaries are acquainting the world
with the customs of the original inhabitants of the New World and
scholarly societies are making people aware of their languages. Thus
the Smithsonian Institution in Washington recently published a dictionary of the Dakota language, a Bible society translated the Bible into
various Indian dialects, and the Jesuits and Methodists preach the
word of God to the heathen. But either the Indians do not succumb
to this influence and flee from enlightenment, fearing for their freedom, or they seemingly yield to the words but in fact prefer to hunt,
and being lazy, die of hunger, privation, and sickness. Particularly
pernicious are smallpox, which mows them down mercilessly, and
fevers and scurvy. From the time the first travelers visited and wrote
descriptions of the Indians, not a single tribe has grown, and many
tribes have ceased to exist altogether. The rest vegetate, weighed down
by ignorance and dullness. It is seldom if ever that an Indian can
count to ten, and despite all the concerns of the government for preserving this indigenous race, it is steadily growing weaker and dying
and will ultimately be wiped out. Unhappily there seems to be no
other outcome for a people whom time has passed by and who are
dying because of their proximity to whites. Someone has estimated
that they are diminishing from various causes at an annual rate of
5 percent. I myself remember," continued the agent, "when some
subtribes of the Dakotas had members numbering in the thousands,
but now they have barely several hundred. In general, of the Indians
who at one time—and not so long ago at that—occupied the vast
expanse from the Pacific to the Atlantic Oceans and from the Arctic
Sea to the Gulf of Mexico, there are now hardly 300,000, compared
to the last count when there were still 388,299."

These reminiscences disturbed the agent. However little of the
Indian there was in his face and however beneficial the mixture of

white blood was for him, it was obvious that the problem was not a matter of complete indifference to him. It was even painful for him to give up the thought of the Indians' wilderness. He foresaw only their destruction because they could not exist under any other conditions, scorning dependence on anyone whomsoever. They recall their ancient tradition that when the great spirit Kitchi-Manitu[1] created the red man, the black man, and the white man and wished to determine what the destiny of each of the races would be, he ordered that a pile of books, hunting weapons, and agricultural tools be brought out. The white man threw himself upon the books and therein lies the answer as to why he rules the world. The red man seized the hunting weapons and the black man was left with the agricultural tools. That is why the Indian considers the white higher than himself and thinks that he degrades himself in adopting agriculture and becoming like the Negro. To an Indian's way of thinking, to bind his labor to a lump of earth would mean to deprive himself of freedom. Not for nothing did an Iroquois on the banks of the Niagara say to me in discussing his poverty and how he might avert it with work: "I am poor but free; I am a friend of freedom!" On the other hand, when it comes to hunting it is hard to find better eyes, keener vision, and sharper ears; the slightest rustle in the grass, the most insignificant little bird in the clouds, the snake crawling in the distance—nothing escapes the Indian's notice or his arrow. When he fishes or pursues game, the Indian is the most patient of beings, uncomplainingly enduring hunger, fatigue, and every hardship.

These accounts by a man who was well acquainted with the way of life of his forebears were extremely absorbing, especially since he promised to show me the Indians in their native dwellings at St. Paul where they were coming to meet him. Meanwhile we continued to steam up the Mississippi.

[Lakier's steamboat continued upriver for four days. He comments on the monotony of the prairies and discusses the earliest white explorers of the Mississippi.]

Tree-covered islets are frequently found in the river. Veering left

1. Kitchi Manitu is Algonkian and means Superior Spirit. It is unlikely that Lakier's Dakota guide would have used this term. Letter from Dr. Nancy O. Lurie, May 6, 1975, Curator of Anthropology, Milwaukee Public Museum.

and right, the pilot tried to avoid shoals and find a clear channel. If it were necessary to disembark an immigrant or a farmer, he could put in to shore any place. A gangplank is lowered from the steamboat to the shore and the passenger, shaking and dancing as if on a rope to keep his balance, descends to solid ground, after which his baggage is thrown to him from the steamboat. If it was necessary to take on cargo or stock up with firewood, the steamboat put in to shore and the business was done quickly and smoothly. Firewood cut and sawed was already stacked on shore with prices and quantities posted on a board. From the deck of the steamboat the captain used a telescope to make out the condition of the forest, and if the price was agreeable, he put in to shore. A wooden barge was hooked on to the steamboat and the firewood loaded while underway. The barge was then detached and sent to a moorage along the river.

The stops were rather frequent. On our left was Minnesota and on our right Wisconsin, both lands having new settlements and even greater expectations of immigrants. The latter quite often disembarked—now on one side, now on the other. At Lake Pepin, where the Mississippi flows for twenty miles at a width of four miles, the shoreline scene changes somewhat. The shores are so bare and treeless here that it was thought there was a depression in the river into which the forested islands had disappeared. The agent embellished this opinion of those who had explored the King of Rivers with a story about an Indian maiden. Her parents did not want to give her to her favorite warrior, so she threw herself into the lake from a bluff which to this day is called Maidenrock. It is here that the southern deciduous forests begin to change to the northern coniferous, with spruce, fir, and pine, and the climate appeared to be somewhat colder.

I was particularly delighted when an Indian emerged from the wigwams and tents scattered along the west bank of the Mississippi and boarded our steamboat for St. Paul.[2] My acquaintance, the agent, spoke to him in his native tongue and told me that he was of the Sioux tribe and was going to visit his people. His face and arms were painted in a most fearsome way. He had no beard or side-whiskers, but his long, black, bristly hair fell almost to his shoulders. The young Sioux was distinguished by his height and a sprightliness of gait as well as by his quietness, tenderness, and inoffensiveness. He

2. See below, n. 8.

was wearing moccasins, that is, light boots, that came up almost to his knees. A wool blanket thrown over his shoulders like a Spanish cloak made him look like a woman, but his inseparable companions were a rifle and a pipe. His clothing was plain, being mostly of deer and buffalo hides.

For a long time I peered at the markings with which the Indian was so lavishly decorated. I must confess that I tried in vain to get at their meaning and significance, since they seemed not to have been guided by any principle of beauty. It was the same vogue that, with different forms and devices, exists everywhere. I thought some markings might distinguish one tribe or family from another but this too was incorrect. Each related family group, the agent told me, has its special symbol, some kind of animal, a wolf, a bear, a turtle, a bird, which is sort of a heraldic emblem adopted by the family elders and the clan and tribal chiefs. But here there were straight lines and circles painted with ochre, soot, red dye, clay, and indigo, not only on the cheeks but also on the ears, hair, and even the blanket thrown around his bare muscular shoulders. Seeing how intently I was staring at those un-recognizable markings, the agent pointed out to me their similarity to hands and arrows. He explained that originally a large number of the markings did have meaning, that they portrayed the whole history of the man and his tribe. But bad representations have dis-torted them to the point that they now appear unrecognizable. In the primordial history of the people their meaning was completely dif-ferent and the markings represented a conventional language. Parents now cover the faces of their children with black paint as punish-ment; cowardly men mark up their faces to hide from the evil spirit or to terrify it. Furthermore these multicolored markings help pro-tect the skin against cold, especially in those far-off territories where, thanks to the whites, Indians are now condemned to live. Needless to say, these markings do not convey the rich imagery of the painting of the original natives. By means of these crude outlines and shapes the Indians portray their notions about the divine being and his manifestation in the forces of nature, such as a lightning flash and the fertility of the earth, and his notions of life after death.

Shackles and slavery await the wrongdoer and coward. On the other hand, for the good man and the brave warrior, there is the promise of rich hunting in the vast evergreen forests where wild animals are plentiful and the rivers full of fish, where the sun never

sets and it is alway warm, and where there are eternal joys and
dances. That basically is what constitutes the eternal dream of the
Indian; the things he so often does not have on earth wait for him
beyond the grave as a reward for his suffering in life. My traveling
companion told me that several miles from St. Paul, and not far
from where we were sailing, is Carver's Cave, named in honor of the
man who discovered it.[3] The Indians called it *Wakan-tipi,* "home of
the spirit." Until recently conferences were still being held there by
tribal chiefs of the Dakota, Sioux, and Naudowesioux. Originally
funeral ceremonies for the dead were conducted in the cave; the
deceased was mourned until the living spirit had left the body, that
is, when the body had begun to decompose, and only then was it
covered with earth. There are hieroglyphs on the walls of the cave
which like the Egyptian are now also unrecognizable and indistinct;
with every passing year they become less visible. Doubtless originally
they were artistic representations of Indian notions of life after death,
and of the rewards and punishments waiting for man beyond the
grave. The Indians now also keep their dead in birch-like coffins which
they hang in the forest until the process of decomposition begins. Only
then can the earth receive the dead and the ritual lamentation over
them be ended.

Listening to this poetical account of Indian ideas about death and
the painful parting of the soul from the body, I found myself recalling
the verses of Schiller—the death lament of the Indians (*Nadowes-
sische Todtenklage*) in which the poet sympathizes with the Indians
in their sorrow over the departed, recounts his exploits, to which death
sets inexorable limits, and consoles the grieving with the joys awaiting
the deceased in the afterlife.[4]

The same pleasures the deceased enjoyed on earth wait for him in
the afterlife. Hence Indians do not want to leave him without the
necessities for life beyond the grave. "You bury him with everything
that can make him happy there. Under his head you place the hatchet

3. Jonathan Carver (1710–80) was a Massachusetts-born traveler who
explored the Upper Mississippi area in 1766–67. His *Travels in Interior
Parts of America,* first published in 1778, was a very popular book, and
went through many editions and translations.

4. Friedrich Schiller (1759–1805), the German poet, composed this
"Death Lament" in 1798. It grew out of the German translation of
Carver's American travel account.

he wielded so skillfully and the club with which he hunted the bear; the trail, after all, will be a long one. Don't forget the keenly sharpened knife with which he used to scalp an enemy in three slashes. Put dyes in his hands so that he might decorate his body there."

The notion of life after death, like the religious faith of the Indians generally, has led some to believe that this tribe is one of the ten tribes of Israel. That is how they explain the origin of these mysterious people. Reinforced by other facts, this could turn out to be a convenient means of explaining the origin of the Indians, but it should not be forgotten that there are concepts innate in every people, whatever might be their stage of development, and the idea of a Deity and of the immortality of the soul are two such concepts. Of course both are subject to modifications in the details of manifestation. Depending on what a person supposes bliss on earth to be, he envisions it in the same form beyond the grave. Contrariwise, he sees in his deprivation punishment for a life unworthy of rewards. If a Muslim can be tempted by beyond-the-grave caresses of houris, for an Indian it is enough to have corn-covered fields and vast forests in which he can hunt game with ease.

The great spirit Kitchi-Manitu is supposed to be eternal. But the Indian also believes in good and evil spirits and that each phenomenon of nature, a mountain, a waterfall, a river, has, so to speak, its own special spirit. Indian beliefs are full of the most diverse embodiments, superstitions, myths, and miracles, as one might expect from a people unenlightened by the teachings of Christ.

For all the simplicity of the everyday attire and costume worn by the Indian who came aboard our steamboat at Lake Pepin, there was one small item to which the agent directed my attention. On the belt of the young Sioux was fastened a snake skin which, kind as he was, the Indian would let me look at only with great reluctance. He accorded it some kind of special respect and honor. That, explained my companion, is the Indian's talisman, which he guards with his life. Seldom, if ever, will he part with his treasure which he believes the Great Spirit has designated just for him. When a youngster reaches adulthood he embarks on life's open road on his own. He is sent to a secluded spot in the forest where he throws himself on the ground and lies there without food sometimes for three or four days, praying to the Great Spirit to show him his future guardian and protector. Finally fatigued, he falls asleep and the first animal that appears in his dream is the one that he must choose as his companion for the rest of his life. Whether it be a muskrat, a beaver, a mouse, a wolf, a bird, or a snake, the young Indian sets out to track down the designated animal in the forest. As soon as he gets one, he skins it, decorates the skin as he wishes, and makes a little bag or belt out of it. He then prays and makes sacrifices to it. He resorts to it in times of sickness and sees it as a source of comfort in sorrow and a guardian against misfortune. He will not sell it for anything. Should he happen to lose this precious item, for example in battle, he believes that happiness cannot return to him unless he kills his friend and takes his treasure and guardian.[5]

II

Meanwhile we continued on our way, and upon leaving Lake Pepin we began to anticipate the imminent end of the four-day voyage. We stopped at the city of Prescott at the confluence of the St. Croix and Mississippi rivers and after again passing wigwams[6] of the Sioux, we headed somewhat to the left up the Mississippi toward St. Paul, the main city of Minnesota. The latter is separated from Wisconsin mainly by the St. Croix River and further south by the Mississippi; it is bordered on the north by Lake Superior and its tributaries. The entire area of this new state is 141,839 square miles and its capital city, St. Paul, is one of the most northwestern of the important cities in the American Union.[7] It has only been in existence for seven or eight years and, thanks to its location, already has more than ten thousand inhabitants. Public coaches travel along its wide streets, which stretch for miles. An enormous hotel is ready to receive the traveler and there are five-story buildings just as in Chicago, Cin-

5. Lakier's account of the talisman—more commonly described as a medicine bag (meaning mystery bag)—is correct, except for his last statement. An Indian could replace a medicine bag lost in battle "only . . . by rushing into battle and plundering one from an enemy whom he slays with his own hand." George Catlin, *The Manners, Customs, and Condition of the North American Indians,* vol. 1 (London: Published by the Author, 1841), p. 37. Lakier was probably the victim of a simple typesetter's error, that is, the use of the Russian word *drug* (friend) instead of *nedrug* (enemy).

6. See below, n. 8.

7. Minnesota was admitted to statehood in 1858.

cinnati, and New York. Until recently lonely Fort Snelling still stood on this side, erected for defense against the Indians. One now frequently hears the hope expressed that St. Paul is destined to be the great city of the Far West.

My patron, the agent, suggested that I go with him in a simple Indian boat, a hollowed-out tree trunk, to give the Indians between St. Paul and Fort Snelling the annual payment sent by the federal government for the lands. In St. Paul the agent had already met the chief of one of the Dakota tribes to whom supplies, tobacco, blankets, and so on were being sent. The boats were ready at the appointed time and we set out for the neighboring estuary formed by the Mississippi. Powerful adult Indians did the rowing and calmly smoked their little pipes. They handled the frail craft masterfully and we soon saw the wigwams of the Indians. Buffalo and deer hides were stretched over poles, with smoke coming out of openings at the top.[8] Gathered in these abodes were the silent, unattractive Indian women and their children. In the center of the wigwam was a fire. It was pathetic to look at the women, especially since their husbands and fathers were so brilliantly attired in a diversity of colors and a richness of garb and arms. The Indian chiefs were wearing the most gala costumes. The color red predominated on their faces and clothing and they wore belts and necklaces made of beads, shells, and feathers. Their faces, hands, and hair were covered with markings. . . . The chiefs shook our hands and sat down on the hides spread out on the floor. Tobacco pipes were offered around by the hospitable hosts. While the agent conducted business with them in their language and gave them blankets, arms, money, and supplies, I was peering at those quiet, apathetic faces in which there were no traces whatever of brutality. But by some strange contradiction of human nature it is difficult to find a being who would be more merciless toward an enemy, who would more cold-bloodedly scalp an adversary and then all his life wear the bloody trophy taken in battle. Besides arrows, quivers, bows, and rifles, eagle feathers warm with blood protruded from the head of

8. Lakier has confused the wigwam with the tepee (tipi). The former is a domed or loaf-shaped lodge made of bent saplings; the latter is a conical dwelling made of poles and hides. The Dakota Indians used tepees, not wigwams. Letter from Dr. Nancy O. Lurie, May 6, 1975, Curator of Anthropology, Milwaukee Public Museum.

each Indian, and from each belt hung scalps taken from victims, along with some rattles and the omnipotent bag—the talisman.

The Indian woman is completely removed from male society and is left not only with domestic work but labor in general. The man only wars, hunts, and fishes; he never performs tasks he finds degrading—those he leaves for his poor wife. It is the complete opposite of the contemporary American, who honors a woman above everything, spares his lady the slightest trouble and unpleasantness, and leaves her to concern herself with clothes, theaters, and pleasures; despite the money matters that besiege him the livelong day, he is not reluctant to take care of his baby and even to do the cooking, while his lady thinks about clothes and parties.

In general the Indians behaved with decorum and nodded their heads as a sign of approval. I understood nothing more and was pleased when the agent finished his business and we began to set out on the road for the neighboring fort. It had gotten cold and it was impossible to spend the night in the wigwam. At departure the Indians expressed their gladness by loudly beating on a kind of tambourine, chanting songs, and dancing. There was much that was warlike and shrill in this whole scene and the agent assured me that they celebrated victory over an enemy with the same loud noises.

Fort Snelling was close to the place where we had met the Indian chiefs. In the evening, when we were among the American officers who served there and we were able to warm ourselves by the open fire and hear and tell stories, I felt that the white man had acted well when of the blessings offered him by the Indian Great Spirit Kitchi-Manitu, he chose books. For with them he chose the possibility of improving himself, escaping from the elements, and living in conformity with his wants.

The officer to whom the agent had introduced me indicated that the fort was built about forty years ago when all of Minnesota was Indian territory and it was impossible even to foresee a time when the impassable forests and limitless plains would be ceded to whites for settlement. The fort is built on a rather high rise, a bluff, for security and better observation of the Indians. It contains living quarters for officers and soldiers (a good half of whom are German) and kitchen gardens for growing vegetables. Until quite recent times these forts were essential for the protection of immigrants. In the course of time cities were created around or near them so that at present, with

the existence of St. Paul and St. Anthony, the maintenance of the fort
has become quite superfluous and there are rumors that it will be
moved one hundred miles further west. In recent times the United
States government has sought to make the Oregon and California
Trails through Utah safe against Indian attacks, a policy which requires the building of forts. What will they do with the present
buildings? They are thinking of using them to establish a military
academy for the far northwest similar to the one that exists for the
east at West Point on the Hudson.

The next morning I thanked my host and the agent and set out for
the town and falls of St. Anthony, which were still further north.

After Niagara Falls, the memory of which was still so fresh, the
Mississippi at St. Anthony was not striking. But the American knows
that the power of these waters was created not only to admire but to
take advantage of. With a speed understood only in America, lumber
mills have been established here. Thanks to that industry, which the
forests will continue to sustain for a long time on the Upper Mississippi, the flourishing and wealthy town of St. Anthony was laid out on
the higher shore near the waterfall. It was here that the University
of Minnesota was founded.[9] Rich shops of various kinds have already
burgeoned on the streets of St. Anthony with its more than three
thousand inhabitants, and a huge hotel is ready to accommodate
strangers who come to these cool healthy places to rest and spend the
summer.

9. In 1851.

II

St. Louis and Slavery

I

The return route from St. Paul on the Upper Mississippi took me
downriver past the same settlements I had seen on the way to St. Paul
from Dubuque. Now that I had traveled about a thousand miles on
the Mississippi, the King of Waters earned far more of my respect,
despite the fact that it still flowed ceaselessly through endless plains.
But when I saw the colorful towns and villages along the shore, I
did not grumble about the monotony. Settlements have sprung up at
every suitable inlet, with steam flour mills and sawmills operating
here and there. If no thought has yet been given to manufacturing and
industrial establishments, it is because the entire population is devoted to agriculture, which brings abundant rewards. It is perhaps
also explained by the scarcity of capital for acquiring land and establishing farms, and capital still carries a heavy interest charge in these
parts.

We had to leave the steamboat at Burlington [Iowa] in order to
get around the lower rapids of the Mississippi. I took advantage of
the occasion to acquaint myself with the former capital of Iowa; it had
been selected as the state center at a time when a choice between cities was not possible because there simply were no other cities. Burlington has a picturesque location, which is true of most of the cities
on the Upper Mississippi, standing as it does on a green hill. As
everywhere in this region, it is surrounded by wheat fields. A railroad
line runs from Chicago to Burlington and thus links it to all the
eastern transportation routes; it is planned that this line will go all
the way to Nebraska. The population of the young town is now about
eight thousand, but already a historical society has been formed and
foundations have been laid for a public library and a geological and

mineralogical office for a collection of fossils found in Iowa. Needless to say, there are many newspapers and schools here.

The road leading around the Mississippi rapids went past well-cultivated fields and prosperous farms. We left Burlington by mail carriage in the morning and by evening reached Montrose [Iowa], where the rapids really begin and interrupt navigation on the Lower Mississippi. At this point there are twelve miles of rapids. Goods and passengers are transported over the hill; that is the way the inhabitants of Montrose earn their living. It is strange that Americans, who spare no expense on improvements, should have neglected this most important transportation route. The explanation for this lies in a dispute over who should assume the quite considerable expense for clearing the rapids. The central government in Washington has put the responsibility on the state, which stands to benefit generally if not exclusively. But the state has shown that the Mississippi is a great waterway for the Union as a whole and therefore all states should participate. Hence the expense cannot but fall upon the central government. Whatever the truth might be, the rapids continue to exist and to interefere with trade.[1]

It is at Keokuk, situated on the opposite shore of the Mississippi in the state of Iowa, that the lower rapids cease and uninterrupted navigation extends down to the mouth of the King of Rivers. Steamboats to St. Louis are always ready and waiting for passengers. Traffic is generally heavy; along the shore, needless to repeat, one finds a solitary farm or a town just getting started. And if one meets up with a loquacious American (which is less likely on a steamboat than on a railway train), the latter can hardly avoid talking about every town and its advantages, and what kind of future it has in store. One town, he says, is flourishing, another is capable of improvement, a third will be a great commercial center; for every one of them he has a flattering hope.

After having passed by Alton and the lower falls of the Illinois River, the general attention of even those who were not first-time visitors to this part of the Mississippi turned to a phenomenon similar to the confluence of the Ottawa and St. Lawrence Rivers. Up to this point the waters of the Mississippi were bright and clear, as in the

1. The federal government finally built a nine-mile-long canal to bypass the rapids and opened it to river traffic in 1877.

purest mountain brook: the bottom was almost everywhere sandy, clayey, or rocky. You could easily distinguish the place where the muddy, turbulent waters of the furious Missouri poured into it. Its power is so great that the Mississippi for the rest of its course retains a muddy color and turbulent character. Trees torn out by the roots and clumps of land ripped from the shore float down from the Missouri, and the opinion of those who thought the Missouri the source of the Upper Mississippi was hardly unjustified. Thus the strong resemblance of these two rivers is below their confluence.

The greater part of the Missouri River belongs to the state of Missouri, which is bordered by Iowa on the north and is separated from Illinois on the east by the Mississippi River. The city of St. Louis is located in Missouri and for a long time was the central point for commercial activity in the West for the North American Union. Ask anyone you please why this city prospers and he will almost always give the same answer—that it is a very old city. That is at least understandable and comes closer to a European explanation for the maturity of a city. Well, turn to history, what then? If one considers that the first log cabin was built here in 1764, the city is not even a hundred years old and is "very old" compared only to Chicago and St. Paul. But the real colonization of the area and the subsequent history of St. Louis properly begins at the time when Napoleon sold the territory to the North American Union in 1804 and settlers moved out from the eastern cities of America. Here again the same Yankees laid down the first seeds of civilization and already by the 1820s there were ten thousand inhabitants in St. Louis, while the arrival of the first steamboats dates from the same time.

This then is what is meant by an old city in America. Today it is amazing that hundreds of steamboats arrive here and are strung out along a three-mile-long levee. The straightness of the Mississippi shore makes it possible to survey at a glance the whole mass of goods either transported and unloaded here, or waiting to be loaded. There is an eternal crush of people among the sacks, boxes, barrels, casks, wagons, horses, and Negroes. As at Cincinnati, the St. Louis levee is paved, and beginning at the river the city rises to its downtown. The view of St. Louis from the Mississippi is picturesque. The first level of the levee is surrounded by large buildings, stores, and offices, and there is constant bustle and movement. This is a purely commercial and industrial city and today it is as if the French with their natural gaiety had never been here. All one hundred thousand inhabitants are exclusively concerned with the clinking of dollars. In this sense St. Louis occupies an extremely favorable position between the mouths of the Missouri, the Ohio, and the Illinois, which flow together from three different directions. Despite the development of other branches of trade, St. Louis has kept its faith in the one trade through which it first attained wealth and prosperity—the fur trade. The Chouteau family to this day controls this profitable industry.[2] Agents and hunters sent out by this house roam far up the Missouri and its tributaries to the Rocky Mountains. To provide for their security and the protection of goods being brought to the Indians, as well as for the storing of furs supplied by the Indians, they built forts. Doubtless in time cities and towns will be formed around them, just as Chicago, Milwaukee, Dubuque, and others had their origins in similar forts. The main item of trade is buffalo skins, which in some years come to one hundred thousand pelts. The hair of many of them is extremely silky and fine. The skins of young, unborn buffalo, from which fur coats are made, are highly valued.

The buildings in St. Louis are rather monotonous, being almost all of unplastered brick. It is a rare story that is not enclosed by balconies and verandas and, except for them, virtually no exterior ornamentation is to be seen, the latter being something for which Americans generally have little regard. Here too there are occasional empty lots and log cabins, as in other cities of the West, an indication that immigrants are still moving here. More than one-third of the population is German and they have assumed the same occupations as in other cities of western America. They are farmers, coachmen, shopkeepers, and artisans, but major trade is in the hands of Americans. Quite often the same mixed German-American speech that startled me in Pennsylvania is heard on the streets of St. Louis. The buildings of the Germans, in distant neighborhoods of St. Louis, are in striking con-

2. René Auguste Chouteau (1749–1829) helped found St. Louis and became the wealthiest fur trader and largest landowner of the area. His brother, Jean Pierre Chouteau (1758–1849) formed the St. Louis Missouri Fur Company in 1809, the first important organization to exploit the beaver regions of the West. Jean's son, Pierre (1789–1865), became an even more successful merchant, fur trader, and financier. Pierre's company, formed in the 1830s, dominated the fur trade in St. Louis through the 1850s.

trast to the huge buildings of the Americans. If the Americans have the large stores, or rather depots for various goods which they sell wholesale, the Germans have the retail trade. It is a rare German house that does not have a bookshop with simple works of German literature, or a tavern selling wine, beer, and liquors, or a tobacco shop.

That the city does not count on one hundred thousand inhabitants but on five times that number, is evidenced by the boundaries which are projected for it on the map. I had a chance to test this myself by walking to the city park, which of course one imagines to be if not in the center of the city, then at least close to it.[3] This is how it is shown on the map. But the park is at least five miles from the courthouse. And in walking to this place designated for strolling by city inhabitants, I had to pass by large empty lots next to huge buildings erected for schools or factories, lots on which corn was growing in its pristine beauty; beyond the field was an enormous building and again an empty lot. When I finally reached the park, I wondered if I had not lost my way. An earthen wall and a fence enclosed the huge area for better protection against cattle. Here and there among the planted trees ran a wide road, but it was overgrown with grass from too little use. There is no comparison at all between what we Russians mean by a park and what that word means in America. But then the view of the city in the distance and of the surrounding hills, which in time will also be built up, is magnificent.

I had the same feeling after a trip to the suburban town of Carondelet, laid out along the Mississippi. A major street, Carondelet Avenue, one of the most important in St. Louis, starts out with huge buildings in the central district of the city. Farther out it takes on the appearance of a ramshackle mixture of plain wooden structures, while closer to the arsenal it becomes almost completely empty and livens up again only on approaching Carondelet. In time, when the town merges with St. Louis, which will surely happen when the population spreads out and the city itself becomes too crowded, this avenue of several miles will be the best street in St. Louis. For me, distant Carondelet was interesting for its workhouse, designed to hold short-term criminals convicted of misdemeanors. St. Louis has its own jail for those still waiting to be sentenced by the courts, while the state prison for

3. Probably Lafayette Park, the St. Louis "showcase park" established in 1851.

felons is in Jefferson City, the capital. The burden of the workhouse
fell on Carondelet and several days prior to my arrival it was witness
to a terrible scene: one of the guards shot a disobedient prisoner and
killed him. Of course they dismissed the guard and brought him to
trial. How it will turn out is not known, but he will plead that the
victim was disobedient, that he behaved violently, and so forth. The
St. Louis newspapers have unanimously cried out against this method
of subduing disobedient prisoners. The court will probably not pardon
a man who caused a death where he was supposed to maintain order;[4]
but the very condition of the workhouse and its miserable maintenance explains why such a sad event was possible. This prison is worse
than all the others I have seen in various parts of the United States
and I was glad when I heard that this was only its temporary location.
Two fences, one some distance from the other, prevent prisoner escapes. On the other hand, the magnificent view of the Mississippi
from the hill on which the prison is located must create that much
stronger an urge among the prisoners to leave, since the prison has
neither the order nor the conveniences that human decency requires
even for the greatest criminals. The cells, instead of being singles, are
made to hold eight men even though they have only four bunks.
Moreover the prisoners, regardless of the degree of guilt and the kinds
of crimes for which they are being punished, are all thrown together
and have no work; women are not even strictly separated from the
men. Idleness and the opportunity to freely communicate with one
another about their past, their plans, and their thoughts, is sufficient to
explain the possibility of similar occurrences. And thus, one recalls
with great respect the improvements that have been made, especially
recently, in the condition of American prisons.

The tops of churches and charitable institutions in St. Louis tower
over private homes, while the Catholic cathedral is the most remarkable in size and wealth of ornamentation. Catholics generally predominate here, indeed a large number of the local educational institutions
belong to the Jesuits and are supported by private gifts. Many of them
train missionaries to preach God's word in the Indian tongues. The

4. The guard, Francis Giles, shot and killed William Campbell, a
prisoner, while the latter was supposedly attempting to escape from the
workhouse. Giles was found guilty of second-degree murder. *The Missouri Republican, St. Louis,* October 28, 1857.

leading Jesuit college is St. Louis University, which justly became famous for the Rocky Mountain journeys of Father De Smet, a man who formerly had spent a long time among the Indians in the distant territory of Oregon.[5] He brought with him to St. Louis many remarkable past and present Indian artifacts and presented his Indian museum to the university. Thus the priest's collection has become common property.

The university in St. Louis is more properly a higher gymnasium. But Americans love the words "college" and "university" and lavishly bestow those names on institutions striving to provide their students with an education in various fields of instruction. Independent of this university in St. Louis is another, the University of Missouri, with a variety of specialized schools. But native Americans are not indifferent to the fact that education of the young is in the hands of a Catholic university, and they foresee a future struggle between Catholicism and the different forms and branches of Protestantism. As proof of that belief they cite the intolerance of the Catholic clergy which, on every suitable occasion, raises a hue and cry against heretical dogma and is not training the youth to honor what constitutes, if not principal tenets for Americans, then at least steadfast beliefs, for example, the observance of Sunday. Americans generally complain about a division of society brought about largely by the intervention of the Jesuits.[6] Still, they do acknowledge that the Jesuits in their time, that is, when the local region was uninhabited and uncultivated and when whites came here reluctantly or not at all, brought the word of God to the Indians on the plains and in the forests. In addition, societies of the Catholic Sisters of Mercy established several philanthropic and charitable institutions, as well as the first schools.

Of public libraries, the largest is the Mercantile Library, originally designed for the needs of merchants and tradesmen in various com-

5. Pierre Jean de Smet (1801–73) was a Belgian missionary who emigrated to the United States and became noted for his work as peacemaker among the Indians.

6. American Nativism, an anti-Catholic and anti-foreigner movement, reached its height in the mid-1850s. In August 1854 there were pitched battles in St. Louis between Native Americans and Irish Catholics in which ten men were killed. Ray Allen Billington, *The Protestant Crusade, 1800–1860: A Study of the Origins of American Nativism* (Chicago: Quadrangle Paperbacks, 1964), p. 421.

mercial houses in the city. Founded by private contributions, it is maintained by annual dues of five dollars from each supporter, or a one-time payment of fifty dollars. The good example set by a few donors has been followed by others and thus a public library has been opened for general use. Today it has no less than twelve thousand books and a rich collection of American and foreign journals and newspapers.

II

St. Louis might be thought of as a refutation of the prevailing opinion that a city in a slave state is not likely to prosper. But the fact is that, however industrialized it may be, an observer is left with the conviction that the city's condition would be infinitely better if it were located on free soil. If this city with its natural advantages of location and surrounding fertile lands were not in the unfree state of Missouri, it would prosper even more than Cincinnati or Chicago. But we see a different phenomenon, and it is futile to search beyond slavery for its explanation. If a black slave cannot approach the level of a free white man in the quality of his labor, black labor is nevertheless cheaper and in this respect the white cannot compete with him. The white living in freedom has more needs and does not want to deny himself, while the Negro makes do with what is given him and will not dare ask for more; in the end he gives up wanting it at all.

Another distinctive characteristic of the Negro is slavish obedience to the will of the master; in this respect, too, the Negro is irreplaceable. But the American is still not satisfied. How he disciplines an already obedient slave is exemplified by the ritual which accompanies dinner in a St. Louis hotel. It is well known that there are no better or more faithful servants than Negroes and that is why free Negroes are in great demand in the free states. There the Negro serves on the same level as the white and is called by his first name like everyone else; in a slave state, however, one must say "boy" to a Negro. The unimaginable discipline in the St. Louis hotel consists in the fact that Negroes serving at table must, at the first ring of the maître d'hotel, who is usually white, leave the dining room with measured steps and go to the kitchen for the food. Another ring and they change the plates. They enter and leave in step like precision soldiers; no one takes one step more or less than another. One of them sets a plate on one side of a long table; at that precise moment and with exactly the same gesture another sets a plate opposite it. Whether there is an unoccupied place or even a whole row of such places, the Negro is not flustered. He acts as if someone were sitting there and hovers about the table, all of it being done for the sake of monotonous harmony. When I saw these maneuvers by living black puppets for the first time in Planters House,[7] the biggest hotel in St. Louis, I did not believe my eyes. It is obvious that all these perfectly unnecessary tricks, which added absolutely nothing to the service, the refinement of the cuisine, or the taste of the food, required many extra servants. Indeed there were more of them here than would be required in the same size hotel with white servants, and dinner was interminable. Meanwhile the owner who trained the slaves to march so well was very pleased with these procedures which, incidentally, amused the Negroes no less than the white who devised them. Force a white worker to do the same, and for paltry wages besides, and of course he will reject this marching. He wants to be useful to himself and others in a completely different way.

The same is true among agricultural laborers. The observation I made in Maryland and on the Ohio River is perfectly applicable to the state of Missouri. I am pleased, nonetheless, to find support for my views in the authority of the Americans themselves. In all legislative assemblies of the unfree states there are parties striving—to a greater or lesser degree—to free the Negroes. The champions of this noble idea are supported by facts and statistical evidence that can convince the most obstinate defender of slavery.

In the last session of the Missouri legislature, one of the representatives, a Mr. Brown,[8] sought to prove that slavery must be abolished for the good of the United States, that it could not stand up against civilization and must disappear, just as the Redskins had been unable to resist the whites—a stronger and, of greater importance, more enlightened and industrious race. As evidence of what freedom can accomplish, Brown referred to New England, which had gained so much in giving up slavery. The difference between the unfree and free

7. Built in 1841, it became the leading hotel in St. Louis.
8. Benjamin Gratz Brown (1826–85) was a member of the lower house of the Missouri legislature between 1852 and 1859. In 1857 he made a forceful anti-slavery speech and prophesied the abolition of slavery in Missouri on economic grounds. He was later elected U.S. senator (1865–67) and governor of Missouri (1871–73).

states and the poorer condition of the former compared to the latter
is understandable. Where there is slavery, one finds huge landholdings; conversely, where there is free labor, each person has no more
than a prescribed number of acres, otherwise the land would remain
uncultivated. With slavery, plantations are necessary; with free labor,
only farms are possible. In the unfree states, says Brown, developing
the idea further, the labor of whites becomes unnecessary, even impossible; without the hope of improving their lives, whites must move
out of states where Negroes work. The reverse is also true: a decline
in the number of Negroes is paralleled by a rise in the white population. The orator provided a large quantity of figures to corroborate
this curious and at the same time natural situation, and he asserted
that several counties in the state of Missouri—by virtue of the fact that
the white population has increased so significantly in recent times—
provide factual evidence of the natural demise of slavery at the same
time that other counties are striving to uphold it.

This is the comforting result provided by twenty-five counties where
white population grew while black population declined. From 1851
to 1856, as the number of slaves in those counties decreased by 4,442,
white population increased by 75,797. The increase is so significant
that while five years earlier the ratio of whites to blacks in the designated counties was 10:1, now it is 13:1. From this the orator concluded that there was no need to fear for a lack of workers, only instead of slaves working under the lash there would be an industrious
white population. As evidence he pointed to the remarkable fact that
many people were migrating from Missouri to Iowa so as not to work
in an unfree state, even though Missouri with its natural routes of
communication was destined by nature for prosperity. But since one
might think that the figures provided for the aforesaid counties are
fortuitous and consequently signify nothing, it was necessary to show
that the Missouri counties where the number of slaves increased had
not been so fortunate. This Brown did, basing his conclusions on statistical evidence. He took the population of ten other counties in
which there was an increase in the number of blacks in the same
span of time, 1851 to 1856. And here is what it indicated: when the
number of slaves increased by 10,000 (from 32,414 to 42,644), white
population in the same counties grew by 20,000 (from 108,558 to
129,963). Compared with growth in other states having the same de-

gree of development, and especially with counties where slavery declined, this population growth was insignificant. In Brown's opinion it followed from this that concern for terminating slavery has as its goal the emancipation not of the Negroes but of the white race from competition with slave labor. For only in a free state is it possible to have true industry, an increase in the number of artists, and a flourishing of the arts, sciences, and commerce.

Finally there is still one important refutation which slaveowners raise against those who demand freedom for the slaves. Quite significant sums were paid for slaves and, even if their labor is recognized as unproductive, who will compensate the owners for the expense they incurred? Does it not mean that emancipation of the slaves would ruin them? Not at all, is Brown's answer. The planters will not be in a position to cultivate the huge lands themselves. They will have to sell off sections, and in the competition from those seeking to acquire them, the price of land will rise significantly. Thus while the slaveowners lose on the one hand, on the other they will be more than compensated. And again in confirmation there are inexorable figures. For example, in 1854 in the state of Iowa 3,822,694 acres were sold for $4,741,341, while in Missouri 2,930,199 acres were sold for $1,282,072. Consequently while the quantity of land sold in both states was in a ratio of 4:3, the price of land was four times higher in Iowa. From 1852 to 1856 the value of land in the free states generally rose by 62.5 percent. This result, indisputable for Missouri, applies to other states. But many do not want to give up what they have become accustomed to in the course of centuries and thus are blind to their personal gain. On the contrary, just when new states are being founded and are flourishing north of the Ohio and Missouri rivers, the unfree states lying south of these rivers more than ever insist that they must preserve slavery just as they have the right to defend any other personal property. The unfree states understand that with every passing year faith in the system they so stubbornly support is diminishing. Therefore in every possible way they want to impede the spread of ideas of freedom coming from the north.

They see the chief means of doing so in the absolute segregation of slaves from whites and from emancipated blacks. As a rule this principle has been adopted in all the slave states. For emancipated slaves, an attempt has been made to set up a special area on the west coast of

Africa (at about 7° north latitude), their former homeland. The colony founded for this purpose was given the name Liberia to signify that it is exclusively for free Negroes.[9] Of course no measures can compel planters to manumit their Negroes or can designate a fixed redemption price for slaves. Liberation is more likely to come about from the terrible rise in prices for Negroes and from the spreading belief that the labor of whites, to say nothing of their productivity, is ultimately cheaper, as is all free labor.

How and when will black slavery be abolished in the southern states? In the cold northern provinces of the Union slavery was abolished without any particular trouble; Negroes were few and they did not comprise a necessary instrument for work. But in the South the existence or nonexistence of slavery is a question of life and death for the planters and their wealth. Instead of a decline in Negroes, as might have been supposed with the cessation of their importation from Africa, their number has increased. From nine hundred thousand at the beginning of the present century, there are now almost four million. There are planters with two thousand Negroes, representing a capital investment of more than two million dollars. What will become of the Negroes, they ask in the southern states, if this entire mass of people is set free—an uneducated people who up to now have lived under the eternal rod and supervision of whites? Wouldn't these people perhaps be dangerous to former owners, on whom they might want to take revenge for long-imposed deprivations and constraints? But on the other hand would a white do anything to alleviate the lot of a man who had the misfortune to be born black?

A special code has been formulated for Negroes in America, a code which in its brutality is reminiscent of the Romans and their notion of abolishing all independence of thought in their slaves. Christianity has not mitigated the notion that the Negro is equal to a beast of burden, a chattel, and consequently must be under the control of his master, bound to serve and obey him. The Negro can own nothing and dispose of nothing, in a word he is an object and submits

9. Liberia was established as an independent republic in 1822 on land purchased by the American Colonization Society. The colonization effort was not very successful. By 1860 only twelve thousand Negroes had been transported to Liberia.

to all laws proposed by the master. This idea is reflected as much in the laws of Virginia as in the laws of Louisiana or Carolina. It is the Slave or Black Code and in order not to spend any more time on an institution I have no desire to talk about, I will state the most important points of the code here.

The American legislator, acting on the principle that the Negro is a chattel, has dispossessed the Negro of the right to have a family, wife, and children, and has given the white the right to beat, punish, and even deprive the man-chattel of life. The Negro does not even have the right to complain against the white, and if a matter were to go to court, the white judge would always side with the slaveowner against the Negro. In some ways the judge is an accomplice of the slaveowner, and by penalizing only the slave, he believes he is teaching his own slaves a lesson. But then the courts are seldom resorted to for punishing Negroes. If a slave is found outside the plantation without permission from his master, he can be stopped and punished on the spot; if he resists, he can be killed. As soon as a Negro is brought to court, no matter what the nature of the complaint might be, whether an insignificant theft or the most serious crime, every justice of the peace has the right to arrest him immediately and turn him over to a jury composed of neighboring landowners. Of course all of them are the natural enemies of the poor Negro and a simple majority is enough to impose even the death penalty. In general the determination of punishments is left to the discretion of the jury; they set the conditions and the length of time. In the case of a death penalty, the same court determines the manner of execution, and the landowner losing the slave is compensated from public funds.

The Romans had already said that the escape of a slave was a special kind of theft and that a runaway was the thief of his own person. The slave in America who flees the province where he is settled is punished with death. The law punishes just as severely anyone who has helped a runaway and any accomplice in the crime. Furthermore if a slave runs away from the plantation and is gone for twenty days, he is subject to harsh corporal punishment. If an owner himself does not make use of this right, any judge can impose punishment on a criminal slave on behalf of the owner.

Upon repetition of the crime the slave is branded on the right cheek with the letter R for runaway. Again, if the owner himself fails to carry out the commands of the law he is subject to a fine of ten pounds sterling and any justice of the peace can order the branding.[10] For a third escape the slave's ear is cut off, on a fourth other parts of the body are cut off. If the master does not carry out these cruel punishments within twenty days after the crime has been committed, he loses his property right to the slave, who is then transferred to the one who informed on the owner.

In general a runaway slave is pursued as if he were a wild beast that escaped from its cage: the master himself, the organs of public power, and even outsiders join in the chase. Each one is promised a reward for the slave's capture. In the event a person suffers losses, falls sick, or is wounded as a result of the zealous pursuit, he is guaranteed to be recompensed out of public funds. As precautionary measures against attempts at even thinking of running away, the Negro is denied any means of education. The idea of his humanity and human .dignity, and notions about property or moral and religious enlightenment, are all suppressed. While in the very beginning Americans at least said that the advantages of transporting Negroes included, among other things, enlightening them through Christianity, so that they would not forever remain heathens living in Africa, now even that argument to excuse an evil business collapses in the face of sad reality. It is hard to speak indifferently about the treatment of Negroes, and what has been summarized from the Slave Code is sufficient to make one look with horror at this hateful ulcer in a free society.[11]

But if you carry on a conversation with any owner of Negroes, he starts talking about the care he lavishes upon the Negro and marvels at the "tales of nonsense" a European directs at the American planter. It is strange how a Frenchman or German who has immigrated to Mississippi forgets those ideas of freedom which were so sweet and dear to him in Europe. Now an owner of slaves living off their labor,

10. Many of the basic Slave Codes in use by the individual southern states in 1857 were enacted in the eighteenth century, before independence, and fines were stated in pounds, shillings, and pence.

11. Lakier's notion that a single Slave Code existed for all southern states is incorrect. Each southern state had its own Slave Code, which varied from those of other southern states. However, Lakier's brief summary of some of the key features of those codes is generally accurate. Kenneth M. Stampp, *The Peculiar Institution: Slavery in the Ante-Bellum South* (New York: Knopf, 1956), pp. 192–236.

he will say without a twinge of conscience that he takes care of the Negro as he does an expensive horse or precious furniture, and that he mates Negroes (a technical term used by the French here— *placer les nègres*) who are healthy and strong with healthy Negresses, not because they have a mutual liking for one another—indeed, he does not ask about their loves or attachments—but simply because they will have a healthy litter of children. This practice takes the place of marriage, and from whomever there might be a baby, whether from a black or a white man, the child of a Negress is a slave like its mother.

It goes without saying that a Negress who can obtain the favor of her master receives some indulgence and respect. But her children, however much white blood may be in their veins, can look forward to the same fate that befalls the blackest Negro—being sold into eternal servitude at public auction. One of the most important factors compelling a European to censure the North American Union is slavery. Except for the slaveowners themselves, hardly anyone defends it.

12

Down the Mississippi
to New Orleans

I

The captain of the steamboat *Philadelphia,* which was heading down
the Mississippi, confused me with the prices he asked for trips to various points along the river. A ticket all the way to New Orleans (a
distance of twelve hundred miles) cost twenty dollars for a full week
including meals, breakfasts, teas, a servant, and a private cabin; but
from Cairo, for example, to that same New Orleans cost more, twenty-
five dollars, despite the fact that the distance is two hundred miles
less and nearly two days shorter. The explanation for this is that five
or six steamboats, sometimes more, leave St. Louis daily, but they
either enter the Ohio at Cairo and sail up to Louisville and Cincinnati,
or they stop at Cairo and return to St. Louis; in short, there isn't such
a large competition among steamboats at Cairo and consequently the
price goes up.

In general the cost of a trip by steamboat is not fixed, and depends
on whether many travelers are going in the same direction and on
how many are going to those places where the steamboat makes stops.
But the charge for a short trip is disproportionately high compared to
the price of a voyage from one major point to another. It is calculated
on a purely commercial basis and guarantees that the American will
not be the loser. The captain tried to persuade me to go directly to
New Orleans. But this would have meant either a short time for becoming acquainted with towns along the river or no chance to see
them at all. After long negotiations we agreed that for five dollars
I would go as far as the town of St. Genevieve, where I wanted to
stop to visit Iron Mountain in the state of Missouri.[1] I had long ago
heard stories about its being one of the wonders of America.

1. Iron Mountain was a 200-foot-high hill with a 500-acre base located in the Missouri Ozarks. Once thought to be composed of solid iron,

On a brisk November morning I left St. Louis and sailed south. The shores of the Mississippi were contrasts in vegetation: the left or eastern shore was low with occasional short bluffs rising here and there, and behind them were the distant black-soil prairies of Illinois; by contrast, the right or western shore was high and wooded and it was there that those mineral-rich mines lay containing the still little-worked treasures of Missouri.

It seemed to me that everything in St. Genevieve except the name of the town was German: the drayman who brought me from the Mississippi up into town, as well as the innkeeper who gave me shelter and the coachman who drove me to Iron Mountain, were all Germans. I stopped there only long enough to hire a coachman for the trip to Iron Mountain. But those twenty-odd miles, which I had to travel by way of potholes and a plank road, will long remain in my memory for the discomforts that accompanied me every step of the way. One might at least have expected a restful night after the anxieties of the day. But this too was in vain. In the eastern states there is virtually no town where one cannot find a clean and reasonably decent night's lodging in a tavern far off the main road. Here in Missouri they sleep two or three in each of two beds in a small room, without asking whether you are acquaintances, whether you are healthy, and so forth. There was no choice and I had to spend the night under the same blanket with a feverish stranger whose face, fortunately, I did not see in the evening, otherwise I would not have closed my eyes all night. In the morning I was frightened by the sight of the yellow, worn-out, terribly sick stranger in the bed and I couldn't get out of there fast enough; for a long time afterward it seemed that death itself was pursuing me. There were other, decent night-lodgings, but they asked terrible prices for them, prices which were as high as they wished. Meanwhile, this is the main road to the mineral wealth of the state of Missouri, the route by which the ore mined in these mountains is brought to the Mississippi. However, a stock company has recently been formed which, they say, will get down to business, and there will soon be a railroad here. What would have been done with these places if they were somewhere in Pennsylvania! One instinctively recalls

---

the ore actually contained about 60 percent iron. Some five million tons of ore were mined by the time the deposits began to give out in the mid-1880s.

those gigantic works constructed in the Alleghenies that pull trains
to the top for the mining and transporting of coal.

On my return from Iron Mountain I went to St. Genevieve on
the Mississippi, where I waited for a steamboat headed for New
Orleans. It was enough to wave a handkerchief to have a steamboat
draw close to shore and lower a plank to the ground; in a few minutes
a new passenger was sailing along the Mississippi. They assigned me a
cabin and in several days' time I was living as if at home. The dimensions of the steamboat that fate had thrown me onto yielded nothing
to those which generally sailed the Mississippi, but it was dirtier than
others I had seen. Perhaps the reason for this was the large number
of extremely diverse and varied people that I found on board, along
with a most bitter and heated card game. Except for the ladies, everyone took part, some with their gestures, some with their eyes, and some
by placing bets on one side or the other. Money obviously had little
value. The tables were piled with gold, and in a free moment the
Negroes came to admire the game their white masters were playing.
Grinning at every stroke of luck and bitterly shaking their heads at a
loss, the blacks standing at the table were truly a curious sight. The
captain told me that there are people who do nothing but play cards.
They board the steamboat only for short distances. It is curious that
he would reproach this passion for gambling just as the Mississippi
flows through the slave states. Virtually no steamboat in this area,
although all adhered to the principles of temperance, would forbid
hard liquor and games on board, or order the observance of Sunday
with prayers and the reading of Scripture. Every steamboat has its
own barroom, and drinking-bouts almost always take place alongside
the gambling. That I was not happy in such motley company goes
without saying. Besides, I had to share a cabin with someone I never
even saw: by day he slept, all evening and night he played cards, and
his coming to bed was a signal that it was time for me to get up. In
the mornings the scene in the salon was awful. The whole floor was
covered with torn, bent, and folded cards and tobacco ashes; the place
was dirty and stuffy. Tired Negroes, with brushes in hand and patently
good intentions which their tired bodies refused to carry out, were on
the couches fast asleep. Other players had fallen asleep in the very
spot where since evening they had been playing euchre or poker, two
American games somewhat simpler than our game of simpletons.
From this intolerable atmosphere the only escape was to the gallery.

From that vantage point the view was of the same unchanging wooded shores of the Mississippi, of floating snags that formed islands in the river, and of dense forests. Here one breathed the fresh air in which the first hints of frost could already be felt.

Despite the fact that the company on board the steamboat was extremely mixed, all of the steamboat's conveniences were used on a basis of complete equality without any distinctions of title, rank, or status. There were the same long, lavish breakfasts and dinners that are served in the large cities on shore; the same abundance of courses; fresh bread, cakes, and pancakes every day; the same freedom of choice in dishes; and for the insignificant price the trip costs, you are fed for the entire length of the voyage. If a traveler straight from Europe were to encounter such a steamboat and have one shock after another —rushing to his place at dinner, sitting next to whomever happened to be there—you can rest assured this new arrival on American soil would be displeased with the local equality and would carry away a rather unfavorable notion of the society as a whole. Although I had already managed to get used to this common equality of each and all in America, and to the naturalness with which everyone thinks he has the right to do as he pleases without paying attention to his neighbor, I must confess that in the eastern and western free states there is more decency and morality. If the inhabitants of the southern states reproach their northern brothers for their coldness and dryness, the latter reproach the southerners, and quite justifiably it seems to me, for their luxury and immorality, which are not at all the same as gaiety and nonchalance.

Be that as it may, it is impossible not to submit to the general principle of equality: one must dine at a common table. Except for the sick, there is no service in private cabins, and every American will readily recount what happened to the German prince who took a trip on the Mississippi. Not wanting to be at a common dining-table and sit alongside some farmer taking his pigs to market, the rich prince requested of the captain that dinner be served in his cabin. The captain seemingly agreed and, when dinner time arrived, he stopped the steamboat at an island in the middle of the Mississippi, ordered that a table be set up for the prince, and invited him to dine alone. Then he cast off and shouted to the prince that since he did not want to be with the other steamboat passengers, the latter would easily make do without him. Left on the lonely isle, the prince had to bide his time

until another steamboat rescued him. Legal proceedings were instituted, but the American who related the anecdote was fully convinced
that the steamboat captain had behaved properly and would receive
no more than a light fine.

This incident may never have taken place but Americans love to
tell it for the edification of their guests. On the Mississippi, at least,
the telling of such a story is not inappropriate.

While the passengers of the steamboat that I was on passed the
time gambling at cards, and at long dinners and breakfasts, the industrious population along the shores of the Mississippi utilized our
steamboat for shipping south the fruits of their labor: flour, apples,
potatoes, and so forth. At a given signal from the shore by a miller or
farmer, the captain pulls in close to the shore; they exchange some
words over shipping price, come to an agreement, a plank is lowered
to the shore, and barrels and casks are rolled on to the steamboat. If
they do not agree, the captain just as laconically gets the steamboat
under way and sails on. At various places we took on passengers and
finally at one point on the right bank of the Mississippi, in the state
of Missouri, we stopped to take on board a white man with his black
slave and her two children. The white turned out to be a Frenchman
and an overseer of a cotton plantation lower down the Mississippi.
He had come to Missouri to obtain a slave woman with two children.
By his own admission, all together they cost him fifteen hundred dollars: the mother was a healthy, grown woman, one child was seven
and the other five. Her husband or mate remained on the previous
plantation and the Frenchman was not at all ashamed to state that
he would have bought that slave too but they asked too high a price
for him.

The young overseer was in every sense a Frenchman, polite, courteous, and loquacious. But he expended his gift in vain trying to convince me that slaves in the power of whites were happy, that they did
not want freedom, that they had security in sickness and old age and
received care in case of accident, that on the contrary only whites
could complain because they pay huge sums for their slaves and when
death takes a slave it deprives them of the purchase price and ruins
them. In my view that would be an important argument for the planters to want to free the Negroes; but the overseer, basing his argument
on long experience, assured me that they would not know what to do
with their freedom and maintained that they could be controlled only

by use of force and severity. The lash, in his opinion, was the inescapble stimulant for making the Negro do anything, since by nature he was lazy, cunning, thieving, and rude. The Frenchman was so convinced of this dismal, distorted notion of the Negro—whom he viewed not as a human at all but as something between a human and an ape—that he made his voice as deep as possible when speaking to the Negress and her children in order to seem more severe. The children had already learned how to babble that eternal word *master*, with which Negroes dignify their overseers. This Frenchman took poor Mrs. Beecher Stowe thoroughly to task and had no doubts whatever in citing Holy Scripture to prove that slavery had existed in the economy of the Patriarchs and that the apostle Paul had demanded that slaves be obedient to their masters. And as proof of the injustice of stories about cruel treatment of slaves, he pointed to the way his Negroes were being transported. Whereas the author of *Uncle Tom* painted the transportation of slaves in the dreariest colors possible, the Frenchman pointed out that the slave and children he had bought in Missouri sat the whole day not in shackles or chains but in the first-class anteroom. But this was so that the new owner could keep an eye on them: at every stop and whistle of the steamboat he considered it his duty to check and see whether his property was still there.

By his nature the young Frenchman was hardly prepared to manage and punish slaves, and there was probably a time when his heart was indignant at the sight of a slave crying out under the blows of the executioner. But unhappily his Creole uncle, that is, a Frenchman born in America, did not have children of his own and summoned him to his plantation, where the young man's heart hardened. He was so convinced it was impossible to treat Negroes otherwise or, better, that his treatment of Negroes was as humane as could be, that he decided to invite me to his plantation. I accepted his invitation, not in the least fearing that it would change my ideas and at the same time wanting to satisfy myself as to how just and sound was my innate hatred of slavery.

Thus we sailed down to Cairo, at the confluence of the Ohio and the Mississippi. The steamboat stopped there for several hours and I used the time to step back onto the familiar shore. But the Frenchman remained in sight of his Negress and the two children, guarding his fifteen hundred dollars, a necessary task since Cairo is in the free state of Illinois and escape would therefore have been entirely possible.

At Cairo our already crowded steamboat took on several more
passengers. There were not enough berths in the cabins, so divans
in the salon served as sleeping places, or mattresses were spread out
on the floor at night and then stacked in the corner by day. The card
game became the exclusive occupation of thrill-seekers; this passion
firmly gripped the entire steamboat. Entrepreneurs with limited means
and dirty cards went down to the second deck where the immigrants
were, and there tried to take away from the poor whatever extra they
might happen to have. For me the steamboat's gallery served as a
constant refuge and haven from the stifling atmosphere. But a quarrel reached me even there. It arose as the result of an insult that a
passenger who had lost all his money hurled at the player who had
beaten him and whom he called a cheat. Revolvers, always at the
ready, appeared on both sides and, if it had not been for the interference of others and the fright of the ladies, the matter would have
ended in bloodshed. This is the same as a duel, if you will, but since
the American does not admit the concept of chivalry, which is alien
to him, or all those ceremonies and formalities bequeathed to Europe
by the Middle Ages, reprisal here is quicker; they do not wait for
seconds or measure off paces. Whoever shoots straight first, wins. If
there are no revolvers, a stick or chair will turn up and personal
vengeance, the American lynching, will be carried out by these unworthy means. If the duel is a residue of barbarism, the American
method of avenging an insult and silencing the offender is an indication of barbarism. Which is better? As long as the duel remains in
style and retains some respect in Europe, it is better not to heap abuse
on the American for so often reaching for the revolver and the stick.
But it is precisely for that, incidentally, that Europeans attack Americans and stigmatize them as savages and barbarians.

II

When we left Cairo the next day, the temperature changed significantly and the climate became markedly southern. Whereas in the
north the trees stood bare or with yellowed leaves, they now once
again appeared in full brilliance. A little further down river they
stopped stoking the iron stove which had been making the salon unbearable. Ordinarily it was kept burning all day long to warm the
cold blood in American veins.

The further south we moved toward Memphis, the thicker and more luxuriant the forests became. Although they are cut down mercilessly for the wood-burning steamboats which require thirty to thirty-five cords of firewood daily, the forests grow back quickly, nature's bounty effortlessly restoring what the forests lose to human hands. It is by and large a young forest and the principal species of trees are the invariable oak, the magnolia, sycamore, and a pine similar to ours. The oaks here are almost all covered with long strands of gray moss falling from every twig and branch like huge ribbons, so much so that the trees lose their foliage from the embrace of these uninvited guests and die. The moss has the appearance of beards, so the local inhabitants call it Spanish beard. From the steamboat these gray trees strike the eye rather strangely and with a little imagination one might easily see them as the mysterious shapes of mythical creatures. Although the moss grows strictly in damp places, the roots do not touch the ground and it lives off the trees it clings to. All southern states that are inclined toward the Gulf of Mexico are filled with this Spanish beard. The Negroes use it for making mattresses, the beard serving in place of horsehair. It is first dried out and assumes an absolutely black color.

At Memphis, which is picturesquely laid out on Chickasaw Bluff, named after the Indians who formerly lived here, we found about ten steamboats standing by, idly waiting for cargoes. The French built Memphis in the last century under the name of Fort Assumption to provide protection for the local settlers against neighboring Indians. Today it is one of the most important depots on the Mississippi for cotton, which is brought here from surrounding areas for shipment to New Orleans, and from there sailing ships carry it to Europe. Bales of cotton were stacked up all along the Memphis riverfront, the cotton having been grown on plantations in Tennessee, Alabama, and Georgia. This is the western terminus of the railroad that begins in Charleston, South Carolina, and is to cross the southern states, but it is not quite completed yet. Cotton arrives here by steamboat, but marketing conditions are not favorable this year since trade generally and foreign trade in particular is in a depressed state and credit has fallen off. One hears about it in every conversation and reads about it in every newspaper. Planters are holding off marketing their cotton and are waiting for more profitable times to sell it.

There are several depots along the Mississippi that prosper because of their favorable location in relation to cotton-producing areas.

The town of Napoleon and the city of Vicksburg are examples, but everywhere there is the same halt in trade. In past times, when the cotton picking was finished in the interior of the country, steamboats loaded from top to bottom with bales of cotton were barely able to keep up in transporting their cargoes. At the present time the cotton plants south of Memphis were still maturing and their precious fibres still whitening. With small interruptions the plantations extended for several miles, and each one, occupying a relatively small stretch along the Mississippi, pushes deep into the interior. The planter's house, invariably built of wood with balconies and verandas, was almost always visible from the steamboat. This is where the planter lives with his family and domestic servants. Behind that is a series of low squat little houses for the Negroes who comprise the planter's wealth and enable him to wallow in luxury and comfort. The planter's domicile often has a garden and other landscaping around its construction sharply distinguishing it from the Negroes' shacks, which stand at a fair distance from it.

At one of the sharp bends in the Mississippi the Frenchman ordered that we be let off. A plank was thrown down and two whites accompanied by three blacks left the steamboat. Without a murmur the Negress dragged her two children up the steep bank and walked behind the Frenchman, as domestic animals follow behind their master, not knowing where or how she would be placed, what she would be forced to do, and with the foreboding that she would have to part with her children. The Negro who watched the arrival of the overseer was given an order that he carried out with the newcomer. He waved her on and she plodded along without tears, complaints, or stops. Such was her fate. She was prepared for it and there was no one to feel sorry for her. Indeed, who knows if this was the first time she was changing masters and mates or through how many hands her children had already passed. In any case it is well that the most recent federal legislation does not permit separating children under ten from their mother.[2]

2. Slavery was regulated by the individual states, not by the federal government. As of 1858 only two states, Alabama and Louisiana, had laws that forbade the selling of slave children under ten years of age without the mother. John Codman Hurd, *The Law of Freedom and Bondage in the United States,* vol. 2 (Boston: Little, Brown and Co., 1858; reprinted by Negro Universities Press, 1968), pp. 153, 157.

If it were not for the Negroes, the home of the Creole planter could have seemed a fine country residence of a wealthy landowner. There was much luxury in the way his daughter was dressed, in the decor of the rooms, and in the lavishly set table. But when you remember whose labor was responsible for all this, and what effort was demanded of slaves so that the planter's daughter could be dressed in silk and the master could entertain a stranger with delicacies from abroad, you begin to count the drops of blood and sweat with which the Negro has watered the land. Indeed, when we are wearing cotton material, how vividly we can imagine the workers through whose hands the inexpensive clothing has passed. One can understand that the many are not wealthy, that the majority work for their daily bread, that equality of status is inconceivable and would hardly even be useful. But while one may become reconciled to the lot of a worker who does not abandon hope of becoming independent and self-sustaining through his own labor, one cannot become reconciled to the fate of the slave, for he has no other future on earth but to be punished at the whim of his master or overseer for every trivial fault.

Nonetheless, the planter turned out to be a hospitable and obliging man. And what was even more important for me, he was able to provide me with figures on how much land in the United States is planted in cotton, and to explain how and when it is cultivated. He told me that this plantation still belonged to his father. Now, however, times are different, the death-rate of Negroes is extremely high, and getting new Negroes requires enormous capital not usually found among Creoles.

In order to explain the necessity for Negroes, the planter more than once called my attention to the millions of bales of cotton produced yearly in North America for the benefit of nearly the whole world. Without their labor, he said, this production would not be possible. But to protect the Negroes and thus his profits, the landowner could maintain the Negroes somewhat better and more spaciously. It is true that each family or several single Negroes occupy a separate cabin, but it is small. The floor is stone or earth, there are shutters instead of glass, and not the slightest attention is paid to the quantity or quality of food. Most sickening of all is the dirt in which the children live who are separated from their mothers; for that matter, their parents live in it too. The habits and the deadening of human feelings that result from long years of slavery, however, have not dulled the Negro; he loves to laugh and joke, and when the occasion presents itself, he will dance and sing to the sounds of a simple instrument similar to our balalaika.[3] He sings songs about his fate, perhaps a whole romance about love, or the work that he has finished or that awaits him.

But if the song is not a song of despair, it cannot be a song of happiness or hope: there is nothing to be happy about, nothing to hope for. The merciless lash can poison the existence of any Negro. Neither the planter nor his overseer goes out without a whip. As soon as the master turns his back, or generally when the slave is not afraid of a beating, the Negro will turn to a passerby and beg for some tobacco.

I spent nearly a whole day on the Creole's cotton plantation waiting for the steamboat to New Orleans. All down the Mississippi I saw shacks similar to the little houses for the Frenchman's two hundred Negroes on plantations that, south of Natchez, Mississippi, and Baton Rouge, Louisiana, grew sugar cane instead of cotton. Their outward appearance is all the same. The planter's house stands back from the shore and the Negro shacks are located closer to the river. Every scrap of land suitable for cultivation is planted with sugar cane which extends for miles on end like a sea of bright green broad-leaved rushes. I did not stop at those plantations because they were sufficiently visible to admire from the steamboat. Also I wanted to inspect more closely one or more of those plantations in the New Orleans area.

III

At the present time New Orleans is one of the most important points for foreign trade in the North American Union, and in that capacity serves the southern and western states, just as New York serves the eastern states. The city I had just reached played an important role in the history of America; it had been the object of various nations contesting for control of the Mississippi, whose significance for trade and industry Europe had early understood.

New Orleans was founded in 1718 by French colonists who were

3. The balalaika is a two-, three- or four-stringed triangular musical instrument with a long neck. It resembles the mandolin in sound and has long been popular with the Russian people.

invited by the French Mississippi Company headed by John Law, a famous French financier of the time.[4] The company was recognized by the French government and granted the right of industry along the Mississippi for twenty-five years, the right to found a settlement, and the privilege of trading the products of this rich area with other countries. In choosing a place for a warehouse the company did not err, although it was necessary to hold back the pressure of the water on the low-lying, marshy land, which is lower than the water level of the river. For this purpose river embankments were built and at great expense a wide wooden levee was constructed on piles driven into the water along the shore. Standing on the levee, one can see the river under it. In any case this was the only condition under which man could make use of the huge half-circular bay formed by the Mississippi here, a bay that can accommodate several hundred steamboats. Because the bay is shaped in the form of a crescent, the city is nicknamed the Crescent City.

However, despite financial assistance from the government, and regardless of the fact that at first immigrants came here readily, the company went into debt, with the end result that it collapsed and its privileges were taken away. The subsequent fate of Louisiana is well known, with its transfer from France to England to Spain, back again to France, and finally to the United States. New Orleans, of course, shared the same fate. But it gained special significance in the war between America and England in 1812, when the latter made every effort to close the mouth of the Mississippi to American trade. To this day there are many streets and squares in the environs of New Orleans and in the city itself that recall that glorious era, just as New York's remind one of Washington and Philadelphia's of Penn. The name of Jackson, the American general who managed to defeat fifteen thousand English troops with six thousand of his own, is immortalized by monuments and by cities named in his honor. The Battle of New Orleans, which the Americans won, ended the war with England.[5]

4. Law (1671–1729) was a Scottish financier who became an influential adviser to the French government. His Mississippi Company collapsed in 1720, a victim of wild speculation in France.

5. Lakier exaggerates. The main battle of New Orleans involved 3,500 American troops against 5,300 British troops. Far from ending the war, the battle was fought on January 8, 1815, two weeks after peace had already been signed in Ghent on December 24, 1814.

From that time on New Orleans, thanks to its favorable location, has flourished and grown to its present status as a commercial city with 170,000 inhabitants.

The very history of New Orleans explains a population mixture that one cannot fail to notice even on the streets of the city. Every one of the nationalities that took part in shaping the destiny of Louisiana left its representatives here, and down to the present day Spanish and French are heard along with English. Even the Americans have adopted foreign words into their language. For example, "picayune" is a small, five-cent silver coin, a word which obviously comes from *picolo* (small); "lagniappe" is something added to a purchase, a reward for some service, for work, or the like. That the character of the local population is not purely American is attested to by the variety of facial types and the liveliness of New Orleans speech. The local Creole women are renowned for their beauty throughout the Union and more than one son of New England has already been carried away by the gracefulness of a New Orleans girl, who is not averse to falling in love with a lean, pale, serious Puritan, if not for his handsomeness, cunning, and loquacity, then for his shiny attractive dollars.

There is no black African blood among Creoles. On the contrary, they are descendants of the first French or Spanish settlers here (hence the distinction between Spanish and French Creoles), whose children have been born and raised under the southern, almost tropical, sky of America. As a result, Creoles combine either French gracefulness, civility, and loquacity or Spanish sharp features and seriousness with that languor toward which the South is disposed. The very color of the face takes on an olive hue, and southern coloring is reflected in the whole physiognomy of Creole women. There are fortunate cities of the world which can count among their sights the beauty of their women: in the East it is Smyrna, in Spain Seville and Cadiz, in America New Orleans and Havana. It is impossible to leave those places without taking notice of their women. A Creole woman usually is not tall. But well proportioned and with black luxurious hair always neat and stylish, she loves to show off her dresses and ribbons, and the colors heighten her natural beauty. Because of that she is accused of being frivolous and coquettish, a point on which Americans generally agree. I can testify only to the fact that they are dressed tastefully, as are true French or Spanish women, and that they love to shop; the best walkways are built under the linen awnings of expensive stores. During the day, until about three or four o'clock, a Creole woman, fearing the heat, will not leave her room; jalousies are lowered and her lovely little foot will not touch the street until the heat lets up.

Having once begun to talk about the beautiful women of New Orleans, I must speak of a class of women who are not absolutely white but at the same time cannot be called black or even mulatto. However white the skin on a person's face may be, an American knows not only by the yellow preserved in that person's fingernails, but in a single touch of the hand, that in his veins there still flows a drop of black blood. To sit alongside, to have relations with, and, especially, to beget a child with the descendant of a slave is considered contrary to social custom and morals. The white takes care not to come too close to a black and therefore always carefully keeps himself apart. Blacks and whites do not even pray together. In the colored theaters there are special boxes for all categories, ranging from the pure blacks to the palest of their descendants.

Such are the requirements of society. But by and large, with the small number of women in America, the mixing of white and black races is quite frequent and mulattoes are not uncommon. The fourth generation of this mixture, the so-called quadroons, live in the same alienation from whites as do Negroes. They are often wealthy and have been educated in Paris or in some other city. They love to dress well and throw their money around, and in vengeance for the fact that whites hold them in contempt, quadroons do not let whites enter their society. An exception is made for a European and the doors to the quadroons' social receptions are more easily opened to a foreigner. Here again you see a series of beauties with snowy white, pale faces, beautifully formed necks and breasts, and the most attractive shapes. Quadroon women are nimble, lively dancers. They still have the innate gaiety and playfulness of the black race, although now somewhat subdued by civilization. These parties have all the decorum of white parties, but are captivating because of the naturalness that quadroon wives and daughters bring to them. The less etiquette, the more fun. The attire of quadroon women is also rich, as with Creole women, and one must have an experienced eye to tell one from another in the street. It is not at all strange that Americans, regardless of all proprieties, fall in love with the daughters of quadroons. But a wealthy quadroon will not always give his daughter to an American, fearing she will be the victim of the scorn that is felt for the black race. There

have been occasions when a white could not receive the hand of a
beauty unless he swore there was black blood in his veins too. For
then it is a different matter: the future husband and wife are equal and
a marriage is possible.

Such a joyful, lively people must necessarily have had an influence
on the character of the city. To begin with, it may be said that as long
as Creoles and quadroons remain in New Orleans in their present
numbers, a Puritan Boston or a quiet Quaker Philadelphia in the South
is impossible. Germans, who are quite numerous here, do not interfere
with the merrymaking since they too love entertainment. However,
danger threatens from another direction, from Americans who have
migrated from the eastern states and would like to have Sunday observed here with the same calm and quiet as in Boston. Their voice
has already been raised more than once in the Louisiana legislature,
arguing that places of amusement, theaters, and public fêtes be forbidden on Sunday and that all merrymaking be banned under strict
punishment and fines. But the other party, the Creoles, have prevailed
and they make merry on Sundays just as on other days, if not more,
and as a result the Americans like to abuse them, calling them an immoral people. However, reconciliation is partly possible without mutual constraint and even without concessions. It happens that the city's
French Quarter, with its buildings, its French-named streets (Condé,
Chartres, Dauphin, Bourbon, Royal, and so forth), and the old Catholic Cathedral of St. Louis fronted by Jackson Square and a monument
to the general, has existed since Spanish times and is separate from the
American part of the city. Between them is the wide Canal Street
where a canal had previously been.

The American part of the city is newer than the French, and until
recently there was still a swamp here which periodically flooded from
the overflow of the Mississippi. The dwellings of poor Frenchmen
had been scattered here and there and the rest of the area was empty.
Today these dwellings have been pushed back to distant streets and
wealthy Americans have erected mansions along the Mississippi.

However, although barrooms selling hard liquors, wines, and soft
drinks, as well as inns selling ice cream, are scattered all over the city,
the greater number of them are in the French Quarter. At every step
you see large, wide, open rooms where gentlemen stand at the counter
providing gin, whiskey, and liquor to customers. A New Orleanian
will seize upon any suitable opportunity to run off to the barroom ten

times a day to drink up his happiness or sorrow. There is no place even to sit down since there are no chairs in the room. It is said this is to avoid any long conversations between the customers and to prevent arguments that do not always end peacefully or without the aid of revolvers. There is nothing here resembling those grand cafés in France, Italy, or the East where a man can rest from his daily labors with a cup of coffee or a harmless game. Still, in every public barroom there is a table loaded with snacks of pretzels, bread, cheese, and sausage to which anyone who is hungry can help himself, free of charge. Such is the custom, and the owner of the establishment makes up for it from the sale of drinks. In addition, in many similar establishments there are games of skittles, of which Americans are generally avid fans. But democracy has transformed it here and it is played without a king. What disturbed me most of all in these establishments were the large signs on the wall reading: "Beware of pickpockets!"—warnings that compel you instinctively to check your pockets to make sure everything is there.

Even the market in the French Quarter is not devoted exclusively to selling produce. Along with stores filled with southern products such as bananas, oranges, sugar cane from which people love to suck the sweet juice, pineapples, and pomegranates, there are establishments in which for a paltry sum people can slake their thirst and satisfy their hunger. At certain hours the common people here form the same motley crowd as do the beggars in the markets of Naples.

The banks, commercial houses, and stock exchange are concentrated in the American part of town. That is where the brokers live, where commercial transactions are carried on, and where there is a constant running about. The French and German merchants, who carry on foreign trade chiefly in cotton and sugar with Le Havre, Bremen, and Hamburg, live somewhat farther out with their families, although their offices are located in the part of town closer to the stock exchange and the levee.

New Orleans more than any other American city recalls the outdoor street life of southern Europe. For example, the Mardi Gras masquerade is preserved here with all the pranks and mischief of a French or Spanish carnival. I did not see it myself but I spoke with people who know the merrymaking permitted in southern Europe at the same time of the year, and they assured me that the local masks, the gala floats, the various amusements, the witticisms and games are as gay and fascinating as at the Roman Circus. Such charming merrymaking by a whole city setting aside work for fun must be strange to Yankees whose motto is work and gain. Negroes and mulattoes, with and without masks, love to mix in the crowd and there is no end to their games, songs, and dancing. The climate, as well as the national characteristics and traditions left to New Orleanians by their forebears, explain this public Mardi Gras holiday. Everyone participates, everyone makes merry as much as he can and knows how, and sad it would be if the increase of Americans and their influence were to disturb this public merriment.

In addition to various places of amusement, there are several theaters in New Orleans, including a French opera, which many Creoles especially attend. Creole women love to show off their rich attire at the opera, so that the latter is a rendezvous for the high society of rich merchants and planters owning several hundred Negroes and thousands of acres of sugar cane.

I arrived at the capital of the South in November, at the very beginning of the winter season. But it was still so hot that only with some effort could one escape the intense heat of the sun. At night, under a muslin bed-curtain, it was impossible to protect oneself against the obsessive mosquitoes; they are much smaller than ours, easily penetrate through the tiniest slit, and torment their victim mercilessly. But for all that, the yellow fever season had already passed. Yellow fever reigns over New Orleans from May and even April to November and sometimes even the beginning of December. Not a year goes by that this plague doesn't descend upon New Orleans. It was brought here by a ship transporting Negroes.[6] The neighboring plantations, where there is much to be done in the summer under supervision of the owners, are the best havens for planters. Some go to the seashore where the heat is less intense, others take advantage of the time to travel to the northern states, to Canada, and even to Europe. Business generally ceases for the whole summer, but with what great ardor the people return to it when the sun begins to burn less fiercely!

6. Yellow fever first appeared in New Orleans at the end of the eighteenth century. In the nineteenth century outbreaks became progressively worse. The climax came in 1853 when a tenth of the population died of yellow fever. John Duffy, *Sword of Pestilence: The New Orleans Yellow Fever Epidemic of 1853* (Baton Rouge: Louisiana State University Press, 1966), pp. vii, 6.

Then the population of the city doubles and triples and everyone, occupied with his own affairs, runs about bargaining and buying. At that time as many bales of cotton are delivered as are ordered in Europe, and every conversation turns on whether the crop is ripe, whether the quality is good, and whether the price is high. Newspapers report these items, and if you go down to the river's edge or the levee, you will see why people are bustling about. Hundreds of steamboats with gigantic funnels are crowded together at the levee. The steamboats have come down from all along the Mississippi and its numerous tributaries. On the other side, closer to the mouth, are anchored seagoing steamships and sailing vessels awaiting cargo and passengers for the Antilles islands, Mexico, Central America, and Europe. The steamboats bring the cotton from various plantations along the Mississippi and the steamships are prepared to carry it overseas. The amount of cotton sold in the New Orleans market exceeds one and a half million bales.

From early morning until late at night work goes on at the levee. Most of the work is done by Negroes who, under the watchful eye of a white overseer, carry bales of cotton and barrels of flour, sugar, and molasses from the steamboats to the shore. The overseer, whip in hand, keeps account of the goods brought ashore and zealously drives the slaves to keep working without resting. If they tarry or daydream, the whip is always ready. But then, a Negro manages to catch a moment when the overseer begins talking with someone, and he knows how to make it look as if he is working when, in fact, he is doing nothing. I often went down to the levee just to admire the ruses of a sly Negro. Seeing that I was not armed with the terrible whip and that I was looking on rather indifferently, the Negro did not feel he had to conceal how he rolled a barrel of apples as if it were as heavy as a barrel of gold, or how he winked at another slave and laughed at the negligence of the overseer, until the latter shouted "Go on!" and suddenly the Negro displayed his lightness of foot and the strength of his arms. With those magic words he is instantly regenerated and begins to work quite differently. Watching these deceptions of the Negroes I automatically recalled our proverb: "Work be not done, from work one can't run."

There were times when the New Orleanians brought up evidence to prove that slavery was essential for the South. They asserted that only the black race can endure working on the levee in a hot sun and

that whites would collapse from exhaustion in the broiling sun. If
that is so, why would they not put up white linen awnings over the
levee, as is done in Havana? In recent times Irish and even Germans
have begun to share the work of the Negro because of a lack of lighter
and more suitable work for them, although most of it is still done by
Negroes. For the most part the latter are hired from planters who
find this kind of work for them in New Orleans after the harvesting
of the cotton and sugar cane has been completed on the plantations.
The wage for the labor of a strong and healthy Negro is high and of
course is turned over to his master, for whose benefit he works. Generally Negroes must never be left idle. Those who are a little older
and cannot do hard work are set up in town to sell fruit or sweets that
are locally produced on the plantation.

New Orleans is always well stocked with slaves and one can buy
as many as one needs. There is no shortage in this trade. Every day
one sees advertisements in the newspapers that a big shipment of
Negroes has arrived from Virginia or from some other section of the
American Union, and that these Negroes (whose abilities and capacity for work are praised to the skies) are being sold for cash or
promissory notes. To attract attention to the offer and spare a white
buyer the trouble of looking for similar advertisements, there is a
sketch of the unfortunate black. It is not a rare sight to see scores of
pairs of Negroes put up for hire or for sale on a street close to the
levee. There are even depots where Negroes are taken on commission
and put up for sale. Curiosity compelled me to stop by the door of one
of those depots. A gentleman who evidently was the proprietor of the
establishment, thinking that I was looking for a slave, insisted that I
come in. There was a long room with benches along two walls. Upon
my entering everyone got up. I was uncomfortable wearing a hat
among those people with their bare heads, but the smile that lit up
every black face revealing rows of white teeth was a thousand times
sadder for me than the tears and groans I would have wished to hear
as a protest against this base treatment of human beings. The proprietor, to his shame, was a German. If we stopped in front of a Negress,
he turned her around, displayed her charms and spoke in my ear about
her various recommendations. The poor woman, forgetting her natural
shame, smiled and asked that I buy her. If young, she was dressed more
coquettishly than the others, and the seller, it was clear, counted on
her attire to sell her off more quickly and profitably at the depot. But
then, most of the Negroes were rather cleanly dressed and had their

hair combed. Everyone had a white collar showing behind the clothing. How, one might ask, was this market any different from the female slave market in Constantinople? Yet Americans in that part of
the world are fond of ridiculing the Turkish slave market, which generally isn't even shown to a giaour. When the German noticed how
quickly I was taking leave of his contemptible establishment, he began to defend the life of the Negro slaves, which he found far better
than that of European laborers, who are also obligated to work but
who are not provided for in case of sickness or old age. It was a bad
tactic to try to minimize one evil by comparing it with another, and of
course the speaker did not believe in the justice of the argument he
advanced, nor did he convince the listener.

To reinforce the feeling of revulsion one brings to a place where
Negroes are sold, it is enough to glance at the newspaper advertisements on slaves who have run away. A reward is promised to anyone
who brings them back. Usually it is one hundred dollars, seldom
less. The description is accompanied by a drawing of a runaway black
man with a bundle on his shoulder, or of a woman carrying a bundle in
her hand. An attempt is made to describe the skin color and any
blemishes that can be seen on the face, to indicate the clothing, the
age if known, and what languages the male or female runaway can
speak. It is precisely how we in our country describe distinctive marks
when we advertise for a missing dog. But there is one peculiarity here
which perhaps would not be bad to add to our advertisements on occasion—an indication of the weight of the slave. The law does not
spare the runaway. The Black Code grants the master the right to
punish a recalcitrant; only killing the latter without a trial is illegal.
In this respect at least, one must agree that the European worker
is better-off.

There is another factor that speaks in favor of the European worker.
At eight in the evening a cannon is fired in New Orleans. One thinks
that this is the signal for ships to cease entry into the port, as happens
in other port cities. Not at all. It is a signal for all Negroes: from this
hour they must be in their houses and cannot appear in the streets,
if they do not want to be carried off to the police station and be sub-
jected to punishment. When I was at the police station they had a
mulatto on trial who was wont to take advantage of his white skin
color. He was particularly fond of going out at night in the company
of a quite black Negro who was supposed to be his servant and visiting the bars. In short, he loved to enjoy life. But he was found out and

together with his companion was sentenced to corporal punishment. After that he would hardly decide to pay so heavy a price for his evening pleasures.

As in the other unfree states, manumitted slaves are not tolerated in Louisiana. They must go to Liberia within a set time if they do not want to be returned to slavery. No exceptions are made to this rule, not even for black Methodist preachers who explain the Holy Scripture to their brothers. To whom could these preachers belong? And would not the preaching of freedom and equality to people mired in eternal slavery be harmful to the tranquility of a slave state? The church owns the Negro preachers as property and their preaching is limited to exhortations for humility and patience, to which their black listeners reply with heartrending sighs and weeping. And it is said these Negroes do not want freedom! That these Negroes love slavery!

But meanwhile, what a contradiction! In the arcades of the St. Louis Hotel, one of the most magnificent and richest not only in New Orleans but in the entire Union, slaves are daily auctioned off at noon. To the shame of Europe and educated France, I must admit that, if it is Americans who buy Negroes, it is Frenchmen who are the auctioneers and sellers. The specimen being sold is placed on a platform specially made for that purpose and his beauty and qualities are extolled, just as in the depot where slaves are sold. Not sparing his voice, the auctioneer raises the arms of the male or female who is being sold, showing off the chest and muscles. He turns the slave around and adds that, among his other assets, the slave is illiterate, uneducated, and without religion, and consequently will be totally a tool of the master. In other words, he is suited to work not like a well-trained delicate coach horse but like a dray horse, without tiring and without resting. Whenever workers are in demand on the levee or on the plantations, the price of a healthy, well-developed Negro sometimes goes up to twelve hundred or fifteen hundred dollars. There is no greater punishment for a slave at auction than to remain unsold at the price being asked for him. How strange! Does it make any difference, when and to whom he is sold? If a white's pride is expressed in the aspiration to a higher status in society, in the desire to have an influence on affairs and to be highly respected by public opinion, the black is ready to boast that he was bought at a high price, that he cost a great deal of money and therefore had qualities that no one else sold at a cheaper price possessed. That is a form of pride, and I myself was a witness to how sadly an unsold Negro stepped down from the platform. A woman is more shy here, too, perhaps more proud than a man, and for her such disregard from the buyers is even more painful. I thought that during my stay in New Orleans I would attend these auctions more often, but they so revolted my soul that I did not go back again. I regret that the respect I developed for the institutions of the northern states was poisoned by the true ulcer of America.

To give me some idea of the luxurious life of wealthy planters in New Orleans, Mr. M., whom I had befriended on the steamship voyage to the New World and whose company had been so useful and pleasant for me in Boston, served as my cicerone. Although he ran back and forth all day long between the stock exchange and the cotton levee and was busy with cotton bales, he found time to introduce me to several wealthy merchants and planters. For the most part their office furniture gave evidence of exquisite luxury and a passion for spending lots of money which, as the fruit of someone else's labor, was not valued highly.

But, then, it was enough to live and dine at the St. Charles Hotel to be convinced that money was of no concern. In appearance it is a palace, with rows of marble columns, a plush lobby, tens of luxurious parlors and an enormous dining room. Dinner could have satisfied the most fastidious and jaded taste. But to make up for it the daily rate, which is two and a half dollars everywhere else in America, is three dollars here.

[I used] the remaining time to visit the courts, prisons, university, schools, and several charitable institutions in New Orleans. Some observations may be in order here regarding the need for judicial reform. For one thing, it is a pity that a person taken into custody sometimes has to wait so long for acquittal or indictment, since courts are not in session during the summer. Furthermore, the New Orleans prison was built in such a way that this waiting is painful in many respects. It becomes even more onerous when, as is sometimes the case, the court finds the charge totally without substance. If foreigners are placed under guard, or people have no friends or relatives in the city who could vouch for them, they spend the first day in the calaboose or guardhouse until they appear before the recorder, and then they are put in the parish prison to await trial. Here, then, is a prison that certainly satisfies neither the demand for justice nor those scientific principles which are brilliantly applied in places of confinement in the northern states of the American Union.

The New Orleans prison takes up a quite large area, is enclosed by a high stone wall, and is divided into four courtyards. The cells open onto them and have iron gratings in place of windows. Four to six men are placed in each cell. The main rule for accommodating the convicts, as well as for those still awaiting trial, is that the least guilty be put together with the worst criminals and that the young be put in with the old. This practice, I must confess, somewhat startled me, all the more so since it was absolutely contrary to that which I had seen in other prisons which I had so admired. Meanwhile, the warden who was taking me around never tired of praising his prison and the fact that there had not been any escapes, not even attempts to escape, and that he alone, unarmed, was left among three hundred and sometimes four hundred criminals; obedience to his every word was so good that all he had to do was give the order and they all almost instantly left their cells. What he said interested me even more, for I still did not know how this unarmed man obtained such good results. It turns out that the entire system for running the prison is based on spying and is predicated on the fact that a young man, not being an inveterate criminal, will be more quickly affected by some malicious intent or attempt to escape, and will inform on his cellmates. Also, in order to avoid too great a concentration of prisoners in one place, the institution is divided into courtyards. Intending it as praise, the warden said that there was only one prison in the entire United States based on this principle. Thank God for that: there is little enough concern for reforming young people who had the misfortune to land here for a petty misdemeanor or even for a single conviction; but a prison that cages them up day and night in the same cell with criminals waiting for the death sentence manifestly corrupts those who were drawn into a misdemeanor by mistake or thoughtlessness. There is even a wall from which the dangerous criminals are suspended on hooks, further evidence of this unconcern for the effect on the young. No one works; most of the day is spent playing cards, shooting dice, smoking, and jabbering. The cells are not even heated in winter, and food is insufficient. If Sing Sing, or another New York or Pennsylvania prison, can be reproached for providing superfluous workers in competition with ordinary workers, the same charge certainly cannot be levied against the New Orleans prison.

13

Washington

I

I was convinced that, for a true understanding of the city of Washington, it had to be visited when Congress was in session. At any other time it looks like a big village whose wide streets were built Lord knows for whom or what. And when you see huge, white, lonely buildings with hundreds of columns standing in various parts of town, you instinctively ask yourself whether all those buildings are standing there in vain. Even the Capitol, abandoned at the end of town, towers in deathly silence, and you fear that it will be so lonely that it will lumber down the wide and empty streets just to pay a visit at the White House, the president's residence.

One gets quite another view of Washington when Congress is in session. The town livens up from the presence of more than three hundred lawmakers and politicians assembled here from various parts of the United States. Stores try to attract rich and not so rich Americans strolling along Pennsylvania Avenue. All one hears about are dinners and parties given by one or another member of the diplomatic corps, and about serenades and meetings in honor of various members of Congress. The hotels, which in summer are a sorry sight of emptiness, open their doors to hundreds of visitors. In the dining room, in the lobbies, and on the porches of the hotels, where at another time one could see only the boot soles of taciturn Yankees, one now hears lively conversations strewn with words like "Kansas," "president," "Douglas,"[1] "treasury notes," and so on.

A session of Congress is an epoch for Washington but even more for the entire Union of the United States, because Congress serves as a visible link for the states. At all other times they live their own

1. Stephen Douglas (1813–61), senator from Illinois (1847–61), was the Democratic nominee for president in 1852 and 1856.

243

autonomous lives, having their own legislatures, courts, educational systems, even their own money,[2] and are governed by officials elected by the people. Were it not for Congress one might fear for the unity of the United States and predict its disintegration.

But why was this place in particular chosen as the national capital of the United States? Weren't there many cities whose locations would have been more central and convenient, and even healthier? Especially significant is the question of the central location of the city in which individual states choose to establish their government. In the new states of the West these points are measured off by compass, as it were, and in equal distances from the borders. But this advantage in relation to the United States of America is something Washington does not enjoy. Hence one must find another reason for its having been chosen.

General Washington, who established the unity of the United States, was a native of Virginia. Memorials of his private life are concentrated along the Potomac River. He was born in Fredericksburg, Virginia, not far from the place where his mother is buried. Washington himself loved the town of Alexandria on the Potomac, and he spent the last years of his life at Mount Vernon, which had belonged to his brother and where the "Father of His Country" is buried. Down to the present day it serves as a place of reverence both for Americans and anyone else to whom the name of Washington is dear. I think Washington's personal affection for his birthplace more or less determined the selection of the site of the capital.[3] If this is correct, then the first president of the United States should not be heaped with blame for having been seemingly guided by egoism but rather with thanks for his perspicacity. More than once have I heard from Americans themselves that the name of Washington and the principles he bequeathed to posterity, both in the Constitution and in his Farewell Address of September 17, 1796, serve as the main if not the

2. A national currency did not come into existence until the Bank Act of 1863. Before then state-chartered banks issued their own bank notes.

3. Locating a federal city on the Potomac River was approved by Congress in 1790 as a compromise between the conflicting desires of the slave and nonslave states. Since Washington, who was then president, knew the Potomac area intimately from his years at home on the Mount Vernon plantation, Congress asked him to select the exact location for the District of Columbia.

sole link between the northern and southern states. What binds them together is a faith in the good sense of Washington who, foreseeing disagreements, stressed that unity and harmony were the foundation stone of American independence, the bulwark of peace at home and abroad, of security, well-being, and freedom. This faith has saved, and of course always will save, the inviolability of unity. Was it not therefore a beautiful idea on Washington's part to link the national capital of the Union with his birthplace and his name?

Moreover it was difficult to force an old, or at least previously existing city, to submit to the executive branch, give up its customary political municipal rights, and be dependent on Congress. That is why it was necessary to choose a vacant site and establish as suitable a form of administration as possible. It is doubtful that an important city will take shape in the usual way on the site of present-day Washington, for it has neither commercial nor industrial advantages. The Potomac is much too insignificant and the city is too far from its mouth. By the residents' own testimony, the climate in Washington is not healthy; during the summer frequent fevers drive out a large part of the population. In short, the city exists because it was ordered to be here. There is no reason to be apprehensive about improvements, the development of business among residents, or population increase: perhaps in time several more homes will be built, as well as buildings for all the departments of the federal government. At certain times the city will become deserted and at others populated. But those who predict that Washington will not always be the capital of the United States are wrong. So many millions of dollars have been expended on Washington, the Capitol, and the departments that their inviolability is assured. I will say that for a future great center of the western states and even the entire United States, it stands to reason that there be another city, a grand city of the West, the need for which is felt in America. Everyone puts forward his own place, be it Chicago, St. Louis, St. Paul on the Upper Mississippi, Cairo, swampy Memphis, even Kansas City. Circumstances will show who was right in his predictions. Meanwhile such a center is felt necessary and there is no doubt that another New York will have to be created in the West.

Whoever has been in the various sections of the United States will recall how unsettled taste and style still are in the construction of public buildings in America. In this sense the European states are more fortunate: each one of them has inherited through its history an archi-

tectural legacy with a certain style. In America, Gothic buildings with
their towers and flowers are not always appropriate because they are
reminiscent of an epoch quite alien to the young states. In Washington itself one can find architectural works of almost all styles, beginning with the most ancient and ending with an absolutely newly
invented and unprecedented one. It is worth taking a look at the
Smithsonian Institution and then at the Treasury Department across
from it: the former is a true likeness of a medieval Norman castle,
and one simply does not know why it has appeared on the banks of
the Potomac, quite inappropriately for a building designated for the
spreading of enlightenment. Meanwhile, the Treasury Department is
modeled on the Greek temple of Minerva in Athens, as are a large
number of the federal buildings in Washington. Of course the columned buildings scattered around the city are not always appropriate;
nevertheless, the eye is not startled by the ancient classical style that
has been transferred to the new land, for this style, despite its origins
in a particular region, has become the property of the whole world.
One finds many replicas of Greek temples in the United States and
perhaps it would be unjust not to admit that some of them come close
to excelling the models. Girard College in Philadelphia, for example,
is unquestionably one of the finest buildings in the New World and
it is difficult to say anything in reproach of the simple, graceful style
in which it is built.

II

The members of Congress are guided by various principles in their
actions and judgments. And whether elections are held for municipal
officials, state officials, or members of Congress, it is all the same:
groups are formed, meetings are held, each puts forward and praises
its candidate, touts his achievements, his past, and his hopes for the
future. And just as in England either the Whigs or Tories receive
a preponderance of the votes, so in America they look to see which
party—Democratic, Republican, or American—will elect more members to Congress and other offices.

At first glance it may appear, perhaps, that there are no essential
differences between the points of view of these three parties, but in
fact it turns out to be quite the opposite. To begin with, it is necessary
to distinguish the American from the Democratic and Republican

parties: whereas the former permits only exclusively American candidates to run for public office, that is, those born in the United States (even stricter principles guide the Know-Nothings), the Democrats and Republicans do not exclude anyone who has been in the United States for the required number of years and has become a citizen of the Union. It makes no difference what nation he was born in. Furthermore, the National Democratic party wants to preserve the unity of both the individual states and the nation as a whole; it therefore endeavors insofar as possible to see to it that no single city, state, or class of people has more political rights than another, so that peace and harmony may prevail in the entire Union. The Republican party endeavors to strengthen the federal government at the expense of the individual states and is prepared to sacrifice the basic unity of the nation for the predominance of one single principle, for example, the abolition of slavery.

The president himself belongs to one of these parties and acts in spirit with it. Thus there are always people in Congress who are ready to defend his principles, instructions, and proposals, just as the opposition is always ready to rise up against them. This division of the members of Congress partly substitutes for the presence of official presidential defenders, and the success of his proposals depends on whether the majority agrees with him or with the opposition. Congress as well as Parliament has its leading men, and their eloquence and the boldness of their arguments attract a greater or lesser number of members.

The current president of the United States is a Democrat[4] and opposition both during his election to the presidency and in Congress has been concentrated in the northern New England states, which object to slavery. Each party has its journals and organs. A congressman who betrays the principles for which he was elected is considered to have committed a breach of public trust and the members of his party take appropriate action against him. The members of Congress take a position either to the left or right of the president, in accordance with their views.

When the elected members of Congress convene in Washington in December to assume their duties, the president of the United States sends them a message which he has prepared for this occasion. The

4. James Buchanan (1791–1868), president from 1857 to 1861.

opening of Parliament in England is not only a state event but an interesting pageant during which the court, the highest state officials, the king and queen and their family appear in all their splendor and medieval regalia before the people and their representatives. To the magnificent Gothic chamber of the House of Lords, to which the members of the House of Commons have also been invited on this occasion, go the Lord Chancellor and Speaker of the lower house, and as many barristers and clerks as possible, all in their long powdered wigs. Here are appropriate toques of the English ladies, with their fluttering decorative feathers and trains, the whole court etiquette, full-dress uniforms, coats of arms, and finally the genuflecting lord— the chancellor, in rich dress, presenting to the king or queen at the foot of the throne a speech directed to the lords and gentlemen.

There is nothing at all like this in the United States: here there are neither wigs nor formal dress nor decorations. Everyone wears a black frock-coat or tails and sits where he pleases. Had I not felt regret for the nice new furniture and carpet in the House of Representatives, I would not even have noticed the rude, but perhaps comfortable, position of the feet raised by a son of the plains above the head of his neighbor, and the nasty habit many Americans have of chewing tobacco. Instead of all the splendor of the English court and council, the clerk of Congress reads the president's long message which calls the members, simply, fellow citizens of the Senate and House of Representatives. Nothing superfluous, nothing dazzling, and immediately after the reading of the message, someone will very likely begin to refute the justice of the principles expressed by the president.[5]

Never, I think, has the English king given so long a speech to Parliament as the clerk read to Congress this year. And this is not exceptional, it is not an innovation of the current president, James Buchanan; his predecessors did the same. I think this is done so that all members of Congress understand the president's ideas and there is no further necessity to elaborate on them. That is why a collection of presidential messages serves as almost the best source for the

5. George Washington and John Adams personally read their annual messages to Congress. Thomas Jefferson, fearful of an imperial presidency, was the first president to send his annual message to Congress to be read by a clerk. This practice was followed until Woodrow Wilson reinstituted Washington's custom of the president's personally reading his annual State of the Union message to Congress.

internal and diplomatic history of the United States.* After thanking
Providence for protecting the Union, the president in his message ex-
pounds on what Congress must give its special attention to, on the
measures it must adopt to eliminate distress, disorder, and so on, and
in addition acquaints Congress with the secrets of United States diplomatic relations with other states.

In the 1857 message the president aptly emphasized those points
on which the attention and activity of Congress were focused. But
national pride will excuse my citing first of all pronouncements from
the president's message that relate to our fatherland. "Our relations
with Russia," said the president, "are, as they always have been, most
amicable. The present emperor, like his predecessors, has always
shown a kindly disposition toward our country on appropriate occasions, and their friendship has always been highly prized by the
government and people of the United States." These words are really
true and anyone who, like myself, has traveled in America can confirm that a Russian name elicits the most cordial greeting and most
affectionate welcome from Americans. The same sentiment is expressed by the American government toward our whole country. This
is a gratifying phenomenon, and there is no doubt that our direct relations with the United States, rather than through English, French, or
German ports, would serve to profit Russia and its productive powers.
We too are like Americans, we are not devoid of commercial boldness
and enterprise. But we won't forget that when Peter the Great was
sailing on Lake Pereiaslavl, English immigrants had long since sailed
across the Atlantic and occupied the unknown lands of North
America.[6]

As for the relations of the United States with other nations, the
president analyzed in quite some detail relations with France, England,
Spain, Persia, China, Central America, and other smaller powers. One
of George Washington's important rules was: do not needlessly take
up arms against anyone and do not interfere in a neighbor's affairs.

* There is a collection of the messages of presidents of the United
States from 1789 to 1851. (*The Statesman's Manual containing the Presi-
dents' Messages, Inaugural, Annual and Special from 1789 to 1815*, by
Edwin Williams, 4 vol. in 4⁰, New York). [Footnote in the original.]

6. Peter began to build boats on Lake Pereiaslavl in 1688, at the age
of sixteen. By 1692, with the help of Dutch sailors, he had built the first
flotilla in Russian history.

Down to the present day the United States has supported this wise principle, but nevertheless its voice carries weight in the affairs of Europe.

As to the internal condition of the country, the president outlined in a most discomforting light the country's financial position during the last quarter of the past year. Despite the country's productive wealth, commercial distress in the manufacturing and commercial cities and states has reached extreme limits. The most reliable companies and commercial houses have collapsed, carrying hundreds of others with them. Sizeable centers of the working population, and most of all New York, have become disturbing areas of unrest because of the lack of work and bread. New York had to provide public work for its poor. It is well known that this financial and commercial crisis, having begun in America, has not been without influence on the other side of the ocean. The president considered the causes of the crisis and the measures to be taken to eliminate this problem in the future. As the head of the Union saw it, disorder in the financial affairs of American commercial cities was produced by an extraordinary amount of paper money issued by *some four thousand* irresponsible banking institutions in various states without sufficient backing in hard currency for the holders of such paper money.[7] How can the repetition of such a misfortune be prevented? Everyone wants to live and enjoy life and not have to worry about his neighbor. People threw everything they had into an enterprise, not thinking that the financial resources necessary to carry it out were insufficient, and credit rose to unprecedented levels. The young nation, perhaps more than others, got carried away in the rush; but even a more experienced western Europe acted on the same principles. Instances of personal bankruptcy do not serve as a lesson for those who still have money and who can afford to continue a speculation they have already undertaken. True, nowhere is there so much paper money as in the United States, and Americans are so used to it that the executive branch cannot, and does not have the authority to, abolish it all at once. That is why the president proposed that Congress consider this particularly important matter and limit the irresponsibility of banks.[8]

7. Early in his journey Lakier had noted the effects of the Panic of 1857 on New York City. See above, pp. 71–72.

8. This was not done until 1863. See above, n. 2.

The foregoing financial circumstances of course have not been without influence on the condition of the federal treasury, and therefore the president recommended to Congress economy in expenses for public needs, although at the same time he justly remarked that this economy must not mean a failure to carry out programs that may cost money but are essential for maintaining the strength of the Constitution and the defense of the country.

The proposals stated by the president in his message to Congress are discussed in both legislative houses and are either approved or attacked by various members depending on their views on the subject and their party affiliation. Speeches are delivered in complete freedom and, restrained neither in word nor expression, they are sometimes quite unpleasant to colleagues or even to the president himself. But then what does it matter if it is all for the common good? Are there any great orators in Congress? What is the distinctive feature of their speeches? These are natural questions when you know that in nearly every country where public discussion of affairs is introduced, one can detect a certain inflection of speech issuing from the basic character of the people and of the orator representing them. Southerners [in Europe] are distinguished by vivid and picturesque expressions and by a talent for speaking with their hands and eyes or for conveying by these means what they cannot or do not want to say with words. Thus it is that declamations or rather dramatic poses, along with a florid style, distinguish the orators of France, Spain, and Italy. It makes no difference for whom or what the speech is being made, where or for what purpose, whether in the courts, the church, or parliament. Northerners [in Europe] are colder, more sedate, and if their orators permit themselves some movement, it is measured and monotonous. Flowery words wither, as it were, in the cold atmosphere. If the speeches of great English orators, for example, do not captivate the masses, many of these speeches, at least, are models of profound thought. This does not mean that the speeches of French orators possess none of those traits; I only wish to say that it is better, more instructive, and even pleasanter to hear them than to read them.

American orators are probably closer to the English type. Of course this refers to the majority, because the degree of education, to say nothing of personalities in the various states of the Union, are so varied that one cannot and should not draw parallels between the eastern and western states, for example. The representative of New

York is a more educated person, more commercial, and having seen the world is prone to speak ironically about the farmers of the western states, the "western men." One can truly say of the latter that they are almost always self-educated, that they began by working their way through the legislative assembly or senate of their states and then to membership in Congress. Several self-made men were pointed out to me in the Senate chamber. If it were necessary to provide evidence, I would mention [Stephen] Douglas, the senator from Illinois. The son of a poor common laborer, by his own efforts he reached a level where he felt the need to educate himself. He has been abroad and has even been to Russia. Today he is a wealthy man, is one of the leading figures in the Senate, and is said to aspire to the presidency.[9]

In the United States the road is open to anyone to be elected to public office. This is the basic principle of self-government. On the other hand, to get elected one needs to be well known to the people, to flatter them sometimes, to try to gain popularity, to appear at meetings, and the like. Not everyone, especially an educated man, has a talent for this. That is why many Americans, especially young people, prefer law or service in government institutions to public affairs. Most often, however, they enter some productive private business and make a lot of money, far removed from any political party, as if little concerned about the fate of America. That is saddening, especially if one compares the situation with that at the time of the War of Independence, or if one compares it with the present state of affairs in England where there is no greater honor or more rewarding labor for a dedicated man than to be elected to represent his county or city. Returning to the orators in the American Congress, I must therefore frankly say that their speeches are not distinguished by either profound thought or elegant style. Most of the orators are verbose and it seems that more often than not their purpose is to satisfy the expectations of their constitutents and the party to which they belong. As to speech-making itself, for the most part it is inelegant. The hands are used much too freely. The legislators pound the table, cleave the air menacingly with fists, or smack their palms together. The American speaks very easily; he does not have to search for words with which to refute an opponent, and that is much, but not all,

9. See above, n. 1.

that is necessary for an orator. It is said that formerly there were more illustrious orators in the Senate. Of the present group I have at least heard the best and, I must confess, I regret that the patriotic sentiment which inspires every American does not always have a worthy interpreter. The craving to provide for oneself and for one's posterity, to make money quickly, captivates many. The Union has enjoyed about fifty years of peace; this has made it possible for Americans to build hundreds and thousands of miles of railroads and canals as well as incalculable numbers of steamships, and to spread their trade around the world. Those opportunities have diverted the attention of Americans from public affairs. Their motto is Go Ahead! and they act accordingly. Those Americans who see the need for a war to stimulate again a feeling of national pride in individuals, the kind of war that aroused all the vital forces of America at the end of the last century, are correct in their judgment.

A member of Congress hears out his opponent most attentively and calmly, almost never interrupting him, even holding back any approving exclamations. And only when one speech is finished will another member stand up and with the words "Mr. President!" in the Senate, or "Mr. Speaker!" in the House of Representatives, signify his intention to speak. He begins his speech only after the President or Speaker replies "The Senator!" or "The Gentleman!" adding the name of the state to which the orator belongs. If several members rise in their place at the same time, the President either gives preference to the one who stood up first or uses his own discretion. In this instance the others acquiesce to his will, though a skillful or perhaps unscrupulous President of the Senate as well as Speaker of the House can make use of the rules at a critical moment, namely, when the last word is expected, to choose an orator from his own party.

Every member of the legislative assembly has the right to present bills for discussion by his fellow members. If they require preliminary consideration they are referred to committees composed of members of Congress from the Senate or House. Upon conclusion of a committee's work, a bill is brought to the full Congress, which either accepts the committee's judgment or, upon a motion by a member, changes it by majority vote.

Congressional decisions are published daily in a Washington newspaper, *The Washington Union.* Moreover, all important newspapers in the United States have their own correspondents and quickly transmit to their readers the proceedings of Congress, along with an evaluation. The telegraph is also utilized, and for several months the attention of the United States is focused on Washington and feeds on the news from Columbia Circle.

III

But let us move to the residence of today's president. Although a large number of the official or, more correctly, public buildings in the city of Washington are white, the title "White House" belongs exclusively to the house inhabited by the president of the United States. The great and most ostentatious street in Washington, Pennsylvania Avenue, leads from the Capitol to the house of the president. Since the name "White House" is well known to anyone who has read an American guidebook or heard stories about it, one can understand, after the Tuilleries and Buckingham Palace, a desire to have a look at how and where the president of the United States lives. Walking from the Capitol, you come across a huge, marble, columned building and you think that this is surely a part of the presidential palace. One wing is still uncompleted and you turn the corner to look at the facade in front, but do not find it. You ask and find out that this building is the Treasury. The home of the president is farther on; it is barely visible behind the trees, a two-story white house sufficient for a private family and not at all conforming to the expectations of a European. Where, you ask, are the guards? When can one go into the house to look at it? Where does one get tickets? How must one be dressed? As is well known, these are the questions that are essential in Europe. In Washington they simply answer you with: "Walk in!" You want to see the president and talk with him: if he is at home and not busy, you will be admitted without any special formalities or etiquette. There are neither doorkeepers nor glittering liveries, and if you were to enter the White House by mistake, not knowing who lived there, it would be difficult not to think it was a middle-class home. Wealthy Europeans and members of the nobility perhaps will not believe what I have just said; but it is true and has been experienced by everyone who has been the president's guest. Ordinarily there is nothing to see in the White House: there are neither remarkable paintings nor statues, and if you get here on a normal day, they show you a portrait of Washington, marble busts of Christopher Columbus and Lamartine,[10] the two reception rooms, the mirrors in the Great Hall, and the chandeliers, which are in no way remarkable.

Agreed, that is not what you expected in a president's residence, and perhaps you leave disappointed, adding that all the stories you have heard about Washington are American humbug; but do not judge rashly what is so incompatible with our notions and our state and social institutions. Try to come to the White House at New Year's when everyone who is in Washington on that day, from small children to old men, from senators to simple farmers, from wealthy bankers to lowly workers, have the right to enter the White House and trample its soft carpets. They listen to music in the entrance hall until the front ranks pass by and then, having reached the reception room, shake hands with the president and wish him good luck. The same greeting and handshake is ready for everyone; no attention is paid either to the clothes or social class of the American. . . . The only ones kept separate are the diplomatic corps and members of the cabinet, Supreme Court, army, and navy. The glittering formal dress of the diplomats and the military stand out even more among the dark mass of thousands moving about, each one of whom considers it a duty to shake the hand of the old man who is president.

I have never seen how a newly elected president is presented to the people at what is called an "inauguration." But I have been told that, while all the people stand in hats, the president rides by with his head uncovered, signifying his pledge to serve the people. I recalled this ceremony when looking upon Buchanan's white hair and his old face at New Year's. The American, conscious of his equality and his rights, walks boldly up to the president. You are amazed at how thousands of people have descended from everywhere and, with neither police nor troops visible, quietly await their turn while guarding against anyone violating the right of the women and children to be first. The picture was completed by Indians who had arrived several days before New Year's to entreat their grandfather(as they dignify the president of the United States) not to offend them and to pay them money for the lands they ceded to the government. This time plenipotentiaries from the Pawnee, Ponca, and Potawatomie had arrived in

10. Alphonse de Lamartine (1790–1869), French poet and statesman. After the revolution of 1848, he served as minister of foreign affairs and, briefly, as head of the government.

Washington. With all my heart I wished that these poor people, who, as one of the leaders expressed it, have worn out their moccasins (soft Indian shoes) on a road of ill fortune, be satisfied in their expectations and petitions. Because in truth it is painful to listen when the Indian begins to recount how things are good for the white man because the Great Spirit protects him, but that he, the Indian, is both impoverished and unhappy through the unkindness of the Great Spirit, and on top of that the white man also hurts him.

With solemn bearing and self-possessed taciturnity the Indians* appeared at the White House in their native dress of varicolored red and blue cloth blankets on their bare shoulders and variegated moccasins on their feet, above which they wore something like lace-up leggings that covered half the torso; people were amused by the bird tail-feathers in their hair, multicolored bands to hold their long flowing hair in place, and the large number of beads, rattles, necklaces, earrings of various kinds and sizes, and above all their painted faces. To the Americans' credit is must be said that they do not pay any attention at all to dress, so long as it is not Indian dress; but even in the latter case they do not permit themselves to laugh, although they are obviously interested in it.

The Indians also shook hands with the president, having absolutely the same rights as white citizens, and, like the others, could then look around the White House. It seemed to me that aside from the president and his unique position in relation to the people, there was nothing remarkable here. Like the residences of our wealthy landowners in the villages, the president's home is set in a garden: one side faces the Potomac, and the other, with a statue of Jefferson in front, faces Pennsylvania Avenue.

The same simplicity and accessibility that governs the president's home is noted in the residences of his ministers. I speak of them only as state officials, without reference to their personal and social lives, to which European representatives, diplomats, dignitaries, and travelers have managed to bring European etiquette, official calls, cards, and so on. Everyone has his place! Without exaggeration I will say that a person can enter the office of the secretary of war without first encountering a person to announce him. Of guards there is not a trace. I do not know whether this simplicity will last long: it exists at present

* From the Platte River Nebraska Territory. [Footnote in original.]

because every American is himself busy all day with his own affairs and will not disturb the secretary unless it is necessary, and if an American has business with him, the secretary cannot turn him away.

With an extravagance, however, that no American grudges when he has a public goal in mind, buildings have been and are being built for the ministries. They are almost all of the same style and have been copied from the best ancient models. Since the governing of each state is vested in its legislative and executive branches, obviously the ministries of the United States have less authority than do those of other governments in which each ministry's authority reaches to the farthest border and where everything under its jurisdiction is subordinate to the executive of the central department. If it were not for the official sources on which I base this, one could not believe that the State Department has only seventeen officials, namely: the secretary himself, his deputy, the chief clerk, twelve secretaries, one translator, and one librarian. Moreover the Department of the Interior consists of the secretary, one chief clerk, and twelve clerks. Equally uncomplicated are the Departments of the Army and Navy, for the simple reason that the land and even naval forces of the United States are insignificant, especially in relation to the vastness of land and water throughout which they are dispersed and which they are assigned to protect. More complicated is the Post Office Department because it handles the mail for the entire Union and supervises postal officials in all states and cities. The postmaster general has three assistant postmasters-general; each has his own special department with a specified number of clerks: the first has nineteen, the second twenty-six, and the third twenty-one. In addition the chief clerk, who has judicial and supervisory powers, has seventeen clerks. But the largest, both in staff and, accordingly, in terms of the building thus far constructed, is the Treasury Department. Although each state elects its own treasurer and in general manages the finances that do not concern the federal government, nevertheless there is a Treasury official in each seaboard and border city because commerce and navigation are under its supervision and management. In addition, one of the chief sources of income for the federal government consists of duties collected on imports and exports. When one adds to all this the need to keep accounts and deal with the other departments, the inevitable complexity of this department, even in America, becomes understandable.

Incidentally, the Department of the Interior has jurisdiction over the issuing of patents for new inventions, as well as over the collecting and publishing of statistical information on agriculture, crops, land under cultivation, and the like. For matters of this kind there is a special Patent Office; a large part of the building, as the name itself already indicates, is devoted to models and forms of inventions which are both new and improvements over the old. How many thousands of models there are here is difficult to say, but to find another collection like it, I am convinced, is impossible. Suffice it to say that in the last week of 1857 alone, sixty-two patents were issued. It is obvious that a number of them must not be very complicated, and actually in a series of models one sometimes sees improvements for which no one among us would have thought to take out patents. But the American counts on huge sales, and prizes a patent for a new rifle, spring, lock, and the like with which to associate his name as its sole producer. It is true that Americans, compared with Englishmen or Frenchmen, have made few new inventions, but on the other hand all their efforts are directed at simplifying work so as not to require too many hands even for insignificant operations in various areas of manual labor. Steam is employed everywhere: for mills, for machines that load and unload cargo and for the pouring of grain, for doing fieldwork, and so on. The great advantage of the United States is that it has inherited the latest experiments conducted in the Old World and has succeeded in applying inventions already made earlier. This link with the Old World is continuously maintained by the immigrants arriving here and it seems to me that the greatest misfortune for America would be the adoption of the Know-Nothing policy which sees only disadvantages in the influx of foreigners, namely, that they bring poverty and defenselessness in times of hunger and unemployment, and so on. In that connection they point to the Irish and partly to German laborers, forgetting that without those people, in the northern states at least (in the southern states a large number of the laborers and servants are Negroes), there would be no servants: Americans themselves look for independent, self-supporting, profitable occupations, and they do not go into service or work for private individuals. The gathering in a single city, and not infrequently in a single workshop, of workers from all sections of Europe cannot but be advantageous to the bold and resourceful mind of an American; he has the opportunity, without going very far, to compare methods utilized in other lands, and if he can he will adopt and simplify, substitute steam for hands, write out a description—and a patent is ready. It seems to me that this can partly explain the large number and variety of inventions for which patents have been issued in the United States.

14

Conclusion

With Washington I concluded my journey through North America, not counting the return route by way of Philadelphia to New York whence the *Fulton* took me to Le Havre. Thus did I fulfill the program I had set for myself in traveling to the New World. While returning to Europe I more than once asked myself whether reality had satisfied my hopes and expectations. In my essays on North American institutions and the life of the country I have frankly stated the observations I made on the spot. I have praised what seemed to me worthy of praise and have not spared censure in contrary instances.

I certainly did not want to conceal the shortcomings I found. I know that the brighter the light, the darker the shadows. That is a general law of nature, and if one wants light he must not complain about the existence of shadows.

But then the Americans themselves well know the shortcomings of their political system. They are ready to admit that a passion for the dollar prevails among them, that slavery is inhuman, that family life is not developed, and so on. If the shortcomings are rectifiable or considered worthy of correction, there are all sorts of means readily available to the practical patriot-American: the press, the public meeting, the magazine, the state legislature and the federal Congress. Europeans, either because they know very little about the internal life of a distant country or because they purposely misinterpret the meaning of what they see and read, proclaim the disintegration of the Union as a consequence of the excessively mercantile bent of its inhabitants, their immorality, and the decline of a sense of honor. If there were any basis in truth for these dangers, a terrible fate indeed would threaten the United States. The trouble is that this dark vision, the realization of which others might even desire, is neither more nor less than the product of idle imagination. There is no doubt that slavery is bad, as is the single-minded passion for the acquisition of wealth, and that unlimited self-government is harmful. But while many shortcomings of which America is accused are shared by other countries as well, nowhere perhaps is the idea so widespread that morality is the best defense of the solidity of society and the independence of its institutions. While deviations from the rules of honor and justice are unpleasant in private affairs, they are not dangerous for the fortunes of the nation so long as education reaches out to all classes of society and schools follow the principles which now guide them.

Then too, what America has succeeded in doing in some seventy years of its independent existence guarantees that it is in a position to make progress. One need not be a prophet to predict that the United States will possess the entire northern half of the New World and that it will have a strong, almost exclusive, influence on the other parts of America. The basic principles of the Constitution are taking root everywhere, despite the immense size of the country, giving full rein to every community, from the smallest group to the largest state. These principles comprise the invisible bonds that tie together the various parts of the huge whole, which otherwise might disintegrate. As long as Americans support the Constitution bequeathed to them, there is no danger to the safety of the Union. It is to the immediate advantage not only of each state but of every American individually to protect its inviolability. Everyone is convinced that as long as the basic principles of the North American system enjoy the confidence they have had up to the present, there can be no danger from either an internal or external enemy. In the event of an attack, all states will forget their private interests and band together as in the time of Washington. There is also nothing to fear from ambitious schemes on the part of the president. Everyone follows his activities, the lowliest worker can write about them, and no act of his against the Constitution can get by without censure.

But must Americans be confined to America or are they fated to return to Europe, bringing with them the institutions that were regenerated on new soil and were cleared of those excrescences which clung to them for centuries in Europe? Young, active, practical, happy in their enterprises, the American people see no reason to answer the question negatively. They will have an influence on Europe but they

will use neither arms nor sword nor fire, nor death and destruction.
They will spread their influence by the strength of their inventions,
their trade, and their industry. And this influence will be more durable
than any conquest.

Index

263